Anthropological Studies of Britain   No. 4

Armenians in London

Anthropological Studies of Britain
General Editor: Anthony P. Cohen

Belonging
Identity and social organisation in British rural cultures
Symbolising boundaries
Identity and diversity in British cultures
Whalsay
Symbol, segment and boundary in a Shetland island community

Also by Anthony P. Cohen

The management of myths
The symbolic construction of community

Armenians in London

The management of social boundaries

Vered Amit Talai

Manchester University Press

Manchester and New York

Distributed exclusively in the USA and Canada by St. Martin's Press

Copyright © Vered Amit Talai 1989

Published by
Manchester University Press
Oxford Road, Manchester M13 9PL, U.K.
and Room 400, 175 Fifth Avenue,
New York, NY 10010, USA

Distributed exclusively in the USA and Canada
by St. Martin's Press, Inc.,
175 Fifth Avenue, New York, NY 10010, USA

British Library cataloguing in publication data

Talai, Vered Amit
    Armenians in London: the management of social
    boundaries. – (Anthropological studies in Britain:
    no. 4).
    1. London. Armenians. Social conditions
    I. Title II. Series
    305.8'91992'0421

Library of Congress cataloging in publication data

Talai, Vered Amit, 1955–
    Armenians in London: the management of social boundaries / Vered
    Amit Talai.
    p. cm.—(Anthropological studies in Britain; no. 4)
    ISBN 0–7190–2927–9
    1. Armenians—England—London—Social conditions. 2. London
    (England)—Social conditions. I. Title. II. Series.
    DA676.9.A75T35   1989
    305.8'919920421—dc20   89–36255   CIP

ISBN 0 7190 2927 9 *hardback*

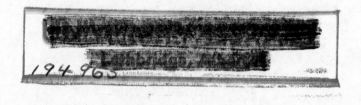

Photoset in Linotron Sabon by
Northern Phototypesetting Co., Bolton
Printed in Great Britain
by Billings & Son Ltd, Worcester

Contents

List of figures   *page*   vi
General introduction   vii
Preface   ix
Introduction   1

1 Armenian associations and institutions   10
2 The self and the Armenian other   40
3 Armenians and non-Armenians   77
4 The historical legacy   115
5 Fieldwork among the Armenians in London   148

Conclusion   154
Appendix: Questionnaire used in household interviews   162
References   166
Index   169

Figures

1 London Armenian voluntary associations   11
2 Distribution of friendships *vis-à-vis* inflection set and association executive committees (Eastern Armenians)   57
3 Distribution of friendships *vis-à-vis* inflection set and association executive committees (Western Armenians)   58
4 Association membership of respondents sitting on association executive committees (Eastern Armenians)   59
5 Association membership of respondents sitting on association executive committees (Western Armenians)   59
6 Popular settings for socialising with friends (Eastern Armenians)   62
7 Popular settings for socialising with friends (Western Armenians)   63
8 Three Western Armenian households   66
9 Establishment of friendships with Armenians upon first arrival in Britain (Western Armenians)   67
10 Establishment of friendships with Armenians upon first arrival in Britain (Eastern Armenians)   68

General introduction

The studies included within the earlier publications of this series have all concerned people who might be regarded as indigenous to the British Isles, and have tended to focus upon the ways in which they distinguished themselves from other indigenous groups. Particular attention has been paid to the symbolic devices with which they marked and experienced these putative differences and through which they expressed their social identities.

Dr Talai's book differs in dealing with a group which is not indigenous to Britain. Caution is needed here: some of the 'Armenians' described in the book may indeed be second-generation or even third-generation residents of Britain, and many are the children of mixed Armenian–British marriages. Most of them are at least two generations removed from their 'native' land. But the book is linked by its topic to others which preceded it in the series. Like the indigenous British, the Armenians lack some of the more obvious and explicit markers of ethnicity that have commonly been noted in studies of ethnic minorities. They are 'white'; they are not concentrated residentially within the cities, and they are not associated with particular kinds of occupation. Although they are members of the Armenian Apostolic Church, they attend the churches of other denominations. Few of the younger Armenians speak Armenian. The longer established residents have English as their first language. Others are most at ease linguistically in the vernaculars of the countries they have lived in previously as *émigrés*: Greek, Arabic, Persian, and so forth. Much of their material culture and tradition has been dissipated by the long years of exile. To the outside observer, the Armenians may thus be apparently indistinguishable from other people of Middle Eastern origin, and may even be indistinguishable altogether.

To complicate matters further, they are themselves divided into 'Eastern' and 'Western' dialect blocs, the members of which have had distinctive diaspora histories; many of the former having settled first in Iran, and, of the latter, in Cyprus, the Lebanon, Syria, and Iraq, before moving on to Western Europe and North America. Their sense of 'Armenian-ness' is thus mediated by extraordinarily diverse experience.

Therefore, their ethnicity within the context of British society is invisible or, as Talai characterises it, 'anonymous'. The Armenians have to render it plausible and substantial by their own symbolic creativity and ingenuity, not only to be able to present themselves as a distinctive interest group (for they are disinclined to this kind of ethnic politics) but also to augment their own sense of identity. Further, they have to do it in ways which do not compromise the expediency of their ethnic anonymity (or, in Talai's telling phrase, their 'part-time ethnicity') so that they can slip in to and out of 'Armenianness', mere 'foreignness', or even 'Britishness' as they judge appropriate. Dr Talai displays in detail the kinds of resource they have developed in their strategic management of identity, ranging from the resuscitation of anachronistic political associations; to the contrivance of linguistic, folkloric, and culinary traditions; to the development within the community of social institutions. She shows how they have created common forms of 'frameworks' of identity which they can inform and make meaningful through their particular and diverse experiences.

But this book gives us more than an intriguing picture of a fascinating ethnic group, more even than an instructive case to enhance the growing stock of diaspora studies. Talai argues convincingly that the modulation of ethnic identity which she observes among the London Armenians should be recognised as a feature of ethnicity as such. Through the ethnographic case and the theoretical discussion which preceeds it, she thus leads us to see ethnic identity as being far more complex than the product of the mere contingency, relativism, or political pragmatism identified in some of the most influential anthropolitical discussions of the subject. In this respect she points the way towards a considerable refinement in the anthropology of ethnicity. Moreov r, she uses her experience of studying the London Armenian community to provide important lessons for the conduct of anthropological fieldwork in the city. The study thus complements other contemporary work (some of it, by Wallman, Charsley, and Young, already included within this series) which is charting innovative pathways in urban anthropology.

A.P.C.
University of Edinburgh

Preface

The fieldwork on which this book is based was conducted in London during 1981–2. It was supported by a scholarship from the Quebec Ministry of Education.

Ever since I chose to study an Armenian community I have been repeatedly asked why I made this choice. Why Armenians? To this day, the truest answer I can give is that, given my research focus on ethnicity, I thought that this would be an especially interesting group. I hope that the book shows that my original motivations were not wrong, the Armenians *are* interesting!

I would like to acknowledge the advice and support of a number of people who helped me in this endeavour. First, I would like to thank Anthony P. Cohen, who as my Ph.D. supervisor and then later as an adviser has always been encouraging and given me invaluable advice. His wisdom and insight have truly been an inspiration. Secondly, I would like to thank my parents, Dr Zalman Amit and Dr E. Ann Sutherland, whose support has always been unflagging. I would like to thank Geoff Kelley, who at a later stage helped with editing a portion of the book and, most important, persistently nagged me to finish it. Most of all I would like to thank the Armenians in London, whose generosity and hospitality made my fieldwork and, hence, the book possible.

In order to preserve the anonymity of individual Armenians, none of the real names of respondents has been used. Instead, I have assigned letters randomly to each individual.

V.A.T.
Concordia University, 1989

Introduction

There are approximately 10,000 Armenians in Greater London. Most are first-generation immigrants, originating principally from Lebanon, Syria, Iraq, Iran, and Cyprus. They also include Armenians from Ethiopia, India, Egypt, Palestine, as well as individuals from other countries. They have, therefore, had various experiences as Armenian *émigrés* before arriving in London.

This diversity of background is reflected in differences occurring between London Armenians. They speak two major forms of the Armenian language; Western and Eastern Armenian. The majority are members of the Armenian Apostolic Church, but there are Catholic and Protestant Armenians as well. Armenians may have different expectations of the Apostolic Church, based on varied experiences of it in their respective communities of origin as well as in London. It has varied in terms of the level of clergy present, the abridgement of services adapted from their original long monastic form, the degree of secularisation of the community, its affiliation to one or the other of two apostolic sees, and so on. The Church as well as Armenian communities more generally have been affected by long-standing political divisions, for example between the Ramgavar, Dashnakstitiun, and Hunchak parties (described in more detail in Chapter 1) as well as more recent movements such as the Armenian Secret Army.

Armenians have, not surprisingly, been influenced by their different host countries. Thus, food, music, language, educational background, and aspirations vary between national subsections of the London Armenian community.

Armenians recognise these differences and allude to them explicitly in such phrases as 'we are divided', or 'the Armenian is an individualist'; as well as to more specific differences between, for example, Eastern Armenian speakers and Western Armenian speakers, or between political parties.

While the kind of differences between Armenians in London may change over time, neither the pattern of settlement in this city nor the nature of the organisation of the Armenian community suggests that differentiation will diminish. Armenians have dispersed residentially and occupationally across wide areas of London. They come together as a group at gatherings sponsored by a constantly shifting network of voluntary associations. As some associations continue functioning, others become moribund, and still others are established. The relationships between these organisations are frequently competitive, identified as they are with different political, national, linguistic, and general orientations.

Armenians do not share a uniform experience of this ethnic identity. What they do share is a set of symbols which provide a framework for their interpretations of their 'Armenianness'. Symbols of the Armenian as an exile from his true motherland in Eastern Turkey, or cultural continuity and antiquity, of individualism, of language and Church gain strength from their ambiguity. Much of the stuff and substance of Armenian community life is debates, discussions, and disagreements over the import of these symbols of Armenianness, but it is a debate operating within a common symbolic framework. As I shall try to show in the following pages, the cohesion of the Armenian community does not derive from consensus or homogeneity. It derives from an acceptance of a symbolic framework which can be shared by people with different interests and backgrounds because its ambiguity can accommodate the variety of views which emerge from these differences.

This framework of ethnic affiliation and identification is not readily encompassed within what is, perhaps, one of the most influential theoretical approaches towards ethnicity in social anthropology, i.e. the ethnic group viewed as an 'interest group'. Its leading proponent, Abner Cohen, argues that ethnic groups emerge and are sustained because of the common politico-economic interests of their members (1969, 1974a; 1974b). Rituals, symbols, customs, and a sense of common origin serve to affirm and strengthen the solidarity of such groups. This is not solidarity for its own sake but as a means to promote common interests in competition with other such collectivities (1969, 1974a; 1974b). According to Cohen, the 'attitudes' of individual Armenians and their interaction with shared symbolic forms would not be a fruitful focus of analysis. The tendency of individuals to offer different and contradictory views over time, according to Cohen, renders such attitudes tenuous as evidence (1981 pp. 321, 322). On the other hand

> A group 'ideology' is concrete, empirically observable, and needs no depth psychology for understanding its sociological import. The subjective factor in ethnicity is significant for sociological analysis only in its objective manifestations. [*ibid.*, p. 322]

However, what the Armenian case indicates is that without understanding the ways in which symbols are manipulated by the members of an ethnic collectivity we cannot understand how a 'collective ideology' operates to support the cohesion of an ethnic group. The assumption in this 'political approach' (Watson, 1977, p. 8), that the functioning of a 'collective ideology' is dependent on the common interests of its members and the intensity of their competition as a corporation with other such groupings, leaves a theoretical vacuum when we approach a case such as that of the London Armenian community.

London Armenians do not cluster in any one industrial or occupational sector. They do not congregate in any particular residential quarter of London. Interactions between Armenians take place for the most part outside their other involvements within the wider metropolitan setting rather than in terms of them. Within these other involvements Armenian ethnic identity may be of little or no immediate relevance. Furthermore, among non-Armenians in London there is little or no awareness of Armenians, either categorically or as a community. Armenians in short, do not compete with non-Armenians in London *as a group* either in terms of the nature of their own occupational, residential, or educational involvements or in terms of the perceptions of outsiders. However, the 'part-time' nature of London Armenian ethnicity has raised rather than weakened the self-consciousness of Armenians about their ethnic identity and community. Because of their dispersal, if Armenians wish to come together as a collectivity, they must make a conscious effort to do so. Armenians can invest a good deal of effort (both in terms of financial cost as well as amount of leisure time) in their participation in the voluntary associations, which are the mainstay of the community, as well as the social functions which these associations sponsor.

The internal differentiation of Armenians and the apparent absence of readily identifiable corporate interests are by no means unique instances in the literature on ethnicity. As David Parkin has noted, ethnic groups like the Luo of Nairobi, who are residentially and occupationally differentiated and compete among themselves, are far more common than those, like the Ibadan Hausa whom Abner Cohen studied, who monopolise certain economic sectors (Parkin, 1978, p. 5). A. L. Epstein pointed out that among American Jews, there were periods in which corporate interests were more readily apparent than in others and yet an identifiable Jewish community persisted in both types of situation (Epstein, 1978). Constantinides, in her study of London Cypriots, also found the concept of the interest group less than immediately applicable to this community, since although clustering in certain boroughs they are still very scattered residentially, and although tending to specialise in catering and dressmaking they do not monopolise these sectors (1977). And similarly Werbner in a study of Manchester Pakistanis found that economic competition was as readily apparent, perhaps even more accentuated, among Pakistani traders as it was between them and non-Pakistanis (1980).

If we continue to insist that the 'political approach' can be generalised as an explanation of ethnic group mobilisation, then how do we deal with such cases as those cited above?' Do we suggest, as A. L. Epstein (1978) has queried that the common interest, in these type of instances, is the existence of the group itself? Or do we accept Light's proposal (1981) that ethnic consciousness may be slumbering in the interval between periods of renewed inter-ethnic confrontation? In short, we can find ourselves in the fairly vacuous theoretical position of arguing that the group exists because it exists, and will promote its common interests when necessary.

If internally differentiated ethnic groups can mobilise and persist, then to suppose that we can ignore the accommodation between these differences, and the development and maintenance of communality or a 'collective ideology' is to box ourselves inevitably into a theoretical corner. The limitations of the ethnic group *qua* interest group approach reinforce Fredrik Barth's point that:

> it is unfruitful to explain a social form, a pattern, directly by hypothesizing a purpose for it. Individual actors and individual management units have purposes and make allocations accordingly [Barth, 1981, p. 108]

Barth, unlike Cohen, focussed his analysis of ethnic groups at the micro- rather than the macro-level. Social patterns were the aggregate result of the choices made by individual actors and the consequences of these choices, intended or not (1981). Instrumentality featured strongly in Barth's analysis of these choices. Actors sought to maximise their advantages in making their respective choices (Paine, 1982a) Thus, the continuity of the ethnic boundary between Pathans and Baluch in Swat, in spite of ongoing transfers of personnel, reflected the advantage for disenfranchised Pathans in identifying themselves with the Baluch (Barth, 1969b). The transfer of personnel, therefore, neither challenged the boundary nor the sets of values operating on either side of it.

The focus in the analysis of ethnicity thus had to be on what was 'socially effective' (Barth, 1969a). Categories were for action and were significantly affected by interaction, rather than contemplation (*ibid*). The difficulty with this emphasis, as Paine has noted, is that Barth's disdain for ideology is not necessarily shared by the people whose behaviour he is seeking to explain:

> [T]he imposition of ideology on ethnographic material by the investigator is one thing; quite another is ideology brought to people by people. [Paine, 1982a, p. 338]

Armenians do discuss and debate the significance and implications of their shared ethnic identity. While the symbolic concepts through which this identity is expressed do not directly determine the actions of individuals, Armenians seek to 'explain' or justify their choices through differing interpretations of these symbols.

The most emotive of these symbols is the view of the Armenian as an exile, brutally expelled from his homeland in Eastern Turkey. This long-standing grievance has been seen as providing a special impetus to the persistence of Armenianness, imparting a moral obligation to perpetuate an identity almost extinguished in the genocide of 1915.

Armenians manipulate this charter concept of a shared moral legacy in a variety of ways. They emphasise it when attempting to assert a commitment to their ethnic identity; they allude to it as an 'explanation' of their individual involvement in the community or in particular activities. Associations use it to argue for their importance, in that they are, respectively, 'doing more for the community'. And it is the basis for a general debate within the community about styles of Armenianness between those subsections and associations which argue for a more militant and vocal agitation for Armenian claims to 'our lands' in Eastern Turkey and those which regard public agitation or any hint of support for organisations (such as the Armenian Secret Army) which espouse armed struggle as irresponsible and unnecessarily provocative.

Therefore, it is in terms of their respective involvements in the London community that Armenians seek to promote and argue for their various interpretations of a shared charter symbol. Barth's stress on action is thus not so much incorrect as incomplete. 'Values', or symbolic concepts and actions, derive meaning and significance from each other. The concepts of exile and past suffering form part of a symbolic framework which Armenians manipulate to make sense of their ethnic identity and community membership. These concepts become more than abstract inchoate forms, and assume immediacy and relevance through these interpretations. These are not isolated and disconnected attempts. Because these symbols are viewed as defining a shared ethnic identity, Armenians seek to persuade one another of their respective views, whether as individuals or as members of associations or factions. The Armenian community is, therefore, more than the aggregate of the choices of individual actors. Its orientation, cohesion, and structure is, at any one point in time, a reflection of a constant push and pull between the different views and stances of its members in the course of their manipulation of shared symbols.

Fredrik Barth and Abner Cohen are in large measure responsible for shaping current anthropological approaches to the field of ethnicity. The distinction between their vantage points is not, however, as Judith Nagata (1986, p. 89) suggested, a distinction between 'circumstantialists' and 'primordialists'. Both Barth and Cohen would probably agree that ethnic groups emerge under certain circumstances and can persist even after the initial conditions prompting their mobilisation have changed. The distinction between them is largely through their entry points into the analysis. Cohen focused his analysis at the level of group interaction and presumed that although specific conditions may change, inter-ethnic distinctions will be perpetuated if competition for politico-economic resources continues on ethnic lines. Barth focused his analysis at the level of individual choices within structural constraints. Ethnic boundaries persisted if the choices of affiliation made by individual actors did not challenge the premises of these distinctions as in the Pathan–Baluch case.

Both of these approaches, however, leave an important gap in the analysis of the process of community building. We do not know from Cohen's emphasis on ethnic communities as corporate groups how the differences of perception and interest between the members are accommodated. We do not know from Barth's emphasis on the individual how these personal choices are synthesised into an ongoing collectivity. In short, neither of these two perspectives provides us with an analytical framework for analysing processes occurring within an ethnic group, i.e. the nature of the relationships between the members and the impact of these processes on the boundary enclosing the community. Between the micro-level of Barth's analysis and the macro-level of Cohen's analysis is a gap which encompasses most of the activities and involvements, i.e. the dynamics of membership in an ethnic community.

Given the predominance of these two approaches, it is perhaps not surprising to find relatively few in-depth ethnographies in the published sociological and anthropological literature on ethnicity. Edited readers abound in this field, but for the most part they provide us with only the outlines of the groupings being described.

In more recent years, the use of symbolic analysis in the study of different forms of community by such scholars as Anthony P. Cohen and David Parkin has focused attention more closely on the management of relations between members of a collectivity. What this work has indicated is that while members of a community, be it ethnic or local, may appear to be saying the same thing, they often attribute different meanings to the same terms or concepts.

> They share the symbol, but do not necessarily share its meanings. Community is just such a boundary-expressing symbol. As a symbol, it is held in common by its members; but its meaning varies with its members' unique orientations to it. In the face of this variability of meaning, the consciousness of community has to be kept alive through manipulation of its symbols. [Cohen, 1985, p. 15]

With this stress, the emphasis on shared values made by Barth, or on common interests made by Abner Cohen can be seen to beg the question of the process of ethnic community development. The very existence of an ethnic grouping suggests, by definition, that its members must have something in common which they perceive as distinguishing them from other collectivities. Otherwise their ethnic identity would remain at the level of categorisation. To say, therefore, that the members of an ethnic group are able to come together because they share common interests or common values is to present us with the form of the symbols used to define community rather than with their meaning. It is, to use Clifford Geertz's terms, 'thin description' rather than 'thick description' (1975), the outline of community rather than its content.

As Anthony Cohen has suggested, to be able to explore the meaning of community, we have 'to look outwards from its core', seeking to understand how the members experience it, and to account for the variable and idiosyncratic meanings they attribute to it (1985, p. 20). The concept of the community as a repository of symbolic forms provides an analytical approach which allows us to link the individual with the ethnic collectivity without requiring consensus or uniformity as a prerequisite for cohesion and communality.

With this kind of approach we would avoid the tendency to treat ethnic boundaries as if they were social phenomena capable of analysis in their own right. A social boundary does not simply happen as a reaction of one system to another. It also reflects the traffic of symbolic meanings occurring within each of these systems or groups, in which the impact of external factors is refracted through the varied experiences of the members.

As Anthony Cohen has pointed out (1982), the kinds of messages which are communicated along the boundary, i.e. the kinds of messages which are communicated to outsiders, tend to be simplifications, glossing over the more subtle and complex interpretations which occur within the boundary. A focus on the inter-ethnic boundary in and of itself gives us only a very partial picture of ethnic groupings.

This is not to say that the internal life of an ethnic community operates in a vacuum. What it does mean is that the account taken of external pressures and perceptions is not uniform throughout the membership. Armenians have come to London from different countries and Armenian communities. Their experiences, both before immigration as well as their experiences within London, have varied. Their perceptions of the outside world vary accordingly and with it their interpretation of the way in which Armenians as a collectivity should manage their relationships with other groups. Many of the internal debates and disagreements which occur within the London Armenian community concern differences in the account taken of external factors. Armenians understand that outsiders have little awareness of the range of views encompassed within their community. The awareness that external perceptions can rebound on the entire membership provides a particular incentive for individuals to seek to shape the image presented to the outside world in ways which conform with their interests and experiences. Thus, associations like the Armenian Cultural Centre in London refuse the use of their facilities to groups which they consider promulgate provocative political views. Associations which are sympathetic to the notion of armed struggle hand out leaflets at community functions urging support for Armenian 'political prisoners', stage public demonstrations, and so on. The focus of this debate concerns the face that the Armenian community should present to the outside world. But this is clearly not a grouping reacting *en masse* to external pressures. What the casual non-Armenian observer sees of this community is but the most visible manifestations of a complex internal debate about how Armenians should manage their position as a minority community within the wider setting of London.

If ethnic groups are, by definition, reacting to other groupings within their immediate socio-economic environment, it is a reaction funnelled through the different experiences and interpretations of its members. The outcome of an ongoing debate within the community in its turn affects the messages which are communicated along the boundary. Thus, what we see at the boundary represents a threshold in a complex traffic of meanings occurring within it.

The present book will, therefore, present the London Armenian community using an analysis that works from the 'core outwards'. It will seek to examine the ways in which Armenians manipulate a shared corpus of symbolic forms to express different views, and it will examine the organisational representation of this variability in a proliferating network of voluntary associations.

The exposition of these aspects will be divided into five main chapters. In Chapter 1 I will deal with the Armenian associations and institutions, trying to chart the organisation of the community and attempting to explore the factors involved in its decentralisation. In this, I will show that the proliferation of associations and their sometimes competitive relationships should not be viewed as signs of the breakdown of the community but as a means by which Armenians seek to become involved in it. In Chapter 2 I will deal with the distinctions that Armenians make between themselves, dealing with some of the major themes of difference which arise, and attempting to show their relevance both to the organisation of the community and to the image of that community in the eyes of Armenians. In Chapter 3 I will set the Armenian community within the wider frame of reference of the way in which Armenians operate in Greater London, exploring the factors which have influenced the dispersal of Armenians and their social anonymity as a collectivity, with its implications for the pattern of interaction between Armenians, the disadvantages of the integration which has been facilitated by this invisibility, and the cultural means which Armenians have sought to develop to maintain their sense of distinctiveness in the face of that integration. In Chapter 4, I will deal with the Armenian charter of exile and lands as a social construct of history which provides meaning for the contemporary location of Armenians, within what they view as the diaspora, and a sense of mission for the perpetuation of 'Armenianness'. In all of these chapters there is the theme of tension between the attempts by Armenians to maintain a low profile as a collectivity on the one hand and the greater visibility and possibly even stigmatisation which is feared to be the consequence of a re-invigoration of the charter of exile and lands. Finally, in Chapter 5 I will examine the methodological implications of anthropological fieldwork within a dispersed urban community.

Chapter 1

Armenian associations and institutions

Introduction

The following chapter provides an overview of the associations which are the mainstay of the London Armenian community. The associations present a bewildering mixture of elements – those specific to the present situation of London Armenians, those reflecting their varied communities of origin, and yet others couched in terms of political rivalries and tensions dating back to the nineteenth century and the Ottoman and Russian Empires.

From one perspective, the associations are simply local organisations sponsoring such undramatic events as dinner dances, teas, literary recitals on Armenian history, and so on. Yet the characterisations of a number of these organisations sometimes appear far removed from the functions performed by them. What are we to make of political movements originating in the Eastern Anatolia and Caucuses of the nineteenth century when applied to associations serving Armenian professionals, entrepreneurs, and students of London in the 1980s?

While the history of political parties such as the Dashnakstitiun, Ramgavar, and Hunchaks acts as a backdrop to contemporary references and claims in London, it is as components of the symbolic repertoire of the Armenian community that these political distinctions become a conceptual framework for Armenian community relations which is recognisable to Armenians of varied nationalities, languages, and lengths of residence in Britain. Like the concept of Armenians as 'exiles' from their homeland (discussed in Chapter 4), the 'political parties' link the Armenian diaspora communities with each other while attributing to them a shared past.

Two major trends are notable in the organisational development of the London Armenian community. The first is the tendency for the proliferation of voluntary associations rather than a concentration of functions and responsibility in one central authority. The reasons for this are both historical and contemporary. Many of the associations being set up in London are branches of associations with which Armenians have been familiar in their respective countries of origin. The London Armenians are

Figure 1: London Armenian voluntary associations

Owner associations

London Armenian Community Church Council (LACCC)
– in charge of St Peter's Church and the Sunday School
– member of Council elected by adult Armenians, resident in Greater London and members of the Armenian Apostolic Church

Church Committee	*Cultural Committee*
runs St Peter's Church	Supervises Sunday School

	School Staff	School Parents' Committee

Armenian House Trust
– runs the Armenian House, a small cultural centre
  Trustees are appointed to the Board

St Sarkis's Church Trust
– manages St Sarkis's Church
  Trustees are appointed for life

Borderline cases

Tekeyan Trust

Society

Armenian General Benevolent Union (AGBU)
– branch of international organisation
– concerned with literary and educational matters
– sometimes identified with Ramgavars

Melkonian Alumni Association
– graduates of the Melkonian, an AGBU school situated on Cyprus

Armenian Scouts Associations
– membership dominated by Iranian Armenians
– reputed to have disproportionate representation of Dashnak supporters among membership.

Non-political associations

Football Club
– largely inactive during period of fieldwork

Ararat Song and Dance Ensemble
– Amateur choir

Anahid Women's Association
– holds monthly coffee meetings

Political associations

Armenian Revolutionary Federation (Dashnakstitiun)

Armenian National Committee
– publishes the magazine *Momentum*

Navarsation Cultural Association
– least controversial of the three
– sponsors such functions as dinner dances including a cultural evening to commemorate the establishment of an Armenian State in 1918.

Armenian Youth Federation
– the least public of the three
– members must be nominated

Popular Movement for ASALA
– ASALA (Armenian Secret Army for the Liberation of Armenia) is credited with underground 'armed struggle' directed against representatives of Turkey and its allies.
– the Popular Movement publishes *Kaytzer* magazine and shorter circulars

Committee in Defence of Armenian Political Prisoners
– advocates on behalf of Armenians imprisoned by Western countries for political 'crimes', often ASALA members

British Armenian Community Association
– small committee
– critical of LACCC
– often associated with the above two organisations although insists on separate identity

essentially reproducing over time the layout, if not the content, of the associational framework of the international Armenian diaspora. But the tendency towards multiplication of voluntary associations is by no means unique to the Armenians. Brotz and Freedman, for example, discuss a similar tendency among Anglo-Jewish associations (Brotz, 1955; Freedman, 1955).

Perhaps the most important factor in the proliferation of Armenian associations is that, being voluntary, they rely on the commitment and labour of individuals who do not gain their livelihood from their services to these organisations. There are, therefore, few serious sanctions which can be applied to independently minded organisers who seek to establish their own offshoot associations. Being unpaid volunteers, most of the organisers of the London Armenian associations carry out their obligations in this capacity in their spare time. There is, therefore, a definite ceiling on the amount of extra work which these people can take on board as new demands are placed on the existing associations for additional services. Although there is a tendency, similar to that described among the Anglo-Jewish community, for some Armenians to attribute status and influence to the officials of certain associations, there is also often (as we shall see in Chapter 3) a considerable reluctance among Armenians to take on new organisational roles because of the time and effort required. In order to accommodate the expanding needs of the community, the organisation of these requirements must, therefore, be spread out over a fairly large number of people. But the necessity for this high level of recruitment in combination with their limited ability to apply sanctions to control their personnel means that as the number of people involved in organisation grows, the likelihood of disagreements and independent action also grows, leading to the process of proliferation of associations. The very multiplication of Armenian associations implies that a large number of people have been successfully attracted towards a commitment to unremunerated service. I would calculate that in the Armenian community, a conservative estimate would be of 200 organisers at any one time serving a clientele of some 1,500 active members, the latter figure including the aforementioned staff. Therefore I consider the proliferation of associations a success story of the involvement and commitment of Armenians towards developing and sustaining their community. This is particularly so when we consider that in such a dispersed population, the voluntary associations and the activities which they sponsor are the life blood of the community. With more organisers, it becomes possible to provide more activities and, hence, more opportunities for Armenians to be involved as participants in their community through their attendance at various gatherings.

The spread of different types of activities becomes additionally important when we consider the heterogeneity of the Armenian community. In this respect as well the decentralisation of the community and the presence of different kinds of associations with a variety of objectives and interests means that potentially more and different kinds of Armenians can be attracted by the eclectic mixture of services and attitudes on offer. It is worthwhile to note here as an example the 'failure' of the London Armenian Community Church Council (LACCC), the supposedly governing body of the community, to attract the youth who are drawn by the more militant and politicised activities of the Popular Movement or the Armenian National Committee. But this brings us to another major trend which will reappear in this chapter: the ambiguity of what is classed as 'political' among the Armenians and the no less significant political debate occurring within the community.

Here again this tendency is due partially to the differing experiences of the Armenians and their uneven exposure to associations operating in their communities of origin which also have branches in London. Armenians carry with them to London an already established but varied baggage of meanings attached to ethnic voluntary associations. The argument over what is political activity is also, importantly, an argument over the course of the future development of the London Armenian community. It is significant because it embodies a fundamental, if not always explicit, disagreement between Armenians about how they can best ensure the health and continuity of their community – through integration or by risking potential confrontation. If politics are, as David Parkin suggests: 'the justifications, exhortations, questioning, and, occasionally, reformulations of a broadly self-defined group's 'moral' code and scale of worthwhileness . . .' (1978, p. 292), then none of the Armenian associations are acting apolitically. But the concept of politics among the Armenians has become associated with public confrontation and militancy, while the non political or apolitical has become associated with an implicit but much more rarely publicly expressed code of collective behaviour. This half-spoken debate runs throughout most of London Armenian community life and will appear not only in this chapter but in succeding ones as well. It represents not so much a reformulation of an Armenian moral code but an ongoing attempt to define it. The lines on which it is run are, therefore, often blurred, containing sometimes contradictory views and, the analysis of it, is an attempt to come to terms with how Armenians view each other, their own ethnic identity, and the implications of these views for the structure and boundary of the London Armenian community.

A sizeable proportion of Armenian gatherings takes place in halls or auditoriums commercially leased by an Armenian association to house a specific Armenian gathering on a particular occasion, and for that occasion only. At the same time several establishments are either owned or leased on a long-term basis by an Armenian association which, in turn, can and does allocate these premises for short-term use exclusively to other Armenian associations. There are only four such venues: the two Armenian Apostolic churches; the Armenian House, which is a small cultural centre; and a local authority school building leased for the Saturday and Sunday of most of the weeks in the school year. These venues I will refer to as the institutions of the Armenian community in London. I do so both because they are the only facilities predictably available to the London Armenian community (and, as such, they serve as the physical landmarks and information clearing houses of the community), and because the primary services which they house (church, general meeting place, and school) are for many Armenians the symbolic landmarks of their community.

The institutions

Two of these venues, St Peter's Church and the school building out of which the Sunday School operates, function under the auspices of the LACCC. According to one of the officers of this council, this association was first established in the mid-1960s as an attempt to diversify control of one of these institutions, the Church. At that time, only one Armenian Apostolic church operated in London, St Sarkis's Church. St Sarkis's Church was established in 1922 mainly through a large donation from Calouste Gulbenkian, a wealthy Armenian businessman. To run the church, Gulbenkian set up a Church Trust Fund, which was supervised by a Board of Trustees whose members were appointed for life. As Mr FS put it:

> At that time, the church was enough. It was a small community then. But then people started coming from Cyrpus, Lebanon and Iran, not the present exodus, I mean, the one before then. Also we had people from Iraq and Syria. They were not happy with the situation . . . At this time, there was Nubar Gulbenkian, Calouste Gulbenkian's son on the board of trustees and people didn't like his attitude to the character of the Armenian people or the Turks. You see, we suffered hardships from the Turks, you may know that and anyone who praises the Turks or is in their favour is unacceptable to us. Maybe this is chauvinist but that is the way it is. And on April 24, we have celebrations and commemorate our dead. This Nubar Gulbenkian, he did not agree with this. He didn't want it to be mentioned in the church. He was chairman of the trustees. Well, Bishop Toumanian, he did mention it and he was sacked. You could say? Yes, they sacked him. Well, we decided to have elections for a community council, a democratically elected body.

The Council, in turn, established a new Armenian Apostolic Church, which is now housed in a church leased from the Church of England, St Peter's. St Sarkis's Church continues to operate under the supervision of its Board of Trustees. Whether or not this account is a fair representation of the events which led to the establishment of the LACCC, it does portray an important aspect of the relationships between London Armenian associations. It indicates the tendency for new demands *vis à vis* existing community associations and institutions to be met by the creation of new associations, a pattern of accommodation which does not necessitate consensus within existing organisational structures. But the proliferation of associations is not matched by a similar rate of proliferation in community institutions.

Shortly before the establishment of the LACCC and the second Armenian Apostolic Church, a small cultural centre, the Armenian House was established, partly with public-subscription but largely with the aid of a large donation from one Armenian, Mr Benelian. A board of Trustees was also set up to administer the fund and maintain the Armenian House. The Armenian House continues at present to be administered by this board of Trustees.

Since the early and mid-1960s when these two institutions were established, only one additional institution has been founded. In 1978, prompted by a large donation from Kevork Tahta of £100,000, the LACCC established the Kevork Tahtayan Sunday School. The Sunday School is housed in a local authority school building leased from Friday evening to Sunday evening most of the weeks in the school year.

This differing rate of increase in institutions and associations is symptomatic of the nature of the associational framework of London Armenian community life. To start a new association only a few members are required; although in order to survive and function effectively the association needs to build up some kind of following. This following can be drawn primarily from only one section of the community, catering to the particular interests of that subgrouping. Some associations cater primarily for youth, others for the middle-aged, some for Western Armenians and others for Iranian Armenians, some for people with particular political interests, others for people with interests in the arts, and so on. However, for a new institution to be established, an association will be required to make possibly substantial material investments as well as provide personnel for organisation requirements, which are likely to be beyond the capacity of its own resources. It then needs either to persuade enough individuals to volunteer contributions of money and/or time, or to persuade other associations to collaborate with it in its venture. In either case it will be unlikely to be successful if it relies only on a narrow following. In short, the establishment of new associations is a response formulated to meet varied demands and interests.

The establishment of a new institution is much more reliant on meeting common interests. But the success of the former trend makes it more difficult for associations to reach a consensus about the formulation of these common interests and makes it less likely that either associations or individuals will accept the authority of one association to run any particular project. The institutions, as they are presently constituted, do attract a cross-section of Armenians but with differing access to and control over the available facilities. For example, the community institutions are used as the venues for gatherings sponsored by other Armenian institutions. It is in the use of these institutions for these kinds of association gatherings that the nature of the power of the owner associations manifests itself. Owner associations are empowered to limit institutional access to other associations. As such, they are unique in the organisational framework of the London Armenian community in their ability to exert their authority over fellow associations, but that authority is extremely limited. As was pointed out previously, the associations conduct a large proportion of the gatherings sponsored by them in venues which are quite separate from the Armenian community. They are, therefore, not dependent on the venues controlled by the owner associations. But the limited authority of the owner associations arouses animosity among the members of those associations which feel discriminated against. It also makes co-operation between associations in projects to establish new institutions more difficult since each is concerned to ensure that the others do not assume this kind of authority *vis à vis* the prospective establishment and themselves.

Organisations which have politicised organisational aims or which wish to sponsor politicised meetings are not permitted to use the facilities of either St Peter's Church annexe or the Armenian House. The definition of which associations or meetings should be classed as 'political' is made ultimately by the LACCC and the Armenian House administrators, who control the allocation of these meeting places. Thus, the Tekeyan Society sponsors a youth group (for those under fifteen) which meets every Saturday at St Peter's Church annexe as well as occasional meetings, at this site, of its adult members. The Armenian General Benevolent Union (AGBU) regularly sponsors small 'literary' meetings at the Armenian House lecture room. The Anahid Women's Association holds monthly meetings of its members in St Peter's Church annexe. The Armenian Scouts association holds weekly meetings of its membership at the school on most Saturdays.

The Armenian Youth Federation, the Armenian National Committee, the British Armenian Community Association, the Popular movement for the Armenian Secret Army for the Liberation of Armenia (ASALA) the Committee for the Defence of Armenian Political Prisoners do not hold meetings at these institutions. However, it should be made clear that members of these associations are not in any way barred from visiting these institutions to avail themselves of the services on offer or the meetings sponsored by other associations.

In spite of the restrictions placed on the use of the Armenian House and St Peter's Church facilities, the 'political' associations do sometimes sponsor institutionally housed gatherings using the auditorium of the school or Gulbenkian Hall. Thus, the Armenian National Committee conducted two lectures on the 'Armenian liberation struggle' at the school auditorium. The British Armenian Community Association, the Committee in Defence of Armenian Political Prisoners, and the Popular Movement for ASALA in conjunction sponsored a meeting on various aspects of the same subject which was held at Gulbenkian Hall. All these meetings were open to the general Armenian public and their intention was to draw as wide an audience as possible.

The institutions as gateways of the community

Only a small proportion of the estimated 1,500 Armenians who participate at some point in the annual round of association-sponsored gatherings in London attend the institutions with any regularity. On most Sundays not many more than a total 300–350 adults and 200 children will be found in attendance at all of the institutional gatherings combined.

Nevertheless, the community institutions remain important focal points for the Armenian community in London. With a population so residentially and occupationally dispersed, the Armenian community institutions (in particular the two churches and the Armenian House, which are reserved exclusively for the use of the Armenian community) are the most visible and permanent identifiers of the presence of an Armenian population in London. They also appear to be traditional landmarks of Armenian communities elsewhere. As Mr VJ, the resident secretary of the Armenian House put it: 'Wherever the Armenians go, first they set up a school and a church and then it spreads from there.' Certainly all of the many Armenian communities from which the Armenians in London originate appear to have had at least a church, and in most cases a school and a community centre as well. In their capacity as familiar and permanent landmarks of the Armenian community, these institutions are able to serve as gateways into the community. As was noted in the Introduction, this is a function which differs from the self-help character normally attributed to ethnic voluntary associations in the literature on this subject. The Armenian institutions play an important function in the establishment and maintenance of contacts between London Armenians, but they have only a small and, at best, an incidental role to play in the integration of Armenians into the wider economic, social, and political system which encompasses the community.

A newly arrived Armenian in London who has few previously established contacts with Armenians in London and no knowledge of the activities of the Armenian associations in this city can be fairly confident that if an active community does exist it will have an operating Armenian church:

> I remember that first Sunday we went to the church. We looked it up in the phone book and they told us about the Haidoon [Armenian House]. That first time we went to the Haidoon, it was very nice. I went every Sunday because I had nothing to do really.

The gatherings at the church or the Armenian House can provide initial personal contacts with other Armenians as well as information about the

activities of other Armenian associations. As newcomers develop the contacts, both personal and associational, to which these institutions introduce
them, they are able to be far more selective about the manner of their participation in the London Armenian community and their dependence on the
institutions is inevitably weakened. Ms A no longer attends the Armenian
House regularly although she continues to visit the church. Her most frequent visits are to the Sunday School in which two of her friends are
involved, as staff and client, respectively. Similarly, Mr H, a 17-year-old
Armenian male of Iranian origin, visited St Sarkis's Church regularly during
his first summer in England and thereby established a number of friendships
with other Armenians in London. By the time I conducted my fieldwork two
years later, Mr H was a rare visitor to the church. He had, however, joined
the Scouts association as a member and his involvement with the Armenian
community at present is primarily through the activities of this organisation.

The institutions not only provide a framework for new relationships to be
initiated they can also, at times, provide the means for previously established
relationships to be reactivated. This role is particularly apparent in the Easter
and Christmas services at the two churches. Many Armenians who would
not normally attend Sunday church services do visit one of the two churches
on Easter, Palm Sunday, or Christmas. Approximately 500–600 Armenians
attended St Sarkis's and St Peter's Church combined both on Easter Sunday
and Palm Sunday. The drawing power of the churches on these occasions can
provide Armenians with an opportunity to meet acquaintances or friends
with whom they have lost contact or whom they have rarely met during the
rest of the year. For some Armenians at least, this opportunity constitutes an
explicit and important part of their motivation for attending church on
Easter and Christmas. As Ms M explained to me, 'Even now we go to the
church on Christmas and Easter. We don't go because of religion but because
its Armenian and that's when I'll see everyone who's come from abroad.' In
short, although only a proportion of the Armenians participating in
Armenian-sponsored activities attend the institutions with any regularity,
many more have been served by them at some point of their stay in London.

The owner associations

As was described earlier, there are three owner associations: the London
Armenian Community Church Council, the Armenian House Trust, and St
Sarkis's Trust. Trustees are appointed to the latter two bodies. The members
of the LACCC Central Committee, on the other hand, are not only elected
but they have a unique position among Armenian associations in London in
that they view themselves as elected by the entire Armenian community in the
city. This view or claim is problematic in that it raises the issue of which

population constitutes the Armenian community in London. Is it that population which participates in association-sponsored gatherings? Is it the entire population of Armenians resident in London? And if so, what is the size of that population? The last is not an easily answered question since Armenians are distinguished on British census records according to their country of birth. Thus, they will be listed as having originated from Turkey, Syria, Iran, Cyprus, Lebanon, Egypt, Britain, and so on, making it virtually impossible to pick out Armenians as an identifiable and quantifiable category. Should Armenians who do not intend to settle in Britain be included in the community's population? And what of the Armenians who participate in the association-sponsored gatherings taking place within the metropolitan borders of Greater London but who are not resident within these boundaries?

The paucity of precise census statistics for the numbers of Armenians resident in London or even in Britain allows figures for this population to be expanded or contracted depending on the argument put forth. The use of population figures as malleable tools for reflecting differing points of view is particularly apparent in estimates of the size of the Armenian population that participates in community activities.

When Mr D, a former officer of the Tekeyan association, wanted to explain why the newspaper of this association had only 150 subscribers, he told me:

> Really, my wife said a very interesting thing the other day. She said that our community is not really 12, or 15,000 but 300 people because when you go to the functions or to the church, you see always the same people.

Mrs D, is a member of St Peter's Church choir. In her own description of rates of participation in the community, she used only the church and its congregation as a measuring stick. When Mr O wanted to emphasise the individualism of Armenians, he told me:

> The associations just mushroom. There must be some 22 associations in London. When you consider that there are 10,000 Armenians in London, 5,000 of which don't care about the Armenian community at all; which leaves 5,000, 40 per cent of which are children, and the rest are making these associations. The Armenians are individualists.

Similarly, when Mr L wanted to emphasise that only a minority of Armenians in London participates in the community, he estimated that no more than 1,000 ever come to the gatherings 'even though they say there are 10,000 Armenians in London'.

At the 1980 election to the Community Council, 1,038 voters were registered on the electoral list of this association, of whom 846 actually cast their votes. Criticism of these procedures has focused on the requirements for eligibility to vote or to stand as a candidate in the 1980 elections to the Council. Critics, such as Ms M, a member of one of the associations classed as 'political' by the LACCC, claim that these regulations unfairly exclude large numbers of Armenians in London from participation in the elections. In making her criticism, Ms M used the figure of 12,000 Armenians in London, contrasting it with the figure of registered voters. In referring to one of the LACCC central committee members, Ms M said that:

> She was elected by a thousand people out of 12,000.
>
> R: But the others could have voted if they wanted to.
>
> M: No, they couldn't because there are so many regulations. You have to live in the Greater London Council area which I didn't because I lived in Surrey. You have to be a British citizen or permanent resident which many Armenians don't have. All these rules and regulations are made to fit those Armenians who have been here for twenty years. I couldn't even stand for the church council because I lived in Surrey.

On another occasion, however, Ms M put the number of Armenians in London at 10,000, of which she said only 3,000–4,000 were actually active in the community.

Ms M was not the only critic. According to a report published in one of the London Armenian journals shortly after the 1980 elections, a 'significant number' of Armenians had been excluded by the regulations to which Ms M had referred. Considerable resentment and bitterness had been caused by their exclusion. Whether or not there had, in fact, been such a reaction, the Community Council has since decided to alter at least one of the regulations so that Armenians who are not permanent residents in Britain will be eligible to vote or to stand in the next election.

In this discussion of numbers Armenians are not simply making a distinction between a population of Armenians and the community of Armenians in London, for this distinction is regularly confounded by the Armenians themselves. On the face of it there would appear to be a contradiction between the claims of some LACCC officers that they are responsible for a number ranging from 10,000–15,000, and the some 1,000 registered on their electoral list. But ultimately this and the acceptance by the LACCC of criticism that it has unfairly excluded Armenians from the electoral list is, in fact, an acceptance of the right of each Armenian, however marginal to the activities of the community, whether he or she be of part-Armenian ancestry (as a number of the total figure of Armenians resident in England certainly are, and are known to be by the Armenians) to participate in the community. But clearly not all Armenians who are invested with this right choose to exercise it. And this is where the argument over numbers assumes its importance. If there are many Armenians who are in no way involved in the community's affairs, then something must be wrong. As we shall see, that something wrong may be attributed to apathy or the excessive demands that the associations make on a person's time and financial resources. But when critics of the LACCC contrast the estimates of the London Armenian population and the numbers listed on the LACCC's electoral list, they are saying that part of what is wrong is the manner in which the LACCC itself operates. It is no coincidence that the people making this criticism most strongly are members of, or supporters of, the politicised associations which have limited access to the institutions governed by the LACCC. It is not surprising that within the context of the election debates they should attempt to emphasise what they see as the LACCC's deliberate attempts to limit the numbers involved in the community. But these people, like most other Armenians actively engaged in community activities, are well aware that this is not the whole problem. For ultimately those wasted numbers haunt all those involved in association-sponsored gatherings. They are the spectre of what is seen as a potential assimilation which could finally bleed the community dry. The strategies which Armenians have developed to counter this threat will form the basis of the discussion in a later chapter.

The bishop and the church

A newly elected LACCC must be confirmed by the Supreme Catholicos of the Armenian Church in Etchmiadzin. There are two catholicosates of the Armenian Apostolic Church, one seated in Etchmiadzin, Soviet Republic of Armenia, whose head holds the title of 'Supreme Catholicos of all Armenians'; the other the Cilician catholicosate, which has been seated since 1929 in Antilias, Lebanon. Each of these catholicosates has responsibility for certain Armenian dioceses. The London Diocese falls under the authority of the Etchmiadzin catholicosate and, therefore, a local Council which seeks as an important part of its mandate the management of an Armenian Apostolic Church in London requires the approval of the Supreme Catholicos. Besides the fifteen elected members of the Council, the London representative of the Catholicos, the bishop, is formally also a member of the Central Committee. Although the bishop does not run for office in Council elections, the council does have some say in his appointment. When in 1981, the incumbent bishop decided to resign from his post and return to Etchmiadzin, the Supreme Catholicos nominated two candidates for the vacancy. The Council was empowered to make a selection for the post from this short list.

I heard few criticisms of the bishop's performance of the religious rituals although, according to Mr S, complaints do occur about the form of the abridgement of services. Most of the lengthy Armenian Apostolic services have been abridged by priests working in non-monastic communities. This abridgement has not been uniform, so that Armenians from different communities have had different experiences of church services. According to Mr S:

> Some of the older people, for example, those from Constantinople, they're used to seeing it done in a certain way and they get very upset when they see it done

differently. They tend to think that the priests are no longer serving the community properly; that they don't care any more; they are just serving their own interest. But this is not the case. It is just out of necessity.

The bishop is also perceived as having a role to play in the wider community and I did hear several complaints that the bishop was not meeting the expectations held of him in this regard. The bishop introduces newcomers into the community and may even be called upon to provide them with assistance in settlement. Nor is this unique to the Armenian community in London. When Ms U prepared to leave France, where she was born and raised, for England, her father offered to write a letter on her behalf to the bishop, 'him being the head of the community. I'll write him a letter in Armenian asking him to protect you.' What is curious about this case is that Ms U, a woman of mixed Armenian and French parentage, is Catholic. Neither she nor her father saw any discrepancy between her membership of the Catholic Church and her approach for assistance to the bishop of an Armenian Apostolic Church. Similarly, when I approached an Armenian resident in Manchester for information about introductory contacts in the London community, I was advised to go and first see the bishop 'because he is the head of the community'. The position of the bishop as titular head of the community is confirmed by his office as President of the LACCC. But how is the bishop to maintain contact with this community? If the bishop perhaps does not, as Ms M and Ms T complained, frequently visit Armenians in their homes, he is a regular participant in public gatherings of eighty or more Armenians although he does not attend 'political' gatherings.

For most Armenians, contact with their bishop is limited to their encounters with him in these kind of gatherings or in the church. Clearly this kind of public contact must be necessitated by the residential dispersal and relative anonymity of the London Armenian population. But, as in the case of the LACCC's electorate, the discrepancy between a formally widely inclusive definition of the bishop's flock and the more limited audience actually approached can lead to the perception that some Armenians are being unfairly excluded. The brunt of both Ms M and Ms T's criticisms was that the bishop had to be asked to come rather than initiating the visit himself.

The Sunday School

The Church is not the only concern of the LACCC. As was pointed out earlier, the Council was responsible for the establishment of a Sunday School in 1978. To deal with this institution, the Council also has a special sub-committee, the Cultural Committee. Although the Cultural Committee is the body ultimately responsible for the school, most of the school's administration, curriculum, and funding is organised by its staff and Parents Committee.

The thirteen members of the Parents Committee are theoretically elected to their position by all the parents of the pupils enrolled in the school. However, at the 1982 committee elections, only forty parents were present even though 200 students were registered in the school at that time. The curriculum's focus, overall, is on the instruction of the Armenian language, both written and oral. To a more limited extent, there is education about the significance of Armenian historical events as well as Armenian national holidays.

The non-owner associations

The political parties

It is not possible to analyse the structure of the associational framework of the London Armenian community without some reference to the Armenian political parties. Since the mass deportations of Armenians from Turkey in 1915, three main political parties have been operating in Armenian communities: the Armenian Revolutionary Federation (or Dashnakstitiun), the Armenian Democratic Party (or Ramgavar), and the Hunchakian Revolutionary Party. All three have their beginnings in Armenian nationalist and revolutionary movements of the late nineteenth and early twentieth centuries which, although often originating in Transcaucasia, sought primarily to address themselves to the situation of Armenians living in Turkey in the last days of the Ottoman Empire.

The first Armenian party to be established was the Armenakan Party, which was founded in Van in the autumn of 1885. The Armenakan Party has not survived but was followed in 1887 by the first Armenian revolutionary party, the Hunchakian Party, which later operated in Armenian diaspora communities. The Hunchakian Revolutionary Party was founded in Geneva by seven Russian Armenian students (Nalbandian, 1963, p. 104; Walker, 1980, pp. 126–30). Its platform was socialist and separatist, dedicated, Hovannisian says, 'to the re-establishment of an Armenian state within the structure of the future world society' (Hovannisian, 1967, p. 16). In 1890, the Hunchaks joined in a coalition of various Armenian groups to form the Federation of Armenian Revolutionaries, in Tiflis, the present capital of the Soviet Socialist Republic of Georgia. The Dashnakstitiun, in its early days, was also socialist, joining the Second Socialist International in 1907 (Atamian, 1955, p. 105), but, while advocating political and economic reforms for the Armenians in Turkey, it did not call for a secession from the Ottoman Empire (Nalbandian, 1963, p. 169; Hovannisian, 1967, p. 16). The Hunchakians withdrew from the Federation shortly after its inception, and at its first general congress in 1892 the Federation was re-formed as the Armenian Revolutionary Federation, the name it still holds (Nalbandian, 1963, p. 166).

Both these parties accepted the resort to violence and armed force as a means of effecting their political aims. The Ramgavar party, which was established in 1908, also focused its attention on the Armenians of Turkey, but unlike its two predecessors eschewed revolutionary aims and militaristic means.

In line with their militant tactics, the Hunchaks encouraged an armed uprising of the Armenian populace in Sassoun, Turkey, in 1894, organised the Kum Kapu and Bab Ali demonstrations, as well as other similar activities. The Dashnaks organised the seizure of the Ottoman Bank in Constantinople in 1896, skirmishes with Kurds and Turks, another uprising at Sassoun in 1904, and so on (Nalbandian, 1963, pp. 118, 120; Atamian, 1955, pp. 108–10). Many of these activities were followed by severe retaliation from the Turkish authorities. Much of the writings of Armenian historians on this period are concerned with trying to establish the degree of cause and effect between the activities of the revolutionaries and the killings of Armenians by Turkish and Kurdish forces in the reign of the last Sultan of the Ottoman Empire, Abdul Hamid. However, all are agreed that the mass killings and deportations which occurred under the subsequent Ittahadist regime were part of a cold and premeditated strategy which required no incitement from Armenian groups.

This ongoing discussion has important implications in two spheres. First, it is concerned to refute the claims of Turkish sources that the regimes of Abdul Hamid and the Ittahadists killed and deported Armenians to counter the rebellion of these subjects. Secondly, differing perceptions among Armenians about the consequences of the activities of the revolutionaries coloured subsequent differences in attitudes to overt and militant politicisation in diaspora Armenian communities.

Activities like the seizure of the Ottoman Bank by Dashnaks, and the Kum Kapu and Bab Ali demonstrations led by the Hunchaks, were designed to attract the attention of the European powers and interest them in the situation of the Turkish Armenians. Supplications to these powers came from less militant forces as well as from the Church hierarchy in Constantinople and the Holy See of Etchmiadzin. Programs for reform were drawn up by the European powers in such agreements as the Treaty of Berlin, the Reform Act of October 1895, and the Reform Act of February 1914. However, there was little concerted effort behind these programmes and most of the reforms proposed in them were never implemented. The notion of the Armenians abandoned by the Europeans to their fate at the hands of the Turks is pervasive. It is the crux of the self-help arguments of contemporary militant groups and forms much of the basis of their criticisms of older Armenian political parties.

In the aftermath of the deportations and killings of 1915, thousands of Armenians fled to Transcaucasia. With the fall of the Tsarist Empire in 1917, the Transcaucasian provinces, including Armenia, initially strove to co-operate with the central provisional government and Petrograd Soviet of Workers and Soldiers Deputies. But the takeover of the Central Government by the Bolsheviks in that same year eventually led to the declaration of independence by Transcaucasia in April 1918 (Hovannisian, p. 106). Continuing military pressure from Turkey during this period and the differing interests of the Georgians, Armenians, and Tartars quickly led to the collapse of the Transcaucasian Federation in May 1918, and the establishment of three separate independent republics of Georgia, Azerbaijan, and Armenia. In Armenia the government of the fledgling republic was overwhelmingly dominated by the Armenian Revolutionary Federation.

The republic had severe problems: it had to deal with the needs of the thousands of refugees from the eastern provinces of Anatolia; food shortages; epidemics; and continuing military conflict with Turkey. By 1920 the Dashnaks succumbed to this pressure and signed over the government to the Bolsheviks. Armenia eventually became, in a smaller form than under the independent republic, what it is today: a Soviet Socialist Republic. The Dashnaks ceased to operate in Soviet Armenia, but continued to operate, as did the Hunchaks and Ramgavars, in diaspora Armenian communities.

Sharp divergences developed between the parties over the relationship of the diaspora communities to Soviet Armenia. The Hunchaks and the Ramgavars, for different reasons, accepted the status of Armenia as a member republic of the USSR, and supported its development, at least in the short term, within this framework. The Dashnakstitiun, which became increasingly 'pro-Western', did not (Walker, 1980, p. 365). These differences became sharpened and at times highly antagonistic as the Cold War heightened in the 1950s, even erupting into violence, as when an Armenian cleric in the USA, who was suspected of pro-Soviet sympathies was murdered during a church service (Lang and Walker, 1978, p. 10). The differences also came to have an influence on the structure of the Armenian Apostolic Church.

Both Armenian catholicosates are elected by a conclave that includes laymen as well as clerics. In 1956, at the height of the Cold War, elections were held to appoint a new catholicos for the Cilician see. The Cilician conclave was dominated by delegates who supported the Dashnakstitiun. The Dashnakstitiun, in turn, felt that the Etchmiadzin see could not function independently of the USSR and, hence, should not operate as the ultimate authority of the Armenian Apostolic Church. The Cilician elections ended in the election of a Dashnak-supported candidate. After 1956 a new constitution was adopted by the Cilician seat which no longer accepted the traditional division of dioceses between the two sees but instead:

> laid down that if a diocese hitherto under the jurisdiction of Etchmiadzin desired to become attached to Antilias, it would be accepted by it. [Walker, 1980, p. 369]

This division within the Church remains until today, but more recently concerted efforts have been made to foster co-operation between the two sees and to encourage a reconciliation. In London today the division does not appear to be the subject of much concern. Although the dioceses of Cyprus, Beirut, Damascus, and others in the Middle East are under the jurisdiction of the Cilician Catholicos while the London diocese is under the jurisdiction of Etchmiadzin this does not appear problematic for Cypriot Armenians or those from the Levant who appear to accept the position of the bishop appointed by the 'Catholicos of all Armenians'.

The Dashnakstitiun itself has considerably modified its stand towards Soviet Armenia. In London its supporters also now speak with pride of the achievements of Soviet Armenia in urbanisation, industrialisation, agriculture, and so on. But the divide which did exist over attitudes towards the USSR and Soviet Armenia no doubt contributed to the development of a common characterisation of the Dashnakstitiun as the most right-wing of Armenian parties, albeit its beginnings as a socialist revolutionary party. It alone continues today to commemorate the anniversary of the establishment of the independent Armenian republic and it continues to mount occasional criticisms of the Soviet systems and the policies of the Soviet government in Soviet Armenia.

Within the diaspora the political parties took on new roles. They set up branches to deal with education, youth movements, literary societies, recreational societies, and so on. Some of these developed a complex infrastructure with branches in communities all over the world, operating without formal reference to the political movements from which they had sprung. However, these offshoots are still identified with these parties, although it is not always clear from such references whether the affiliation continues to be active. Thus, in London, when Armenians talk of the political parties, it is not immediately clear whether they are referring to the party *per se*, or to associations identified with these parties. Although when describing the political structure of the Armenian diaspora Armenian speakers in London will usually refer to all three political parties, in fact, the Hunchakian Revolutionary Party appears to be virtually inactive in this community. It sponsors no activities under this name nor are there any associations in London identified with it. Its name appeared only once, in any formal sense, during my fieldwork period, on a list of associations in London jointly sponsoring a commemoration of 24 April, the anniversary of the 1915 Genocide.

Apart from its supporters, London Armenians almost never mention in such general descriptions a more recently developed political movement. But this movement does indirectly operate through its own set of affiliates and supporters in many communities, as well as in London. In January 1975 the 'Armenian Secret Army for the Liberation of Armenia' (ASALA) was launched. Its aims are the liberation of Eastern Anatolia from Turkish control and the establishment of an independent Armenian State which would eventually unify the 'historic Armenian homeland', including lands in the USSR, Iran, as well as in Eastern Turkey. The ASALA is engaged in what it terms an 'armed struggle', believing that only by the use of force can Armenians achieve their 'liberation'. It has therefore, since its launch in 1975 been involved in a number of attacks on Turkish diplomats and officials outside Turkey and, in 1982, in an attack in Turkey itself. In the summer of 1983 a wave of attacks by such underground Armenian organisations was staged in European capitals. Such attacks appeared to indicate the development of splinter Armenian organisations which advocate 'armed struggle'. This development, in conjunction with the ferocity and concentration of the 1983 attacks, undoubtedly had some influence on London supporters of organisations like the ASALA, but since it occurred after fieldwork had already been completed these events and their consequences for London Armenians cannot be reported. Hence, the description of ASALA as it relates to the London Armenians is confined to the period ending in the autumn of 1982.

The ASALA is critical of its political predecessors, accusing them of failing to deal with the problems of the Armenian people (as defined by it) and of dependence on, and collaboration with, the powers which betrayed the Armenians in the past, i.e. 'Western imperialists'. Thus, they represent themselves as the logical and necessary political alternative to the political parties.

The hiving-off of associations from the major political movements and the diversification of functions of these branches which has occurred in Armenian communities since 1915 has made the issue of politicisation in the Armenian community of London a very complex one. Both the Ramgavar Party and the Dashnak Party operate in London through offshoot associations. Thus, a person is usually not a member of the party *per se,* but a member of an association identified with, or considered to be an affiliate of, the party. Although the members of the associations differ in the degree to which they themselves identify their party links, in none of the cases is the link publicly emphasised or elaborated on, and in one case in particular (the Tekeyan Association), no formal recognition is made by the association itself of any party links.

In classifying the associations for description, I use those categories which I believe best reflect the distinctions that Armenians themselves make between types of associations. But because these distinctions are often ambivalent and reflect very subtle gradations from characterisations of non-political to those viewed as unambiguously political, the categories used in the following section are necessarily to some extent arbitrary and oversimplified. They are not intended, however, as a definition of the Armenian associational framework in London (apart from the owner associations already described), but simply as a tool for organising its presentations.

The non-political associations

Only three associations have never, in my experience, been attributed a political stance: the Anahid Women's Association; the Ararat Song and Dance Ensemble; and the Football Club. During the time I was in London the Football Club sponsored only one major event: a concert by a popular Armenian singer. It is not an association which is frequently brought up in conversation between Armenians, and consequently I have very little information on its operations. The Ararat Song and Dance Ensemble is an amateur choir (despite the 'dance' in its title), which participates in most of the amateur musical and literary recitals put on by the owner associations, although it does not independently sponsor such recitals.

The Anahid Women's Association is the best known of these three and, hence, the most likely to meet either criticism or praise. Formally the association has 200 members, although participants at its monthly meetings rarely number over thirty, the latter figure largely constituting a core group of regular participants. These montly meetings are usually held every second Thursday of the month in the annexe of St Peter's Church. The association is headed by a committee of nine women, elected by its members yearly. Most of the women who come to these monthly gatherings are middle-aged to elderly, with a high proportion of Iranian Armenians, although Western Armenian speakers are also present.

Aside from the meetings organised for its members, the association regularly sponsors gatherings directed towards a wider audience. During the period of my fieldwork these included a lavish New Year's Eve Dinner Dance with tickets selling at £18 a person, and a simpler tea held to commemorate Mother's Day. Most of the association's income comes from these functions as well as from the interest on its deposit account. The fund-raising of the Anahid is principally directed towards an initiative, under the overall aegis of the LACCC, to establish a new community centre.

At the 1982 elections to the Anahid steering committee, the degree to which the association's fund-raising should be directed towards this purpose was the subject of some heated discussion. Several women argued that the funds raised annually should not be diverted towards any other sources (with the exception of the administrative costs of the association) but should be reserved for the one project. Others argued that the committee could not be so limited in its handling of the association's income but had to be free to allocate at least part of these funds where the need was felt to be great. These women particularly emphasised the obligation that Armenian associations had towards the assistance of students in financial distress. Doubts were also raised about the structure of the community centre fund-raising project. Doubts about the LACCC's handling of the fund-raising campaign were voiced more explicitly in a private interview with one of the officers of the

Anahid. Mrs Z and her husband, both Iranian Armenians, felt that the LACCC was trying to appropriate a project which it had not initiated. According to Mr Z, several Armenians had already privately collected large sums of money towards the establishment of a new community centre when the LACCC decided to take over the management of this project:

> But a club had nothing to do with them. They are a *Church* Council! They were elected to take care of the church, not of the club. When they were elected, there wasn't any club. These people already have the money. Let them build the club and you take care of the church. But no, it has to be under them.

Thus, although the fund-raising of the Anahid continues unquestioned in itself, there is by no means consensus among its members about the final destination of the sums collected or the ultimate administrator of these funds.

Anahid is praised by some Armenians, such as Mr FS, an officer of the LACCC, for being one of the most active of the Armenian associations in London in sponsoring public gatherings. But some more militant members of associations such as the Popular Movement and the British Armenian Community Association as well as the Armenian National Committee characterise the Anahid as a collection of 'rich, bourgeois' women, whose dinner dances, teas, and coffee circles contribute very little of any significance to the community. Whatever the view of its work, the Anahid is in the rather rare position of being one of the Armenian associations, defined as non-political by Armenians of almost every political persuasion.

The borderline cases

This is not the case with most of the Anahid's associational counterparts, even those defining themselves as cultural or educational societies, such as the Tekeyan Cultural Society, the Armenian General Benevolent Union (AGBU), the Melkonian Alumni Association, and the Armenian Scouts Association. For the most part, these associations are not attributed a political stance in terms of the actual activities that they sponsor but in terms of their imputed affiliation with one of the Armenian political parties.

It is generally agreed among Armenians that the Tekeyan Society is equivalent to the Ramgavar party. The chairman of the Tekeyan society made no mention of this affiliation in his description of the association. He compared the Tekeyan to the AGBU, which he said was similar 'except we put more of an emphasis on cultural matters'.

The Tekeyan is a branch of an international organisation with headquarters in the USA and Lebanon. In London the association has two separate agencies, the Tekeyan Society and the more recently formed Tekeyan Trust. Most of the members of the steering committee of the society are elected by its membership, which officially numbers approximately 200. On the other hand, the Trustees of the Tekeyan trust hold their positions for their lifetime.

The Trust is formally responsible for the publication of the *Erebouni* monthly periodical, sold by subscription. The Tekeyan has initiated a youth movement for children aged five to fifteen years with an emphasis on painting and music instruction. This youth society meets every Saturday in St Peter's Church annexe, thus overlapping with the meeting times of the Armenian Scouts Association, which also sponsors weekly activities directed at this age group.

Like the Anahid, the Tekeyan sponsors at least one lavish dinner dance annually as well as showings of Armenian films, and, in 1982, it persuaded a dance company from Soviet Armenia visiting England for a dance festival to perform for the Armenian community under its aegis.

The Tekeyan has funds of £100,000 in a bank deposit account (hence the Tekeyan Trust), raised from voluntary donations as well as fund-raising activities. Similar to the Anahid, the money accumulated in the shape of the Tekeyan Trust is primarily earmarked for the development of a new community centre, but unlike the Anahid the Tekeyan feels able and prepared to move on with this project on its own. The chairman of the association rejected the LACCC's project as unrealistic in its collection target of £1,000,000. The Tekeyan, he asserted, had been the first association to start collecting money for a new community centre and would soon be in a position to establish one. As for the other associations concerned with this project:

> I'm sure that when we start it, the other associations will come round us and join in. But in the meantime, we have to start it because there is a need for this centre.

Thus, in this vision of the community centre project, it would be the Tekeyan and not the LACCC or the Anahid which would be the prime mover.

Like the Anahid, the Tekeyan is none the less characterised by critics from the Armenian Youth Federation, the British Armenian Community Association (BACA), etc. as a collection of rich bourgeois 'who don't do anything'. But this characterisation is not wholly a product of the Tekeyan's activities in London. It is inextricably tied up with a view of the Tekeyan as an international organisation and with that organisation's identification with the Ramgavar Party. In *The Armenian Community,* published in 1955, Atamian gave his view of the historical development of Armenian political movements from the nineteenth century to their role in communities in the USA during the 1950s. Atamian, who apparently favoured the Dashnaks, launched a vitriolic attack on the Ramgavar, which he described as the party of 'the Armenian bourgeosie'. In 1982, in London, Mr TC, a member of the Armenian Youth Federation, a Dashnak affiliate, applied the term 'capitalist bourgeois' to the Ramgavars.

The identification of the Tekeyan with the Ramgavars is pervasive at every level. An LACCC officer listing Armenian associations in London, when reaching the name of the Tekeyan, paused and explained 'but now we get to the political parties'.

The Ramgavar Party internationally appears to have maintained little separate identity from its offshoots. In London the Ramgavar Party itself is virtually non-existent. In 1981–2 no gatherings or publications were sponsored under the name of Ramgavar. References to the Ramgavar as a party functioning in London are always, in fact, references to the Tekeyan. But, as we saw in the case of Anahid, activities such as dinner dances, films or operettas, dances, or song performances, are not considered to be clearly politicised. Thus, although in general descriptions the Ramgavar is still treated as an independent entity, a political party with a particular political stance, in more specific references to the present situation even harsh critics of the Ramgavar will admit that 'it is no longer really a political party'. Where the equivalence is made between the Tekeyan and the Ramgavar party it does not necessarily, therefore, imply a perception of the Tekeyan as a politicised association.

The Armenian General Benevolent Union (AGBU), to which Mr HM, the chairman of the Tekeyan society compared his association, is also sometimes identified with the Ramgavar Party, although much more rarely. In fact, the establishment of the AGBU, in Egypt during 1906, preceded the establishment of the Ramgavar Party by two years. According to Ms JV, whose husband Mr LR serves on the AGBU committee in London, the AGBU

> is not supposed to be political, but it always had this image of being Ramgavar. That is why in 1960, it formed the Tekeyan which is explicitly Ramgavar to try to separate itself from its Ramgavar image. But the heads of the AGBU still tend to be Ramgavars.

The AGBU is an international organisation known for the schools it has established in Armenian communities throughout the Middle East – with the exception of Iran – as well as in the USA, for its literary publications, and for its financial assistance to Armenian students in need. Although internationally the AGBU, is occasionally imbued with a Ramgavar-oriented image, its London branch is treated, where it is mentioned, as a non-political organisation with interests restricted to 'cultural and educational matters'.

The London branch of the AGBU has been responsible primarily for sponsoring regular (almost every month) literary meetings at which books and journals are reviewed, and the work and background of Armenian poets and novelists discussed. During 1981–2 it sponsored two dinner dances, one tea party, and apparently it has also been known to occasionally sponsor concerts.

A number of people who are regular participants in the AGBU monthly literary meetings are alumni of the Melkonian School, an AGBU day and boarding school in Cyprus. Several times a year, the Melkonian Alumni association sponsors reunions for its graduates living in London and their families and friends.

There is in fact a general attribute which characterises all three of the associations listed so far in this category (the Tekeyan, the AGBU, and the Melkonian Alumni Association) namely that their membership tends to be dominated by Western Armenian speakers. This is not the case with the Armenian Scouts Association. The Scouts Association is dominated in membership and leadership by Eastern Armenian speakers or more specifically Iranian Armenians. Also, unlike the former three associations, which are identified with the Ramgavar Party (either directly as in the case of the Tekeyan, or more indirectly as in the case of the AGBU and, hence, by implication, the Melkonian), the Armenian Scouts Association is identified with the Dashnakstitiun.

Like the AGBU and the Tekeyan, the Armenian Scouts Association is an international organisation with branches in Armenian communities worldwide with its headquarters in Lebanon. The London branch of the Armenian Scouts Association was established in 1979 by a group of young Iranian Armenian adults who had been members of a similar association in Iran. In London the Scouts Association caters for youths from the age of six years up to and including adults in their twenties. The association has 180 formally registered members, only fifty of whom are in the six to sixteen age category; the majority are over the age of sixteen. Like Scouts associations elsewhere, a strong emphasis is placed on camping and camping skills, but emphasis is also placed on the use of the Armenian language as the medium of communication in Scout activities, observance of Armenian religious holidays, and anniversaries of historical events. Thus, the Association sponsors activities for its members commemorating, among other anniversaries, 24 April and Independence Day, i.e. the anniversary of the establishment of the short-lived independent Armenian Republic in 1918. As I pointed out earlier, only Dashnak associations or associations identified with this party formally mark this occasion with public ceremony.

If the activities sponsored by the Scouts are not in themselves considered to have an explicitly politicised content, organisers of the association are often considered to be supporters of the Dashnakstitiun Party. Like the Tekeyan and the AGBU, the Scouts Association continues to be identified with a political party but at the same time continues to be treated for all intents and purposes as apolitical itself. However, there is a qualitative difference between the two.

Where the Tekeyan, particularly, is equated with the Ramgavars, this equivalence mutes the political character of the latter, but the Scouts Association is identified with a party which maintains a separate identity, if not necessarily a separate infrastructure, both within London and outside it. There is no question in the minds of Armenians that the Dashnakstitiun is a 'political party' unlike the Ramgavars. Futhermore, the identification of the Tekeyan and the AGBU with the Ramgavars has a history outside the London Armenian community in Armenian communities elsewhere. According to some of the most vociferous critics of the Scouts Association, when it was first established in London it was expected to operate as an apolitical association and only latterly did its identification with the Dashnakstitiun develop. Hence, where the identification of the Scouts is made with the Dashnakstitiun, it usually sounds an accusatory note. There is the implication that the Association is unfairly allowing political affiliations to be introduced where they do not properly belong. The controversy over this affiliation may account for the tendency to imply the Scouts Association's imputed political affiliation rather than for it to be openly stated, whereas the Ramgavar–Tekeyan identification commonly occurs in reference to this association without any hint of controversy.

The political associations

The Armenian National Committee, the Armenian Youth Federation, and the Navarsatian Cultural Society are more explicitly affiliated with the Dashnakstitiun Party. But here again definitions of what is political and what is the political line espoused by any one association are fluid. In part, this is due to the tendency to identify politicisation with particular styles of presentation, i.e. with overt and public discussion of political stances and not necessarily with the identification of a particular association or group as 'political'. But, in part, this is also due to the wider Armenian setting of which the London community is a part.

Most of the associations described so far and those to be described shortly are branches of international movements. But although there are important inputs from one branch to another or from the headquarters of the movement to its branches, particularly in terms of an exchange of ideas and publications, this does not mean that all the branches of one movement are simply copies of each other. In the first place, an association which is dominant and influential in one community may have a sister association in another community which is not similarly placed. On the other hand, because these communities are positioned in different countries, associations in them may have to develop their own approaches and styles of presentation in response to elements in the host society which influence not only them but the community which they are addressing. What this means is that Armenians in London who originate from many different countries may have had different experiences of branches of the same associations, and developed different perceptions of them. Thus, perceptions of the nature and stance of particular associations do not depend solely on the way in which these function in London but also on the experience of their functions in other communities. At the same time the activities and statements of these associations as a whole, i.e. on an international level, may continue to affect perceptions of associations in London. Thus, criticism may be directed at particular associations in London not because of what they themselves have done but because of what their sister associations or headquarters have done in other communities, in the past and in the present.

The characterisation of associations within the London Armenian community is, therefore, the product of a complex interplay between past experiences in other communities, continuing input of information into the community from the international Armenian diaspora, the particular circumstances of Armenians in London, and the details and style of the operation of the associations in London. Since Armenians come from different backgrounds, enjoy different circumstances in London, have uneven access to or interest in what goes on in the diaspora outside London, and uneven and different relations to the associations in London it is not surprising that a uniformity of attitudes to and categorisations of the associations has not developed and that contradictory behaviour and attitudes also occur.

The Armenian National Committee is chiefly responsible for the publication of an English language journal, *Momentum*. *Momentum* was initiated in 1980 but from autumn 1981 until autumn 1982 only one issue of the journal was published. In the first edition of this journal issued in April 1980, its leader defined the aims of the journal as well as the aims of the Armenian National Committee publishing it.

> We launch this publication in order to present to our readers – friend and foe alike – topical news and views about Armenian National Affairs in general and in order to promote the Armenian cause here in the UK in particular with a view to bringing about a comprehensive understanding of the ARMENIAN QUESTION.

As for the Armenian National Committee itself:

> The ARMENIAN NATIONAL COMMITTEE in London and in other major capitals of Europe and the USA, together with other Armenian organizations throughout the world, exist to serve the Armenian ideal: to preserve the heritage, to demand restitution of Armenian rights and ultimately establish an integral Armenia on Armenian ancestral land now under the grim rule of Turkey.

The only other major service sponsored by the Armenian National Committee during the period of my fieldwork was a series of four lectures held in the month leading up to 24 April, focusing on the subject of the Armenian liberation struggle and a protest march on the day of 24 April.

The Navarsatian, which, along with the Armenian National Committee, is identified as an affiliate of the Dashnakstitiun party, does not focus as intensively on the 'Armenian cause'. The events which it sponsored for the Armenian public at large tended to have a significant recreational component. Like the Tekeyan, the Navarsation sponsored a lavish dinner dance. It sponsored a summer picnic two weeks after the Sunday School Parents Committee sponsored a similar picnic on the same grounds in the same park. It also sponsored a cultural evening to commemorate the anniversary of the establishment of an Armenian State in 1918.

The Armenian Youth Federation, another Dashnakstitiun affiliate, expressly seeks to address itself to Armenian youth. It is not only more selective in its target audience in terms of age range but within this range as well. It holds regular meetings of its membership but these meetings are open only to members; they are held at a private location and the subjects discussed are secret and not to be discussed with non-members on other occasions. Potential recruits must first be nominated by a member and the choice approved by other members before they can be included in the meetings and there appears to be a bias, although my evidence for this is very limited, towards candidates with a personal or family background in the Dashnakstitiun.

According to some of the Dashnakstitiun critics, the rhetoric of armed struggle and revolution, which characterises many of the meetings and publications in which young Dashnak supporters are involved, is an artificial contrivance designed to appeal to young Armenian adults and is not born out of any political conviction. Such allegations generally come from members or supporters of associations more sympathetic to the ASALA than the Dashnak version of armed struggle. In fact, the most explicit antagonism which occurs between associations in London is that between the Dashnak affiliates and associations such as the Popular Movement, the Committee in Defence of Armenian Political Prisoners, and the British Armenian Community Association, whose members tend to be the most vociferous critics of the Dashnaks. Both sets of associations focus much of their attention on the 'Armenian Question', the issue of armed struggle, and Armenian national self-determination. Both call themselves socialist and progressive, and both tend to have high proportions of young adults in their late teens to early thirties involved in the organisation of, and participation in, the respective events and publications sponsored by them. Both sets recognise and emphasise the special appeal of their political focus to Armenian youth. Paradoxically, it is probably the similarity of their approaches which has the greatest influence on their mutual antagonism for they are competing for much the same audience, using similar rhetoric in their attempts at persuasion.

The Popular Movement for ASALA in London functioned until 1982 as an Armenian students' society, under the title 'Union of Armenian Students in Europe, London Branch'. Under both titles the association was active in disseminating information about the activities of organisations such as the

Armenian Secret Army, the detention and trials of members of such organisations, in particular those considered to be ASALA members, and, more generally, political rhetoric about the 'Armenian liberation struggle' and the 'Armenian armed struggle'. The major publication in which such writings appear is the *Kayzter,* a journal printed primarily in Armenian but with sections also in English. Besides the *Kayzter,* which is issued and distributed for sale regularly (approximately every month), the association is also involved in the distribution of shorter circulars which, unlike the Kayzter, are generally offered free of charge. Like the youthful Dashnak supporters, members and supporters of this association can be found at almost every Armenian public gathering distributing these publications and, like the Dashnaks, many of these members are young adults of Iranian Armenian origin. However, unlike the Dashnakstitiun publications, which focus blame for the failure to provide a solution to the 'Armenian Question' on international silence and apathy, the Popular Movement for ASALA focuses much of the blame for the continuing dispersion and assimilation of Armenians in the diaspora on its political predecessors, in particular the Dashnakstitiun itself:

> For over sixty years our traditional leadership, in particular the political parties, sat next to the leaders of oppression and world imperialism, bargaining for our rights, knocking on every diplomatic door, imploring for a solution to the Armenian Question. The solution never came and it could never have come because their diplomatic and peaceful politics was aimed at begging our rights from our enemies. A *policy of begging* which they simultaneously presented as the *only means* of solving the Armenian Question. In this way they denied the most important determining factor in any liberation movement, namely the strength and will of the people . . .
> Therefore, the birth of the Armenian armed struggle was due mainly to the failure of the traditional political leadership, in its ideological bankruptcy and policy of begging.

Such views appeared in the editorial of a 1982 issue of the revised *Hayastan-Kayzter Organ of Popular Movement for the ASALA (Britain).* In this issue, the publishers formally announced their support for the ASALA and their intention to work towards mobilising support among Armenians for a political movement focused on the ASALA. Hence, from then on, they would cease to function only as a student organisation and operate as the Popular Movement for ASALA, one, it is claimed, of several such movements springing up in different Armenian communities.

The explicit militancy of the Popular Movement's written and verbal pronouncements disturbs many Armenians. Few ever refer to the association by its proper title. References are to the 'Communists', the 'Leftists', 'those people', 'his group'. The association remains, for most, an association which is variously puzzling, discomforting, or even alarming because of its unequivocal line of support for armed militancy.

The Popular Movement is not the only association in London to support the ASALA movement. Ostensibly, the Committee for the Defence of Armenian Political Prisoners works for the release of Armenian political prisoners anywhere. Although the Committee does not officially address itself only to cases of imprisoned ASALA members, much of its attention is, in fact, focused on this organisation.

The Popular Movement, and the Committee tend to be identified as part of a cluster of associations which also includes the British Armenian Community Association (BACA). Members from these three associations tend to be friends, to cluster together in meetings, to refer to themselves as 'our people', 'we', 'us', and people who are neither members nor supporters as 'they'. All three associations also co-operate at times in the organisation of joint gatherings and even publications.

In spite of this, the members of the BACA are even more insistent on the separate identity and aims of their association *vis à vis* the Popular Movement than the Committee. It should be pointed out here that two of the organisers of the BACA were also members of the Committee. The BACA, it was explained to me, is concerned with the internal politics of the London Armenian community in distinction to the focus of ASALA on the international political framework of the Armenian diaspora. According to Ms M, one of the founders of the BACA, the association was formed in 1981 to act as a watchdog of the LACCC. In particular, the association is critical of the policy of the LACCC and the Armenian House Trust which refuse access to St Peter's church annexe and the Armenian House to politicised associations, and is bitter at their characterisation as more politicised than other associations allowed to use these premises for their gatherings.

Conclusion

There is one characteristic common to the majority of Armenian associations in London (with the exception perhaps of the Ararat choir or the Sports Club). Each one claims to be, if not the most active, then among the most active in working for the community's needs, or for Armenians in general. Criticisms of other associations generally rest on the claim that they either have not done anything for Armenians or the community, are not doing anything for them, or will not be able to do anything for them. There are two strands of discourse about the contents of this 'doing'.

One centres on the kind of projects which would benefit the community: a community centre, independent and/or day school, extra-school activities for Armenian youth, and so on. Within this strand of discourse runs the question of who is best equipped to develop and administer these projects. Although the LACCC is referred to, even by its most vociferous critics, as the governing body of the London Armenian community, this does not mean consensus about its ability, or right, to manage the institutional development of the community, or about even its present institutional framework.

The ability of each association, including the LACCC to initiate new projects depends on its ability to attract the interest of a section of the community's population, prompt participation in its fund-raising events, and encourage the contribution of voluntary donations. The larger the project is, the more labour intensive and the greater the funds involved, the more dependent an association is on enlisting the co-operation of other associations, and the support of a wide cross-section of the community's active members for its realisation. Hence, the community centre project is particularly difficult to realise.

There is very little public debate on the issues discussed heretofore. Most of the scepticism, aspirations, and disagreements are expressed in private, or in association membership meetings. This is a particularly salient feature in the issue of associations and politicisation, upon which the second strand of discourse about 'doing' centres. The degree to which an association is likely to be treated as politicised has become bound up with the extent to which it issues public statements concerning its political stance.

There are, no doubt, historical reasons for the reluctance of some Armenian associations to enter into public debate. Many Armenians remember deep divisions in their communities of origin between associations affiliated with competing political movements. As these movements became involved with non-Armenian political movements (in particular, the Cold War rhetoric between the USA and the USSR), these divisions were seen to be sharpened and exacerbated. But there is also, as we shall see in the next few chapters, a view among a number of Armenians that continued open public debate brings unwelcome outside attention to the Armenian community, attention which is seen as having been in the past, and potentially in the future, dangerous.

As a result, however, politicisation has become bound up with discussion of, and support for, violent political movements. Such movements are alarming and frightening to quite a number of Armenians. This has helped to reinforce the view of explicit and public politicisation as dangerous and best avoided. The response of a number of Armenians to the rhetoric of the Dashnaks and the ASALA supporters has been to ignore it and avoid it as far as possible.

What is being discussed in this line of discourse is what needs to be done to preserve 'Armenianness' as a whole and who is *doing* more to meet that need. Supporters of the ASALA movement and the Dashnakstitiun often dismiss the activities organised by associations such as the Anahid or the Tekeyan – their bazaars, films, dinner dances, and concerts – with phrases such as 'they're not doing anything'. These are seen as either irrelevant or of secondary importance to the necessity of doing something to move Armenians out of the diaspora into a concentrated resettlement in a nation-state, a movement considered to be of vital necessity if Armenianness is to be preserved. The other strand of argument within this half-spoken debate which sees the institutional and associational development of the community, and educational and recreational activities as vital to the preservation of Armenianness within the diaspora, short-term or long-term, remains largely bereft of public organised expression.

In short, the only fundamental issue which has the consensus of all the Armenian associations, and which forms the basic postulate upon which this framework is built, is that Armenian ethnicity should be preserved and that organised voluntary collective action must be taken in order to preserve it. What form this organisation should take, what actions it should undertake, who is best equipped or most committed for the undertaking of this task are issues by no means agreed upon. Each requirement tends to be defined in the development of a new association and as new associations are formed, struggle to maintain themselves, and acquire a following the possibility of, and the means to effect, a consensus becomes more remote. What this associational proliferation does do, however, is to increase the numbers of Armenians actively involved in organisation and increase the number and kinds of activities on offer to Armenians in London. In a population so dispersed and heterogeneous as the London Armenians, where a community is defined and manifested in terms of collective public gatherings, this enhances the very existence of the community rather than hastens its dissolution.

Chapter 2

The self and the Armenian other

Introduction

In Chapter 1 I outlined the organisational framework within which there is an ongoing and significant political debate between Armenians that represents an attempt to define a code, or more correctly codes, of Armenian ethnicity. The lines of this debate are often blurred and sometimes contradictory but are none the less, crucial for an understanding of how Armenians perceive their ethnic identity, their community, and their participation in this community, and, hence, for an understanding of how Armenians manage the social boundaries which define this community. Accordingly, in this chapter I will attempt to look more closely at the lines of this debate by picking out several of the most important and recurrent themes in the arguments between Armenians about being Armenian before going on, in Chapter Three, to look more directly at the ethnic boundary maintained between Armenians and non-Armenians. Although for the purpose of discussion I have separated these themes under several subheadings, this expositional division should not be treated too literally since, as will become clear, such themes shade into and overlap one another, while the categories used by one Armenian to describe and analyse a particular situation will not necessarily be those used by a fellow Armenian to analyse a similar or same situation.

When Armenians talk about what it means to be an Armenian in London and how they believe their community should be organised and developed, they very often do so in terms of contrasts between kinds of Armenians. Discussion of the differences between Armenians can be used as a means of distinguishing between the various subsections of the community and thereby making sense of (at least for the individual concerned if not to the agreement of his Armenian cohorts) what can sometimes appear a confusing jumble of associations and self-proclaimed leaders. But in making such contrasts, Armenians also implicitly or explicitly evoke judgements of, and thereby set up standards for, how they believe an Armenian should behave in respect to his or her ethnic identity and membership in the London Armenian community. It is for this reason that I have referred to the debate between

Armenians as an attempt to define a code of Armenianness. However, this ongoing discussion between Armenians does not represent a chorus of voices speaking out in united deliberation. There is often conflict, disagreement, and misunderstanding between the speakers. The categories which are used to locate people within the framework of the community and to draw standards for their behaviour as Armenians can also be used to pressure individuals into alignment with one or the other of the subgroupings within the community. But the tension and potential fractionalisation which results from these pressures are contained by a shared acceptance of all these different kinds of people as, after all, Armenians. In seeking to define sometimes conflicting codes of Armenianness and even in seeking to pressure individuals into explicit sectional affiliation, the respective protagonists are still seeking to persuade, cajole, and push those that are unsure or those that disagree to accept their respective viewpoints. They are still seeking to address themselves ultimately, if not always successfully, to all Armenians. The discussion is still of what we can or should do for the community and not only for a section of it. What is important about this discussion is that it goes on and not whether it finally ends in a consensus, for it is in the attempt to come to terms with that different but none the less *Armenian* other that Armenians become conscious of, and thoughtful about, their community and the roles they play or seek to play in it.

The following chapter will be divided into two sections. In the first, I will present the accounts which Armenians themselves give of the differences between them. A major theme in this discussion concerns the differences between Armenians in terms of their countries of origin and the inflection of the Armenian language that they speak. This theme relates to the generalised explanations that Armenians give of the divisions between them, their appraisals of which inflection and national grouping most closely approximates to true and authentic Armenianness, and their different evaluations of the effect of such distinctions on the organisation of the London community. This theme of national and inflection differences overlaps with a series of interlinked themes concerning the rich, the intellectual, or poor Armenian student, the militancy and volatility of the youth, and traditional political differences between Armenians. Within these latter themes particularly, I return to an issue first encountered in Chapter 1, namely the issue of the way in which the organisation of Armenian ethnicity should take account of the potential responses of non-Armenians to the actions, and particularly public and visibly militant actions, of the Armenians in their midst (see pp. 36–9).

In the second section, I seek to recontextualise these self-accounts by looking at the ways in which the general differences alluded to influence the patterning of relationships between Armenians within the London community. I look at such factors as differences in the organisation of and contacts between communities of origin of London Armenians, as well as variations in the patterns of migration from these communities which have contributed to the tendency towards the establishment of friendships and identification of particular associations in terms of inflection sets. Finally, I will attempt to show that the selection of categorical distinctions by Armenians in their description and analysis of trends in the community should not be treated over literally but as a kind of shorthand.

Why are we divided?

It is important at this point to make clear that it is not I, as the outsider, who emphasises the internal differentiation in the Armenian population, rather it is the Armenians themselves who stress this aspect. The negative aspects of this divisiveness are often stressed. They are stressed on two levels: as an aspect of the Armenian population as a whole, i.e. on an international level; and as an aspect of the London Armenian community specifically. Statements like:

> I'm sure you have realised we have many committees . . . I don't agree with that, I'm on a committee but I think we should be united and forget about the past. I don't mean we should forget about our history, but we shouldn't think what this committee did or that committee, we should think about the future.

recur often in discussions, particularly as stated to an outsider. But, as this statement indicates, this kind of fragmentation is seen as an aspect of Armenian history. It is an inevitable characteristic produced by the historical conditions in which Armenian culture developed. In an explanation which was repeated to me by five different speakers, on five different occasions, with only slight variations between them the Armenian was represented as virtually ungovernable:

> The Armenian is an individualist. You see Armenians lived in mountainous areas and because of this villages were cut off from each other and had a high degree of autonomy. There was no central authority organising all these separate groups. This continues to have an influence till today. As a result, the Armenian is an individualist. He finds it very difficult to listen to a central authority. He wants to keep his independence and he does this at the beginning by starting an enterprise, in his family and then on a higher level, perhaps in an association.

If not all Armenians wish to go so far back in their history to explain their contemporary fragmentation, there is widespread agreement that at the very least, the more recent dispersion of the Armenians, after their deportation from Turkey in 1915, has caused inevitable differences between subgroups of Armenians. The fact that for several generations at least Armenians have been part of communities separated from each other by their positions in different host countries is inevitably produced as an explanation for their internal divisions when this issue comes up in a conversation, both spontaneously and in answer to a direct question. But agreement breaks down over the nature of the process which caused this differentiation and also about the extent to which these divisions as they manifest themselves in the London community are typical of Armenian communities in general.

The complaint that the London community is not a 'good one' recurs often. In comparisons with communities in other countries and other cities, in almost every case, the London community is viewed unfavourably. As to why the community is not good, there is a myriad of explanations offered which often involve sectional cross-accusations.

National/inflection differences and authentic Armenianness

As is probably clear by now, national difference is the most frequent theme to come up when Armenians reflect on their community and the divisions within it. But very often discussions of nationality refer to differences in inflection. Because in London only Armenians of Iranian origin employ the Eastern inflection, reference to Eastern-Armenian speakers is often synonymous with Armenians originating from Iran. On the other hand, Western Armenian speakers originate from a number of different countries so that when reference is made to Western-Armenian speakers it encompasses a wide range of nationalities. But here again reference to Western-Armenian speakers is often synonymous with reference to Cypriot Armenians and to a lesser extent Lebanese (Beirut) Armenians, who are commonly believed to be predominant among users of this inflection. This is particularly the case in references made by Iranian Armenians, who commonly use the term Cypriot when, in fact, referring to Western-Armenian speakers generally and *vice versa*. When the discussion is about actual instruction in the language then both Eastern-Armenian speakers and Western-Armenian speakers tend to use the terms Eastern and Western in making a distinction, rather than the national grouping which, in London, is identified with that inflection.

Very often the difficulties in communication caused by the differences in the inflections were stressed but in almost all cases the stress was made by Western-Armenian speakers.

One of the reasons suggested by Western-Armenian speakers for their difficulty in understanding the Iranian Eastern-Armenian speakers is the tendency of the latter to include Farsi words in their speech. In Soviet Armenia, explained one, where the Eastern inflection is also used, they do not use such alien words and so we have no difficulty in understanding them. This too forms the basis of an ongoing debate among Armenians, i.e. which dialect is more correct, more truly Armenian.

I was in the Armenian House about five to six years ago and there was a terrible argument going on. When I came in, they stopped and said, here's [O], he can tell us which one is right. And do you know, they are arguing about which dialect is the more correct one, the Eastern or the Western. I said 'is that what you were arguing about, it sounded so fierce, I thought you hit someone. Look, there isn't a right or wrong one dialect. So long as you have a language and you can communicate; thats all that matters. If you ask me which one is more correct phonetically, then I have to say the Iranian because they pronounce all the letters in the alphabet, the Western Armenians don't . . . But what does that matter? The important thing is that you're all Armenians, you belong to one nation.'

The speaker is a Syrian Armenian, i.e. a Western-Armenian speaker, but it should be pointed out that he prides himself on being able to speak classical Armenian, Farsi and Kurdish, all influences on the form of Eastern Armenian as spoken in Iran today. The stress that he lays on a common national identity is verbalised by members of every national subgrouping but the issue of which inflection is the 'correct' one is not so easily resolved among his fellows.

Although I heard from quite a number of Western-Armenian speakers the complaint that Iranian Armenians used too many Farsi words, thus making communication and understanding difficult, the claim that theirs was the more 'correct' inflection came more usually from Iranian Armenians. In almost all cases it was related to the use of the Eastern-Armenian inflection in Soviet Armenia. Soviet Armenia as the standard-bearer of true Armenian culture is a pervasive concept among all Armenians and will be discussed in greater detail in later chapters, suffice it to say, for the moment, that in this context it is used by some Iranian Armenians to legitimise their use of the Eastern inflection as being more authentically Armenian. It is clear by now that the distinction drawn by the Armenians between Eastern- and Western-inflection speakers is not just a question of communication but has a great deal to do with the ongoing discussion among Armenians about what it means to be Armenian.

In the context of national divisions, it sometimes takes the form of an accusation by some Iranian Armenians that the Cypriot Armenians have become too Westernised, too like their British hosts. More commonly, the distinction is made in terms of length of residence, i.e. those who have been in Britain longer have become Anglicised and Westernised in contrast to the more recent arrivals. But since the Cypriot Armenians are commonly believed to be the longest settled national subgrouping in the present composition of the London Armenian community and the Iranian Armenians the most recent, the distinction between old-timers and newcomers and national subgroupings often overlaps in expression, as in this analysis by Ms PY, an Iranian Armenian woman:

Also the Cypriots don't attend the meetings. They seem to be very individualist. They've absorbed the British way of life, especially those who have been here for many years, but we Iranians are still culturally very different. We like to be with each other, in groups, talking and doing things. But they appear to have become more assimilated, in particular if they've been here for a long time. Seven or eight years ago, there were no community activities here. You could go to the Haidoon on Sunday but there weren't any other activities. Its only five or six years ago, when Iranians started coming here in large numbers.

The view that Iranian Armenians are somehow more authentically Armenian than the Western Armenians was most forcibly and explicitly expressed by three Western-Armenian speakers but none of these is Cypriot in origin. All three also feel themselves to be somewhat marginal in the community. Mr F tied the authenticity of Iranian Armenians to their resemblance to the Armenians in Soviet Armenia, thereby legitimising it. But both Mrs W and Mrs JV attributed it to the greater boisterousness of the Iranian Armenians, in particular to their tendency to dance in group dances, in contrast to the Western Armenians who either did not dance at all or danced in European style (i.e. in pairs), an indication as they saw it that the Iranian Armenians had retained more of the Armenian 'customs'.

But, as Mrs W pointed out, it is these very characteristics of Iranian Armenians which may be derided by other Western-Armenian speakers, in particular Cypriot Armenians. It is certainly the case that in their description of Iranian Armenians, Cypriot Armenians sometimes characterise them as loud, boastful and vulgar Armenians who drink and eat too much. They characterise themselves in contrast, as calmer and more cosmopolitan.

This kind of attitude drew a bitter response from Ms C, an Iranian-Armenian woman who works as an employee in a shop owned by a Cypriot-Armenian woman and frequented by a number of Cypriot-Armenian women as clients:

> The Armenian Iranians, they are taking over everything and they don't like that, but the Cypriots, they think they know everything. They think we are stupid because we come from Iran and because our English is not so good because in Cyprus, they were under Britain or something like that but really, Vered, if you saw Iran under the Shah, it was really modern, and our education is better than they are. You saw [LX]; you saw the people that come and go, their education but the Armenian Iranians, I can't say all of them, some of them maybe was not so good, but we have better education than them. Cyprus is very small, like a village but they think they are better than us. They think we are stupid but we are not. All of the Cypriots, no, I can't say all of them but I hear the Cypriot ladies that come into the shop.

But this kind of response is relatively rare. As was indicated earlier, if Iranian Armenians do refer to the Westernisation and Anglicisation of the Cypriot and Lebanese Armenians, they usually represent it negatively, as a diminishment of Armenian culture. However, the theme of the Iranians taking over which appears in Ms C's speech is pervasive in the attitudes of Armenians from every national subgrouping. More often than not it is implicit, commonly occurring in an analysis of the national composition of specific gatherings at organised activities such as dinner dances, concerts, the Sunday

School, and so on. Statements like '80 per cent of the people here are Iranians', 'there are only three Cypriot Armenians here' when twenty individuals are present are frequent and come from Armenians of every nationality. But if there is consensus with Ms PY's view that Cypriots do not attend the meetings, and a more general perception that Iranian Armenians are very often in the majority among the participants of organised activities and at the institutions of the Church, Armenian House and Sunday School, the relevance of national distinctions to the organisation of such activities is far more contentious.

National/inflection differences and the organisation of community

Two strands run in the exposition of this issue by Iranian Armenians. One of these is that expressed by Ms PY, i.e. that it is the Iranian Armenians who have been most active and productive in organising community activities. In this view, there were few or no committees and, hence, few organised activities before the arrival of the Iranian Armenians. 'The Western Armenians don't do anything, the Scouts, the disco, that's all the Iranian Armenians', I was told by Ms V, a young British-born Armenian woman of partly Iranian origin. Another strand in the argument is that the Western Armenians (i.e. the Cypriots and Lebanese) have deliberately been monopolising the agencies for decision-making in the community and are trying to exclude the Iranian Armenians from their rightful share.

There does appear to be a vague but general recognition that community facilities and organised activities have developed and proliferated in response to the growth in population with succeeding waves of immigrants. However, an event or a process which involves national subgroupings can be interpreted by one speaker with the stress laid on these national distinctions, whereas another speaker, while recognising this relationship, will place an emphasis on another set of contrasting categories in his explanation. To illustrate this point, the case of the last elections to the Community Church Council is useful. As discussed earlier, during the last election Armenians who did not hold permanent British-residence status or who were domiciled outside the boundaries of the Greater London metropolitan district were not eligible to stand or vote. Mr RW, an Iranian Armenian, interpreted these criteria as an attempt to exclude Iranian Armenians – the most recent of Armenian immigrants to London and, therefore, considered to be the most likely to be outside these criteria – from direct influence in decision-making. The general reaction to these regulations was interpreted in terms of national antagonisms:

> The Western-inflection speakers, in particular the Cypriots who had been here the longest, wanted to keep control of the community's affairs but after the last

election, about four years ago when so many Armenians, especially those from Iran, were excluded because they weren't permanent residents, there was such a hue and cry that they're going to change it and the situation should be quite different after the next election.

Mr FS, an officer of the Community Church Council and a Cypriot Armenian, while admitting the intention to change the regulations, presented it as an attempt by him and like-minded members of the Council to allow 'other' Armenians to participate and be active in the community, without any mention of any national grouping or of any partisan response which might have prompted such a move. Ms M, and several other young Armenians of Syrian and Lebanese origins who are either members or supporters of the British Armenian Community Association, rendered a passionate account of the same issue in which the exclusion of Iranian Armenians was presented as incidental to the main issue of the monopoly of power by a small handful of Armenians.

We have seen that the emic explanation for the national distinctions between Armenians can be related to a variety of other differentiating processes: the historical individualism of Armenians in general, difficulties in linguistic communication, assimilation and Westernisation, length of residence in Britain, political control and responsibility. But the most generally held view is that Armenians living in different nations were affected by the culture and customs of their countries. It is natural, therefore, I was told, to feel closer to those Armenians who share your background, language, and customs, i.e. those Armenians who share your country of origin. But although 'natural' and understandable, it nevertheless evokes a quality of defensiveness. It was repeatedly explained to me by Iranian Armenians that it was the Cypriot and Lebanese Armenians who kept to themselves and did not want to mix with other Armenians, and similarly by Western-Armenian speakers of Cypriot, Lebanese and Syrian origins that it was the Iranian Armenians who did not want to mix with them. Why this defensiveness? 'Because we are all Armenians', a statement which in a variety of forms can be heard from Armenians of every national origin.

As has already been indicated, there are several themes of internal differentiation which occur even in discussions of national distinctions. These themes do not appear only in the context of such discussions as have already been recounted but also independently differentiating Armenians in terms of criteria such as young and old, rich and poor Armenians, powerful and powerless, and so on, which can, but do not always, cut across national subsections.

Opposition between the rich Armenian and the intellectual Armenian

There are many references to 'rich' Armenians in comments by individuals. These can be general references without specifying particular individuals or groups of individuals, or they can be applied more precisely to a particular individual or association. When Armenians talk about the 'rich' they do so in terms of attitudes and behaviour which are attributed to this category rather than in terms of discrete measurable criteria such as property assets, size of income, and so on. To the rich is generally accredited a concern with material things: money, the material objects that money can buy, particularly nice houses and the sources of money, i.e. jobs and businesses. As a consequence, the counterpart to the rich Armenian is not so much the poor or destitute Armenian but the intellectual, and in particular, the student. In fact, the student is the only kind of Armenian who is consistently represented as poor and in need of support from his or her fellow Armenians.

The rich are often represented as unwilling to give to the worthy projects sponsored by the associations. Ostentation, which is sometimes attributed to Iranian Armenians by Cypriot and other Western-Armenian speakers, is another characteristic which is often attributed to the rich in general. On every occasion when names of donors of large contributions to a particular association were announced at fund-raising dinners by the recipients, there was always someone to be found accusing the donors of 'showing off', of faking generosity in a bid for public acclaim and attention. The implication is usually that if the rich do give, they do so only to show off. There is also sometimes condemnation of the exclusivity and snobbery of the rich, as in this account by Mrs W of a woman who had only shortly before had her name announced at a Scouts Garden Party for a donation of £200:

> Just she give because she want to show she give. You see that woman is my mother's cousin. Her husband was [AG]'s [husband of W] best friend. In fact, they met in my house in Cyprus. Then they came here and they hit the jackpot, their business did very well and they became very rich and since then, she's ignored me. She told a friend of ours that [W] can't equal me in any thing. I sent a message back to her, maybe not in money but in other things.

Two attitudes of the rich are, therefore, most generally criticised: snobbery and selfishness. But selfishness in relation to whom? As Mr BY explains it, to the young, the students:

> There are no young people at these dances because obviously a student can't spend thirty pounds on a ticket. They should think about the young people, about the students. They're the ones that are important, not the old people. I have never seen them give half-price tickets for students, so they can't go.

Politicisation and youth

Mr BY thus introduces another dimension into the distinctions attributed to
the rich. When the distinction is made only in terms of the young and old,
there is general approval for Mr BY's stress on the young as important, that
they should be included in all events. Almost every head of every Armenian
association in London expressed a desire to increase the participation of the
young in his or her organisation. But when a political dimension is added to
the distinctions, the young are no longer always appealing.

Militancy is consistently associated with the young or the students.
Members of the Dashnak affiliates and the Popular Movement and other such
organisations without fail represent their movement for a campaign of armed
force as appealing to the young but as having little impact or influence on the
old. However, such public support for 'armed struggle' is often viewed as
dubious or irresponsible:

> You can look at the youth organizations, at the student societies, they are trying to
> politicize it. I was at a meeting. They were discussing the terrorist activities and the
> so-called revolutionaries. But I told them: What are you going to do about this
> fascist Turkish government? There are 100 fascist Turkish organizations in
> Europe, the 'Grey Wolf' and that kind of thing. What are you going to do if they
> decide to do something against the Armenians because of the terrorist actions?
> Have you talked to the leaders who run the Armenian House and the School? Who
> will be the . . . yes, voice who will protect the Armenians? Who is going to talk to
> the government and tell them this is the danger? Some of the students, they are
> aware of this but the others, they don't think this is an important issue.

More commonly, criticism of militancy is directed towards the damage which
could be inflicted on the reputation of Armenians as viewed by non-
Armenians. Several Armenians made reference to the difficulties already
created in their relationships with non-Armenians by the activities of such
organisations as the Armenian Secret Army.

> What they are doing is only hurting the Armenians. All that people know about us
> is that Armenians kill the Turks. Every time there's a report in the newspaper about
> one of the killings, when I go to work, they say 'you guys are at it again' and it
> makes me feel very uncomfortable.

Militancy and overt politicisation are seen as enhancing the possibility of
negative reactions from non-Armenians towards Armenians not only in
Britain but in other countries as well.

Militant young Armenians can also represent themselves as vulnerable.
The Armenian Community Church Council was represented by one of these
'militants' as primarily spies for the British government who eliminate their
opposition by reporting them to the Home Office as subversive elements.
Another supporter represented Mr FR, who is 'not like us,' the 'young
people', as a 'spy' for the Home Office:

Wa call him the 'spy in the community' because he has a lot of contacts in the Home Office. If a student or anyone with visa problems doesn't get along with him, he calls the Home Office. No, I'm sure he doesn't but that's what people say.

The Armenian Youth Federation meets in secret and recruits new members secretly because as one youth, who is not himself a member, explained 'they say the rich people want to use us'.

It is these rich people who are represented as effectively controlling the London Armenian community. As such, militant Armenians represent them- selves as vulnerable to their opposition. This opposition is most commonly referred to by aspiring militants by using the labels of 'rich', 'businessmen', or 'old' combined with such terms as 'conservative' or 'reactionary'. But to whom these labels are applied depends on the context of the argument. They can be narrowly applied to the LACCC when the point is to show how politicised associations are denied access to the few permanent meeting places for Armenians in London. Or they can be applied to all those associations which define their organisational aims as cultural and not political, and which are seen as disapproving of the overt politicisation and militancy of associations which theoretically support the use of armed force. They can further be applied to all Armenians in London, save the few supporters of the guerrilla organisations, when the point is to show the relative powerlessness and marginality of these militant associations and their supporters.

Similarly the labels 'young' and 'students' can be used generally by less militant Armenians to include all young Armenian adults or all students when the argument is for their greater involvement in the community's affairs as the future standard-bearers of the Armenian culture in the hinterland of Britain or Europe. It can be used even more generally to represent an attitude which places intellectual concerns above material interests. But it can also be used more narrowly, in conjunction with labels such as 'extremist' and 'revolu- tionary', to represent that group of Armenians considered as potentially dangerous, not only because they may support the use of a campaign of armed force but also because they draw attention to the grievances of Armenians through overtly politicised and public militancy.

It should be clear by now that a particular individual can find him or herself classified under one or other of these labels not according to his or her own particular circumstances or life-style but because of his or her participation in certain associations or certain events, or support for, as well as opposition to, a particular political strategy. Thus, the women of the Anahid association were referred to by several young Armenians as 'rich men's wives', although among its members are women like Mrs F who is herself a secretary-typist and whose husband is a construction worker. Similarly those young people or students who support the strategy of armed force or participate in public demonstrations can, in application, include individuals who are in their forties, employed full-time and, in some cases, own their own homes.

Traditional political differences

These rather general distinctions centring on public militancy and support for a campaign of assassinations overlap with more traditional political distinctions. If you ask almost any Armenian in London about political differences between Armenians he or she will relate that there are three Armenian political parties: the Ramgavars, the Hunchaks, and the Dashnaks. As was pointed out in Chapter 2, the issue of how these political parties actually function within the contemporary London Armenian community is a subject which has by no means this degree of clarity or agreement among Armenians. But the confusion relates not only to which association is affiliated with which party, and whether this affiliation actually embodies politicisation in the nature of the operation of that association, but also relates to individual membership in these parties. Although certain associations such as the Tekeyan may be commonly referred to by non-members as Ramgavar or the Armenian National Committee as Dashnakstitiun, members of these associations themselves will not usually (and in the case of the associations identified with the Ramgavars, almost never) make such an explicit reference in conversation. More to the point, in conversation with non-members, members will almost never refer to themselves personally as Dashnak or Ramgavar. If it appears then that this avoidance of direct reference in combination with the complexity of identification of associations with traditional political parties might create some confusion about who precisely is a Dashnak or Ramgavar, then that appearance would not be very misleading. As Mr LR, a member of the AGBU explained:

> At the top, all the political parties are very secretive. Very few Armenians know what their policies are or what kind of decisions they make at the top. You know that this man or that one is a Dashnak but you don't know for sure and you don't know what position he has. But at the top, they all know each other and co-operate with each other.

In fact, as one Armenian woman explained, it would be very bad form to ask someone directly whether he or she was a Dashnak or Ramgavar. But allusions and speculations are constantly made as to the political affiliation of individuals, particularly whether a person might be a Dashnak.

As Mr LR pointed out, there is no greater clarity about the policies of these parties and he would not be alone in this opinion. Ms C pointed out that:

> I don't know what the Dashnak is. I asked many people but they couldn't answer me. I asked [M]. She said this, that, but she didn't tell me what it is. My uncle, my father's brother, he is a Dashnak but I never understood what he is. My family in Iran, we were never Dashnak or the other group, we were always in the middle. I am the same here. I am not for Dashnak and I am not for [M]'s group.

Although Ms C has no idea what the Dashnaks represent, she is quite emphatic that she is a neutralist. Several Armenians complained to me that they were constantly being pressured to take sides but that they insisted on maintaining their neutrality. One of these, Mrs W, a young Syrian-Armenian woman, pointed out that the people pressuring her to take a stand and align herself with a particular political group, did not know themselves what the policies of these groups were.

These disputed political loyalties become further complicated in their overlap with national subgroupings. Because the membership of the Dashnak-imputed associations is dominated by Iranian Armenians and the membership of the Ramgavar-imputed associations is dominated by Cypriot or Western Armenians, loyalty to a particular political group, or to an association considered to be aligned to it, can be interpreted in terms of national differences. This comes out very clearly in the case cited earlier where Mrs W, a Syrian Western-Armenian speaker married to a Cypriot Armenian, who has her child registered in the Armenian Scouts, was invited to shift her child to a recently developed club for the same age group sponsored by the Tekeyan.

> A man came up to me in the school and he said 'You're one of us. I think your children would be much better with our club'. I said: 'How do you know what I am and what I think?' He said: 'But we're paregorzagan [AGBU] and they're right'. I told him: 'I don't care what they are, you should join the Scouts. Then, we can have one large club, not two clubs and don't you ever come to me and say that again . . .' Its not necessarily Western Armenians who would join them. They say it's because they're Western Armenians but really it's because they don't belong to the same political group.

It is clear that it was assumed that because Mrs W was a Western-Armenian speaker, she would prefer to have her children enrolled in the club sponsored by the Tekeyan, although 'we' in this context was demarcated as AGBU, i.e. Ramgavar; in distinction to they, who are 'right', i.e. Scouts, Dashnaks, Iranian Eastern-Armenian speakers.

Differentiation and community

This case indicates how difficult it is for an organisation to identify itself in the Armenian community in neutral terms with equal sympathy to all Armenians in London. Inevitably the organisation and its actual and potential membership will be differentiated by one or other of the criteria of political strategy or affiliation – nationality, 'rich', or 'student', – which, in the references of Armenians, are woven together in a complex multi-stranded web. Similarly, as was pointed out earlier, individuals find it difficult to maintain a neutrally generalised identity as 'just' Armenian. They are either ascribed a label or pressured to align themselves with one or other of the subgroupings identified

by these labels. Armenians are aware of this, hence, the insistence of individuals on neutrality even when the lines of partisanship are so blurred as to be
barely decipherable. Similarly, Armenians of every background are found
denouncing the presence of a plurality of committees in statements such as
'We shouldn't have so many committees, because after all we are all
Armenians.' Such statements are not a denouncement of the many activities
and facilities sponsored by these committees but of what is perceived to be the
inherently antagonistic and partisan character of the relationships between
them.

The London community is represented by many Armenians as being
particularly rife with these sorts of divisions, and they are responsible,
according to a number of Armenians, for the failure to organise permanent
institutions such as the community centre. Virtually every other Armenian
community is represented more favourably by comparison, as at least having
a large and adequate community centre. Armenians from Iran, in particular,
stress that their community of origin was far more united and, therefore,
more productively organised than the London community of which they are,
at present, members. As was indicated earlier, in the statement of Mrs Z, an
Iranian-Armenian woman, one of the explanations offered for this is the
greater monetary generosity of Iranian Armenians towards the associations
and institutions of both their present and particularly their past community.
Another reason suggested for this by several younger and more militant
Iranian Armenians is the monopoly of one political party, the Dashnakstitiun, in Iran. Cypriot Armenians, on the other hand, rarely claim that their
community of origin in Cyprus was more united than the London community
although they will claim that it was 'better'. But Cypriots and Western-Armenians speakers in general, as well as Iranian Armenians, complain about the
apathy of Armenians in London and their reluctance to participate in community activities. Iranian Armenians are more likely to attribute this apathy
specifically to the Lebanese and Cypriot Armenians and not to themselves.
Western-Armenians speakers are more likely to attribute this to a generalised
apathy of all Armenians without specifying a particular national grouping.
However, several Armenians attributed their own reluctance to participate in
a particular event or a particular association to the competitive repetitive
nature of the activities sponsored by the associations. 'If I go to one, then I
have to go to all of them, so I don't go to any', explained Mr O, a Syrian
Armenian who has been attending activities in the community only very
sporadically for the last five years.

Armenians do admit that in comparison with Armenian communities
elsewhere the London community is relatively recently established and, in
fact, not yet firmly consolidated. It is seen as inevitable that many of the most
recently arrived Iranian Armenians will move on to other destinations, either
because they never intended to settle in London in the first place or because

they have been unable to obtain permission to stay.

Thus, explanations for why the London community is not 'good' may refer to such characteristics as its being relatively recently established, its transitory nature *vis à vis* many of its present members, the apathy of many of its members, and its factionalisation, which is extreme even for the 'individualist' Armenians – all generalised attributes which affix no blame on one section or another. But, as we have seen, equally prevalent are explanations for the situation of the London community which approtion blame cross-sectionally.

The fluidity of the categories and labels which Armenians use in making distinctions between themselves, and the variety of interpretations and explanations for these distinctions is not surprising considering the heterogeneity and relatively recent establishment of this community, which the Armenians themselves allude to in explication. The majority of Armenians in London whom I encounterd are first-generation immigrants. They originate from over seven different countries, speak two major inflections of Armenian and a number of subdialects. Finally, the present composition of the community dates no further back than eight years when many of the Armenians from Iran and Lebanon started arriving in London. One could say that Armenians in London are still trying to make sense of their new ethnic neighbours and define the tone of their interactions. It is paradoxical that these very attempts of Armenians (at times at cross-purposes) to separate and define a distinctive but circumscribed domain of relationships from the myriad of relationships in which individual Armenians are involved suggest that it is unlikely that a uniformity of behaviour and attitudes within the community will develop. For, as Armenians continue to involve themselves in a variety of relationships and interests outside the community, they are likely to continue to bring different interests and expectations into the community. For the Armenian community to thrive its framework must be able to encompass this variety. We have already seen the tendency of associations to proliferate and the more limited growth of institutions as potential centralising influences in response to these varied interests. Similarly, an exposition of Armenianness which defines appropriate behaviour and attitudes too explicitly and too narrowly would be incapable of accommodating the variety of interests and experiences outside the community. Thus, although the nature of these differences may change over time, the differentiation itself is unlikely to disappear.

Contextualising the account of differences

One should be careful not to exaggerate the importance of national distinctions in the pattern of interaction of Armenians in London lest the picture of community life be distorted. Armenians in London from every national subgrouping can be found at most gatherings organised by the various associations and at the institutions of Church, Sunday School, and Armenian House. Nevertheless, differences are apparent even on such occasions and can be clearly discerned in the organisation and participation in such activities.

To examine more closely some of these elements, in particular those relating to national distinctions, I will first refer to a series of structured interviews conducted with these issues in mind. Twenty households were interviewed on the subject of their attendance at the institutions of the community, their participation in Armenian associations and the gatherings these associations sponsored. Ten of the households had at least one member, and in most cases all, who was an Eastern-Armenian speaker, i.e Iranian Armenian in origin. The remaining ten households had at least one member in each, and again in many cases most or all, who was a Western-Armenian speaker. But in the latter ten households country of origin was varied among the respondents. I would like to make it clear that I am not suggesting that these households are representative of the London Armenian population in general. But I do think that their responses indicate certain trends in affiliation which extend beyond the twenty households themselves and which I was able to observe among Armenians not included in this sample. These twenty households also each had one or more members who were at least marginally involved in community activities. As such, their responses should be set within the context of that population of Armenians who participate in at least some of the community events, and not within the wider context of Armenians in London where many are not involved in these activities in any way.

As far as possible, in each household every household member aged fifteen years and over was interviewed. The composition by national origins of the respondents was as follows:

Iranian-Armenian households
17 first-generation immigrants from Iran
 1 first-generation immigrant from Cyprus
 3 British-born to Scottish mother and Iranian-Armenian father
 2 non-Armenian spouses: both Scottish

Western-Armenian households
18 first-generation immigrants from Cyprus, Syria, Iraq, Egypt, Lebanon, Ethiopia, Greece
 2 British-born, one with a Cypriot-Armenian father and English-Danish mother, and one with a Cypriot-Armenian father and an English mother
 1 non-Armenian spouse: English-Danish.

In outlining the responses elicited in the interviews, I have included the Cypriot-Armenian wife of one of the Iranian-Armenian respondents among the first-generation Western-Armenian immigrants. In this group I have also included one of the British-born Cypriot Armenians since although born in England, at the age of five, his family resettled in Cyprus and he emigrated back to England on his own at the age of fifteen. The second British-born Cypriot Armenian I have not included in the following analysis of responses since although her parents wished me to interview her she was only thirteen years old, two years below the limit I had set for the respondents interviewed. Finally, I have not included the responses in this context of the non-Armenian spouses listed above, although these were all interviewed and two of these have fairly close links with the Armenian community.

In Figures 2–5 I have listed the responses of Eastern Armenians and Western Armenians, respectively, regarding the proportion of their Armenian friends within the same inflection set as themselves and measured this against their own involvement and the involvement of their Armenian friends in the executives of London Armenian associations. If we compare the two groups of responses, we see that they differ markedly in two important respects. While only two Eastern Armenians out of twenty had friends serving on the executive of borderline political Western-Armenian associations (Tekeyan, AGBU especially), eleven out of twenty Western Armenians had friends sitting on the executives of these associations. Similarly, while no Eastern Armenians reported sitting on the executives of the Tekeyan or AGBU, four out of eight Western Armenians who are members of association executives did sit on the executives of such borderline political associations. Another important difference is that while only one Eastern Armenian replied that half of her Armenian friends were in the same inflection set as herself (the other nineteen having more than half or all of their Armenian friends within the same inflection set as themselves) eight of the Western Armenians had half or less than half of their Armenian friends within the same inflection set as themselves. Seven of these eight, with only one exception, reported having friends on the executive of politicised Armenian associations.

Among the Eastern Armenians, eight respondents also had friends serving on the executives of politicised Armenian associations but here there was no similar correspondence with the proportion of Armenian friends within the same inflection set, with seven of the eight reporting that more than half or all of their friends were in the same inflection set as themselves. It should be remembered, as was pointed out in Chapter 1, that politicised associations such as the BACA, Popular Front, Armenian Youth Federation, Armenian National Committee, Navarsatian, and so on are dominated by Iranian Armenians.

Thus, there appears to be a significant clustering in friendships, particularly with respect to contacts with those associations which are identified with an

Figure 2: Distribution of friendships *vis-à-vis* inflection set and association executive committees (Eastern Armenians)

Proportion of friends in same inflection set	On committee of association committee	Not on association committee	Politicised associations	Borderline case Iranian–Armenian	Borderline cases Western Armenian	Non-Western political Armenian	Owner association	No friends on any association executive
			Friends on executives of†					
All		X		X				
All		X		X				
All		X				X		
All		X	X			X*		
All		X	X			X		
All		X						
More than half	X							
More than half	X		X					
More than half	X							X
More than half	X		X					
More than half		X	X					
More than half		X				X		
More than half		X				X		
More than half		X				X		
More than half		X		X				
More than half	X							X
More than half	X		X	X	X	X		
More than half		X	X	X		X*	X	
More than half		X	X			X		
Half	X				X	X		
	7	13	8	5	2	10+*	1	2

† Borderline case – Iranian–Armenian = Scouts Association; borderline case – Western Armenian = Tekeyan, AGBU, Melkonian Alumni
* Listed Football Club which could be either one of two associations, one a branch of the Scouts and the other independent of the Scouts. Uncertain which they were referring to.

Figure 3: Distribution of friendships *vis-à-vis* inflection set and association executive committees (Western Armenians)

				Friends on executives of					
	Proportion of friends in same inflection set	On committee of association committee	Not on committee	Politicised associations	Borderline case Iranian–Armenian	Borderline cases Western Armenian	Non-Western political Armenian	Owner association	No friends on any association executive
1	All		X						X
2	All		X				X		
3	All		X			X			
4	All		X				X		
5	All		X						X
6	All		X			X	X	X	
7	More than half		X				X		
8	More than half	X				X	X	X	
9	More than half	X				X		X	
10	More than half	X				X	X		
11	More than half		X			X			
12	More than half		X	X		X	X		
13	Half		X	X					
14	Half	X		X					
15	Half	X		X	X				
16	Half	X		X		X	X	X	
17	Half	X		X		X			
18	Less than half	X		X		X		X	
19	Less than half		X			X			
20	Very few		X						X*
		8	12	7	1	11	8	5	2+1

* Uncertain of which association executive her friends were members

Figure 4: Association membership of respondents sitting on association executive committees (Eastern Armenians)

	Politicised organisations	Borderline cases Eastern (Scouts)	Borderline cases Western (Tekeyan, AGBU)	Non-political (Ararat, Anahid, Sunday School)	Owner associations (LACC and its sub-committees)
1				X	X
2				X	
3	X				
4				X	
5	X				
6					X
7				X	
	2			4	2

Figure 5: Association membership of respondents sitting on association executive committees (Western Armenians)

	Politicised organisations	Borderline cases Eastern (Scouts)	Borderline cases Western (Tekeyan, AGBU)	Non-political (Ararat, Anahid, Sunday School)	Owner associations (LACC and its sub-committees)
1	X				
2			X		
3				X	
4	X				X
5			X	X	X
6			X		
7			X		
8				X	
	2		4	3	2

Armenian political movement. But this is not the case with associations considered to be apolitical such as the Anahid Women's Association, the Ararat Song and Dance Ensemble and the Sunday School. Ten out of twenty Iranian Armenians reported having friends on the executives of these latter associations, and eight out of twenty Western Armenians reported the same. There is also an indication that Iranian Armenians are more likely to concentrate their friendships in their own inflection group than are Western-Armenian speakers. This orientation becomes understandable if we put it into the context of the public gatherings which make up the substance of community life in the London Armenian community, remembering that these respondents all have some involvement, although some only marginally so, in these gatherings.

Earlier it was pointed out that Armenians of every inflection set and national origin are generally agreed that Iranian Armenians are more highly represented at public gatherings sponsored by the associations. According to my own observations this appears to be the case. In fact, when I set out to organise these interviews I realised that I knew fewer Western-Armenian speakers than Eastern-Armenian speakers, having garnered many of my acquaintances through my own involvement in these gatherings. In a similar way, a Western-Armenian speaker who wishes to be actively involved either in the organisation of, or attendance at, these gatherings is likely to come into contact with a large number of Eastern-Armenian speakers. This would be the case particularly if he or she wishes to be involved with an association with a more youthful or more politicised membership. All the politicised associations (as are almost all of the associations catering for young adults) are dominated by Iranian Armenians. Thus, out of the eight Western Armenians who reported that they had half or less than half of their friends within the same inflection set as themselves and also had friends on the executives of politicised associations, only two were over forty; the rest were in their thirties or twenties. For Iranian Armenians it is far easier to restrict a greater portion of their interactions to members of their own inflection set, for, with the exception of the Tekeyan, the AGBU, Melkonian, and the LACCC, Iranian Armenians are well represented in the executive, membership, and participation in the London Armenian associations and the gatherings they sponsor. In fact, it may be more difficult, as some Iranian Armenians claimed, for an Iranian Armenian to establish relationships with Western Armenians than with other Iranian Armenians because of their differential rate of participation in the gatherings sponsored by the associations. It should be pointed out, however, that both in the Sunday School and in the Ararat Choir, at least until the end of my fieldwork period, Eastern and Western Armenians were fairly evenly represented. Although the Anahid tends to be dominated by Iranian-Armenian women, Western-Armenian women do attend, and out of the three original founding members, two were Western Armenians. On the other hand, Iranian Armenians do not appear to have made any significant inroads into the Western-Armenian-dominated associations. Western Armenians appear more easily able to establish contact with people involved in both the Eastern-dominated associations and the Western-dominated associations. Six out of the eight Western Armenians who had friends on the executives of politicised associations also had friends on the executives of the Tekeyan, or the AGBU, or both.

Why do Western Armenians appear to be under-represented in the gatherings sponsored by the London Armenian associations? As we saw earlier, some Iranian Armenians claim that Cypriot Armenians, in particular, who generally have been resident in Britain for longer than Iranian Armenians or other Western Armenians, have become the most Anglicised, the most assimilated of the Armenians in London, and, hence, the least likely to make an effort to maintain involvement with the community. This may or may not be a factor, but I have not been able to verify it with sufficient cases. On the other hand, it may be that Iranian Armenians now outstrip the Western Armenians in numbers altogether in London, but here again I do not have sufficient data to verify this. It is possible, however, to examine another factor which may influence this rate of participation, particularly among Cypriot Armenians.

Fifteen of the Western Armenian respondents, including all the Cypriot Armenians, reported that more than half or all of their friends were Armenians. Even among the remaining five respondents, none of whom were Cypriots, only two replied that less than half of their friends were Armenians, the others claiming an equal balance between non-Armenians and Armenians among their friends. Thus, although Western Armenians collectively are not perhaps as frequently present at the public association-sponsored gatherings, this does not necessarily mean that they do not have significant contacts with Armenians. Rather, the indication is that their interaction with other Armenians may take place more frequently in a private context than a public one. Armenians of every nationality are involved in informal interactions with other Armenians taking place in private settings, usually involving visiting between homes. Seventeen of the Eastern Armenians reported that they socialised with their friends at each other's homes, as did eighteen of twenty Western Armenians. However, eighteen Iranian Armenians reported that they also socialised with their friends at Armenian association-sponsored gatherings. One other respondent did not report this as a setting for socialisation with her friends but she is, in fact, extremely active in the associational life of the community, sitting on the executives of three associations and had earlier complained that the cost of entertaining in London had decreased the opportunities for the exchange of visits between homes. Thus, with only one exception all the Iranian Armenians questioned do appear to socialise with their Armenian friends within the context of Armenian public gatherings. Among the Western Armenian respondents, only eleven out of twenty listed an Armenian association gathering as a common setting for their interactions with friends (see Figures 6 and 7).

So, it would appear that Iranian Armenians may be more dependent on the Armenian public functions and meeting places for meeting their Armenian friends than their Western-Armenian counterparts. To understand why this is so we must look at the structure of their communities of origins, the relationships between these communities, and the nature of the migration from these communities to London.

Although Cypriot Armenians in London originate from several different sites in Cyprus, mainly Nicosia, Larnaca, and Limasol, there appears to have

Figure 6:   Popular settings for socialising with friends (Eastern Armenians)

	Armenian association gathering or institution	Each other's homes	Non-Armenian public setting
1	X	X	
2	X	X	
3	X	X	X
4	X	X	
5	X	X	
6	X	X	X
7	X	X	
8	X	X	
9	←————————	X*	
10	X	X	X
11	X	X	
12	X	X	
13	X		X
14	X	X	
15	X	X	
16	X		
17		X	
18	X		
19	X	X	
20	X	X	
	18	17	4

* Did not report meeting with friends at Armenian gatherings but known to be an extremely active community member and participant in these gatherings

been extensive contact between the Armenian communities in these different cities. This is not entirely surprising considering the small size of Cyprus and its relatively small population. One Cypriot-Armenian woman told me how she had lived in Nicosia in the home of her husband's parents while her husband commuted daily to his work place in Limasol, which was also her birthplace and the home of her parents. Armenians from these different communities often attended one Armenian secondary school, the Melkonian school, which accommodated boarding students as well as serving local day students. And even where there was no personal acquaintanceship, Armenians from one community often knew of Amenian families in other cities on Cyprus, their names, occupations, number of offspring, and so on.

At the same time, there appear to have been regular contacts with other Western-Armenian speaking communities in Syria, Lebanon, and even as far afield as Ethiopia. To judge from the life histories of Western-Armenian speakers in London, contacts appear to have been based on four main forms of interaction. In the first place, many of the Armenians in communities outside Iran originate from Turkey. They are the Armenians deported from

Figure 7: Popular settings for socialising with friends (Western Armenians)

	Armenian association or institution	Each other's homes	Non-Armenian public setting
1	X	X	
2	X	X	
3	X	X	
4	X	X	
5	X	X	
6		X	X
7	X	X	X
8	X	X	
9		X	
10		X	X
11		X	
12		X	
13		X	
14		X	
15	X	X	
16	X	X	
17	X		
18	X		X
19		X	X
20		X	X
	11	18	6

Turkey in 1915 and their descendants. In a number of cases families appear to have split, members settling in different countries. Thus, an Armenian in Cyprus may have relatives in Syria, Lebanon, Turkey, and so on, and may have maintained a correspondence with these relatives and exchanged visits. Secondly, a number of Armenian schools in different communities were established by branches of one or the other of Armenian associations. Thus, the Melkonian school is an AGBU school and there are other AGBU schools in Lebanon and elsewhere. Teachers in schools run by the same organisation sometimes moved from one branch to the other. Thus, Mr FS, taught both in Jerusalem and in Cyprus and has ties with former students from both of these regions. Similarly, Mr D, a Cypriot-born Armenian, was sent to Ethiopia as a teacher and later married and settled there, starting up several businesses. On arriving in London he was able to renew relationships both with former Armenian schoolmates and friends from Cyprus as well as friends met in Ethiopia and now in London. At the same time Armenian children were sometimes sent from Syria and Lebanon, for example, to be educated at the Melkonian school in Cyprus. Thus, Mrs G was born in Lebanon, educated at the Melkonian school in Cyprus, and later taught at another AGBU school in Beirut. On arriving in London she met former friends and schoolmates from Cyprus as well as from Lebanon. Thirdly, there appear to have been holiday visits to and fro between these Western-Armenian speaking communities in the Middle East. Several Cypriot Armenians I knew in London had met their spouse while holidaying with friends or relations in Syria, Greece, or Lebanon. Finally, a number of Armenians appear to have moved from one community to another in search of better economic prospects. As an example of the kinds of contacts which existed between these communities let us look briefly at the background of Mrs LX, a Western-Armenian speaker in London.

Mrs LX was born in Mesene, in what is now Turkey, to which her parents returned after they were deported from there in 1915. When she was six months old, her parents migrated to Cyprus. Her maternal grandparents also moved there. In Cyprus she attended the Melkonian school. When Mrs LX was twenty-eight years old, she went with some friends to Lebanon, where she met and married her husband and eventually settled. In Lebanon, she renewed her acquaintance with her father's brother's daughter, who had migrated from Turkey to Lebanon after the troubles in 1915. Mrs LX enrolled her son and daughter in an AGBU school in Beirut. Several of the teachers who had taught Mrs LX in the Melkonian school in Cyprus now taught at the AGBU school in Beirut so that her children received tuition from some of these same teachers. In addition, one of her daughter's teachers had been educated at the Melkonian school in Cyprus. When her daughter completed her secondary education in Beirut, Mrs LX acceeded to her wish to be educated further in Europe. In the meantime, one of Mrs LX's brothers and her sister and parents had migrated from Cyprus to London. Mrs LX decided to send her daughter to Britain where she could be supervised by her sister and mother. In Britain Ms M, Mrs LX's daughter, met and married Mr NM, an Englishman, and settled in London. When her husband died, Mrs LX left Beirut and came to live with her daughter in London. Mrs LX's present set of friends in London consist primarily of people she had already met in Cyprus or in Lebanon, and to a smaller extent their Cypriot and Lebanese friends.

As is indicated by Mrs LX's life history, the movement between Western-Armenian speaking communities in the Middle East can provide Armenians with contacts in several different communities. Thus, when a Western-Armenian speaker arrives in London, he or she may potentially have previously established relationships with a number of Armenians in Britain emanating from several different countries. In fact, it is likely that they will be drawn to London because they already have Armenian contacts there. Thus, Mrs LX sent her daughter to Britain because her sister, brother, and parents were already there. Similarly, the only sibling of Mrs LX still in Cyprus, her brother, sent his own daughter to Britain to be educated because his siblings and parents were already there as well as his wife's parents.

Another factor indicated by Mrs LX's story is the tendency of Cypriot Armenians particularly to move as extended families to Britain, to be joined later by additional family members. Parents follow children, siblings follow siblings, and so on. In fact, a large proportion of the Armenian community in Cyprus appears to have migrated to London just before or just after Cyprus achieved its independence. London was a particular drawing point because most of these Armenians had received British passports just before the independence of Cyprus, which had been a British colony. Thus, it is highly unusual to find Cypriot Armenians who do not have any family or friends from Cyprus in London. In fact, when Mrs LX met Ms DS, a young Cypriot-Armenian woman studying in London, the former was astonished to hear that the latter had no family with her in London. At the same time, because of the previous contacts between Western-Armenian speaking communities, many Western-Armenian speakers who are not Cypriot-born nevertheless had previously established relations with Cypriots and other Western-Armenian speakers when they first arrived in London. However, it is more common to find Western-Armenian speakers of non-Cypriot origin who, like the Iranian Armenians, have experienced separation from close family members. According to the Armenians themselves, this is because of the much smaller proportions of the Lebanese, Syrian, and Egyptian communities which migrated to London, but I have not been able to verify this with any independent figures. The relationships between Western-Armenian speaking households in London can be highly complex, involving previous commercial and school ties as well as affinal ties. As an example, let us look at the relationships between three households in London, the AG, BT, and P households. As is shown in Figure 8, Mrs P is Mrs LX's sister.

Mrs P is married to a Cypriot of Greek and Armenian parentage. In Cyprus Mr P ran a business in partnership with Mr BT, his sister's son. Mr BT's wife was introduced to him at the home in Cyprus of his 'best friend', Mr AG. Mr AG is married to Mrs W, who is Mrs BT's cousin's daughter. Mrs W was born in Syria and met Mr AG while he was holidaying with Armenian friends in Syria. Mr AG is Mrs P's mother's sister's son's stepson. In fact, Mr AG's stepfather, who was orphaned by the troubles in Turkey, was partly raised by Mrs P's father. At present all the aforementioned individuals are now in London, but Mrs W's siblings and parents now reside in Toronto.

Iranian Armenians in London also originate from a number of different places in Iran, principally Tehran, Isfahan, Abadan, and Tabriz. However, in contrast to the situation of Armenians in Cyprus, Armenian communities in these Iranian cities were separated by hundreds of miles. There was no common school attended by Armenians from all these communities. In fact, there were thirteen different Armenian day schools in Iran in the various

Figure 8:   Three Western Armenian households

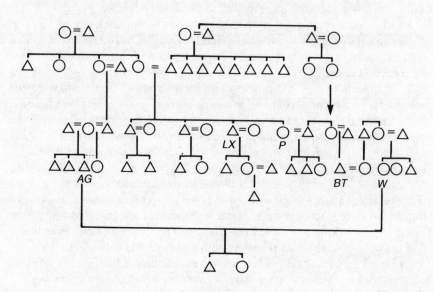

communities. The Armenian population in Iran was a relatively large one, numbering approximately 200,000 individuals. It is common to find that Armenians in London from the same community in Iran did not even know of each other before their arrival in Britain and subsequent acquaintance. It is rare to find Armenians emanating from different communities in Iran who had a previously established relationship with each other before their arrival in London.

A much smaller proportion of the Armenians in Iran were deportees from Turkey. The majority of Iranian Armenians are the descendants of Armenians who arrived in Iran during the course of the last two or three centuries. Contacts with Armenian communities outside Iran appear to have been focused on the community in India and that in Soviet Armenia. I met several Iranian Armenians who had received some part of their education in Armenian establishments in India and/or in Soviet Armenia.

Like the Cypriot Armenians, many of the Iranian Armenians in London whom I knew had followed a relative or friend to London. But it is more common to find Iranian Armenians who had no friend or relative in Britain upon first arrival than it is among Western-Armenian speakers (see Figure 9 and 10). It is also much more common to find Iranian Armenians arriving in London singly or in small nuclear family groups than among the Cypriot Armenians. Unlike the Cypriot Armenians, few of the Iranian Armenians in London previously held British passports. The bulk of Armenian emigration from Iran to London has taken place within the last ten years. With the

Figure 9: Establishment of friendships with Armenians upon first arrival in Britain (Western Armenians)

	Proportion of friends in same inflection set	Friends or relatives already in Britain	No friends or relatives already in Britain	Through Armenian association or institution met friends	Through old friends met new friends	N/A
1	All	X		X		
2	All	X		X	X²	
3	All	X		X		
4	All	X	X¹			
5	All	X	X¹			
6	All	X			X²	
7	More than half	X	X¹		X	
8	More than half	X	X			
9	More than half	X	X	X		
10	More than half	X				
11	More than half	X				
12	More than half	X				
13	Half	X	X¹	X		
14	Half	X	X¹	X		
15	Half	X		X		
16	Half	X		X		
17	Half	X		X		
18	Less than half	X	X	X	X	
19	Less than half	X		X		
20	Very few	X				
		19	1	10	10	4

[1] Primarily renewing relationships previously established outside Britain
[2] No new friendships established; relying only on friends and relatives from Cyprus

Figure 10:   Establishment of friendships with Armenians upon first arrival in Britain (Eastern Armenians)

	Proportion of friends in same inflection set	Friends or relatives already in Britain	No friends or relatives already in Britain	Through Armenian association or institution met friends	Through old friends met new friends	N/A
1	All	X				X
2	All		X			
3	All	X		X	X	
4	All	X			X	
5	All		X	X	X	
6	More than half	X		X		
7	More than half	X		X		
8	More than half	X		X	X	
9	More than half		X	X	↓	X[1]
10	More than half	X		X		
11	More than half	X		X		
12	More than half	X		X		
13	More than half	X		X	X	
14	More than half		X	X		
15	More than half	X		X	X	
16	More than half		X	X		
17	Half	X			X	
		12	5	12+1[1]	8	2

[1] When first arrived in Britain, resident in Manchester where he was attending university; when he moved to London, he relied on Armenian associations and institutions for meeting new friends

tightening of immigration regulations in Britain during this period, a number of Iranian Armenians found it difficult to acquire permanent residence status or British citizenship. Some of these have since moved on to the USA, Canada, or Australia, leaving friends and relatives behind. At the same time, those still domiciled in London have found it difficult to arrange for family members still in Iran to join them in Britain. Thus, Mr BJ, a young single Iranian Armenian, has been under intensive pressure from his parents, still in Iran, to emigrate to the USA, where they hope he will more easily be able to obtain permission to have them join him. His brother, who was living in London with Mr BJ, has already moved on to Los Angeles. Similarly Ms C, an Iranian Armenian who has managed to acquire British citizenship because of her British-born Scottish spouse, is considering emigration to the USA where she hopes to be able to arrange for her parents, sister, and brother to join her. Not surprisingly, it is very common to find Iranian Armenians speaking with great sorrow of their separation from close family members, a complaint more rarely heard, at least with the same degree of intensity, from Western-Armenian speakers.

As such, Armenians arriving in London from Iran often had relatively few previously established contacts with Armenians already in London, unlike the Cypriot Armenians and many of the Western-Armenian speakers in general. Because the London Armenian population is so residentially dispersed, about the only way in which a newly arrived Armenian can establish contacts with other Armenians, if he or she has few or none to begin with, is to visit the permanent meeting places of the Church or Armenian House, and to attend the functions sponsored by the associations. Several Iranian Armenians described to me how in their early days in London they would wait with longing all week for Sunday to arrive so that they could go to the Church and to the Armenian House (which is open to the public only on Sundays) and meet Armenians there.

Thus, Armenians from Iran appear to have initiated most of their relationships with other London Armenians in Britain. Cypriot Armenians, on the other hand, appear to have initiated many of their present relationships with other London Armenians outside Britain. Western Armenians not born in Cyprus also appear to have initiated more of their relationships with other London Armenians outside Britain than have their Iranian-Armenian counterparts, but perhaps to a somewhat lesser extent than their Cypriot-Armenian counterparts. As such, the Cypriot Armenians particularly would not be as dependent in establishing these relationships on the association functions or the institutions. It is, in fact, possible to find Cypriot Armenians who have not extended their set of friendships beyond those relationships initiated outside London, even though they have been resident in Britain for as long as twenty years.

However, we should make one thing very clear. All of this is not to say that

Western Armenians did not attend the associations meetings and visit the church or Armenian House when they first arrived in London. Most of them did, and because of the nature of the population I studied (i.e. those Armenians who have some involvement, however marginal, with the annual round of community functions) most of the ones I met still do. However, as we already pointed out, at present Western Armenians are more likely to do this less frequently than Iranian Armenians. As for their earlier involvement in these activities if we look at the responses of first-generation Western and Eastern Armenian respondents (Figures 9 and 10), there does not, at first glance, appear to be any sharp discrepancy between the two sets in the use they made of association sponsored gatherings, as opposed to friends for establishing relationships on first arrival in London. Some ten out of twenty Western Armenians reported relying on the introductions of old friends (i.e. friendships established outside Britain), and eight out of seventeen Eastern Armenians reported the same. Some ten out of twenty Western Armenians reported meeting friends through the association-sponsored gatherings, compared with thirteen out of seventeen Eastern Armenians, a somewhat higher figure. However, out of the ten Western Armenians relying on association-sponsored gatherings, five reported that in attending these gatherings in their early days in London, they were meeting only or primarily friends known outside Britain. Another two Cypriot Armenians reported that they established no new friendships with Armenians in Britain, relying only on relations and friendships derived from Cyprus. Thus, in combination with the six who reported that they did not use the association sponsored gatherings at all but relied rather on the introductions of old friends this means that some thirteen Western Armenians out of twenty relied extensively, when first arriving in London, on previous contacts for establishing relationships with Armenians in London. In contrast, only three Iranian Armenians relied primarily on previous friendships for establishing contacts with Armenians in London, most of the remaining fourteen relying on meeting friends through the association sponsored gatherings with five (out of these thirteen) in addition using introductions from old friends.

It may be that having used the association functions or institutions for initially meeting Armenians in London, Iranian Armenians continue to be motivated to participate in them because of those very relationships they have established. That is to say that the prospect of attending a gathering may be more attractive if one is fairly certain that friends will also be in attendance. And, as was pointed out earlier, frequent participation or contact with regular participants ensures better access to information about future events, thus facilitating continuous participation.

It would seem, therefore, that the greater use made by Iranian Armenians of Armenian public settings for initiating and maintaining friendships with other London Armenians, and the greater use made by Western Armenians of private settings may have contributed to the continuing tendency to focus friendships within the respective inflection sets. But as we saw earlier (Figures 2–5) even when Armenians of every national subgrouping either participate themselves in the associations or have contacts with others who do, their involvement may also be differentiated according to the inflection set of which they are members, with Iranian Armenians much less likely to either be members of, or to have intimate contacts with members of the Tekeyan and the AGBU. This differentiation may be at least partially due to the tendency of London Armenians to establish or affiliate themselves with branches of associations with which they were familiar in their country of origin. And in this respect there is an important difference in the experiences of Western-Armenian speakers and Iranian Armenians.

In Iran only one Armenian political 'party' held sway: the Armenian Revolutionary Federation, or Dashnakstitiun. The associations which operated in Iran were almost all affiliates of this party. Although the Dashnakstitiun operated in other Armenian communities outside Iran – in Lebanon, where its headquarters are situated, Cyprus, and so on – it existed side by side with associations independent of its control and in fact imputed to have affiliations with the two competing parties, the Ramgavars and the Hunchaks. These kinds of associations, such as the AGBU and the Tekeyan, had branches in virtually every Western-Armenian speaking community but not in Iran. As was pointed out earlier, the AGBU in particular established a number of schools in these communities, such as the Melkonian school in Cyprus.

In London, Western-Armenian speakers established branches of the AGBU and the Tekeyan, whose membership and executive is overwhelmingly dominated by Western-Armenian speakers. They have also established the Melkonian Alumni Association, which *de facto* excludes Iranian Armenians from membership. On the other hand, Iranian Armenians have established the Armenian Scouts Association, which is identified with the Dashnakstitiun. Not surprisingly, considering their past familiarity with this association, they also are prominent in the other branches and associations of the Dashnakstitiun in London: the Navarsatian Cultural Association, the Armenian National Committee, and the Armenian Youth Federation. Thus, in London, membership and organisation of Armenian associations, particularly those identified with political movements, has become in some cases almost congruent with inflection set – on the one hand, Iranian Eastern Armenians, and on the other, Western Armenians. And hence, the equivalence as we saw earlier between the AGBU or Tekeyan, Ramgavar and Western Armenian. But what prevents this tendency from polarisation is the straddling role played by the non-political associations, in particular the balanced commitment of Eastern and Western Armenians to the Sunday School, as well as the involvement of some younger and/or politicised Western Armenians in the political associations which are otherwise dominated by Iranian Armenians. This latter may be encouraged by the previous exposure of Western Armenians to the Dashnakstitiun, but it is also, and perhaps more importantly, encouraged by the virtual monopoly which the politicised associations have on organised activities for young Armenian adults in the community.

Polarisation, at least within the context of association-sponsored gatherings, is also offset by the fact that congruence between inflection set and particular associations does not hold equally well for attendance at the functions organised by these associations. Iranian Armenians may certainly be well represented at events organised by associations with a high proportion of Iranian Armenian membership, but at the same time they may be highly represented in events open to the Armenian public at large, such as concerts, dinner dances, and so on, even when they are organised by associations such as the Tekeyan. However, they are extremely under-represented at events organised by the Melkonian Alumni association which are directed at an audience of former alumni of the Melkonian school and their friends.

In this respect, the nature of the advertising of particular events has an influence on the groupings which may be found in attendance, and this is related, in turn, to the membership of the association which sponsors the events. Meetings of the committees which run the associations are not advertised at all; meetings intended primarily for the paid-up members of the associations are advertised primarily through personal correspondence; and for meetings open to the Armenian public at large, members may be informed of the impending event through personal correspondence but the function is also more widely advertised through leaflets and posters circulated at the institutions and at preceding association-sponsored gatherings. In the first two cases, the high representation of one or the other of the inflection sets in association membership will obviously influence their representation at the meetings. In the third case, this influence will be muted by the more open advertisement of these events, but this tends rather to work towards a greater representation of Iranian Armenians than of Western Armenians.

But if there are associations which are dominated by Iranian Armenians as, or perhaps even to a greater extent than, there are associations dominated by Western-Armenian speakers, why do some Iranians complain that the Western-Armenian speakers are trying to keep control of the community's affairs? As was pointed out earlier, there are only four regular public venues for Armenian gatherings – the two Armenian churches, the Armenian House, and the Sunday School. One of the two churches, St Sarkis's Church was established by Calouste Gulbenkian in 1922 and has been run since then by a trust set up by Gulbenkian. The trustees are appointed for life. Similarly, the Armenian House, established in 1961, is also run by a trust with appointed trustees. During the period in which these institutions and the trusts to run them were established, the bulk of the Iranian Armenian migration to

London had not yet begun, so it is perhaps not surprising that the majority of the trustees are Western-Armenian speakers. On the other hand, St Peter's Church is run by the LACCC and members are elected to the governing committee. But as was indicated above, until the last election to this Council, only Armenians domiciled in London, holding British citizenship or permanent residence status in Britain were able to stand for election or to vote. As Iranian Armenians are among the more recent of Armenian immigrants, these criteria tend to exclude more of them, in particular more than the Cypriot Armenians. As a result, out of fifteen Council members, only two are Eastern-Armenian speakers. One should point out that it is doubtful that these criteria for eligibility in the elections were deliberately devised to exclude the more recent of the Armenian immigrants to London. It is likely that they were devised at a time when the majority of Armenians in London were British passport holders, as is the case with the Cypriot Armenians. The Sunday School is, for the most part, run by its parents committee and staff. Until recently Western-Armenian speakers and Eastern-Armenian speakers were fairly evenly represented on both these bodies. However, officially, the Sunday School is ultimately under the formal control of the LACCC, and the staff and parents committee are expected to report to this body. Thus, the few permanent meeting places for London Armenians *de facto* are under the control of trusts or organisations with a high representation of Western-Armenian speakers and this, no doubt, has contributed to the view of some Iranian Armenians that they are not as equally represented in the control of community affairs as their Western-Armenian counterparts.

Until now, I have been speaking about the way in which national differences influence affiliation and friendship sets within the London Armenian community. We have seen that this factor has an influence both on the way in which Armenians perceive one another and on the way in which they form affiliations in this city, with particular associations and in more informal friendship sets. However, as has also been indicated, other kinds of distinctions also operate, sometimes independently of and sometimes overlapping with national differences.

If we place these kind of distinctions within the context of the associational framework discussed in Chapter 1, they become much easier to understand. If the differentiating criteria which Armenians use to distinguish themselves from one other are often woven in their references in a multi-stranded web, this is because the phenomenon itself is indeed multi-componential.

There is a generational demarcation between the London Armenian associations. Political associations like the Dashnakstitiun affiliates, in particular the Armenian Youth Federation and the Armenian National Committee, and the triad of associations supporting the ASALA movement are dominated in membership and participation by young Armenian adults under the age of thirty-five, many of whom are students. Non-political associations and marginally politicised associations such as the Tekeyan, Anahid, AGBU, etc., but with the exception of the Scouts Association (which is identified with the Dashnakstitiun if not openly affiliated with them) tend to be dominated in their membership and in their organisers by Armenians over the age of thirty-five.

But, as should be clear by now, these associations are also distinguished in terms of their approach to overt and public politicisation. For those Armenians who find explicit politicisation offputting or even alarming, the young who are engaged in overt political activity in support of armed militancy become in this context alarmingly irresponsible.

Non-politicised associations tend to interpret their role *vis-à-vis* the London Armenian community in terms of the provision of the arts (or what they term 'culture') and education. Many of the gatherings which they sponsor for a non-membership audience have a strong emphasis on entertainment, which often involves conspicuous consumption and display of one kind or another, for example, consumption of food, alcohol, elaborate dress, and so on; and since these are usually fund-raising activities as well they often involve expensive admission prices. Such activities are interpreted by a number of Armenians, and not only young militant adults, as an over-preoccupation with consumption and material things, and, as we saw earlier, in some cases with conspicuous display of wealth. Reference to this issue is usually couched in terms of the 'rich'.

In contrast, many of the gatherings sponsored by the political associations are in the form of lectures, with relatively little or no food; participants tend to be casually dressed and admission is usually free of charge. There is, with the exception of the Navarsation activities and the Scouts disco, rarely any conscious effort made at entertainment.

Non-politicised associations are provided with a range of access to the community institutions which is denied their more politicised counterparts. The organisers of the owner associations are usually also in the over thirty-five age bracket and the gatherings which they sponsor also often have strong emphasis on entertainment and consumption.

Thus, we have a concentration of a number of elements which together can produce two different styles of collectively organised and public Armenianness. On the other hand, there is middle age, avoidance of explicit public politicisation, a recurrent feature of consumption and display, and a wide scope for institutional access and management. On the other, there is youth, student militant politicisation, public preservation of political views, and limitation of institutional access. This is not to say that the Armenian community is ranged into two opposing sections with members of each identifying with the style associated with that section. Quite the opposite, most Armenians are constantly manoeuvring between these two poles, combining and recombining elements of each. The most militant of young

Armenians can be found happily consuming at the Scouts disco, at a dinner dance, watching a film or concert, elaborately dressed. Older, more cautious, Armenians can be found studiously and patiently listening to a lecture on Armenian history or linguistics, discussing education in Soviet Armenia, arguing about the need to financially support young Armenian students, or even being involved in the organisation of gatherings or publications with a more controversial or politicised content. But when Armenians want to contrast, disassociate themselves from, or criticise a particular feature of a gathering, association, or even an individual, they will often do this not by actual precise reference to the element under scrutiny but by reference to a feature which is associated with that element at a conceptualised structural extreme. Thus, when Mr BY wanted to criticise the expensive admission prices to dinner dances sponsored by associations such as the Tekeyan, Anahid, etc., he did so by reference to the young, the students, who were being excluded. When Mrs CW wanted to point out the irresponsibility of overt militant politicisation, she did so by reference to those emotional excitable young people. When members of the BACA wanted to criticise the attempts to exclude politicised activists from St Peter's Church or the Armenian House, they did so by making reference to the 'rich' who control the community, the old people, or through assertions that the Community Council is composed only of businessmen.

In other words, the Armenians appear to be using a shorthand to refer to particular patterns of grouping that tend to be more identified with some attitudes and behaviour than others. Necessarily, therefore, the terms are ambiguous and fluid in their application, since no one attitude or behaviour is specific to one individual, or one association, or one kind of Armenian, and yet these attitudes are being identified and discussed in terms of groupings and kinds. Thus, different themes or terms converge in their use as references for particular attitudes or behaviour (refer to use of 'rich', 'old', 'businessmen', and 'Ramgavar' to address the same issues), while each of these themes in itself can be extended to identify a series of attitudes associated with a range of narrower and more inclusive groupings (refer to the range of groupings referred to as 'rich', in different contexts).

However, this shorthand is not merely a passive tool for locating particular attitudes or behaviour. It can be used to organise groupings, place individuals within them, and structure relationships between them. But an ambiguity and fluidity that was useful for identifying and referring to particular areas of concern or disagreement can become oppressive and appear arbitrary when it is used to pressure individuals to align themselves with one group or another. It is within the context of this use of the shorthand that Mrs W complained that she was being asked to align herself with groupings whose policies neither she, nor its members were clear about. It is within this context that Ms C complained that she did not know what the Dashnaks were and no one appeared able to explain satisfactorily to her what they were. It is within this context that Armenians insist on their neutrality, although apparently unable to identify the groupings between which this neutrality is maintained. This is not such a paradox as it seems, since it is the very ambiguity and lack of clear consensus about who these groupings are that leads to the insistence on neutrality.

More generally still, Armenians frequently express disapproval of the disunity caused by this pressure and the proliferation of associations. The axiom on which this disapproval rests ('we are all Armenians') implicitly sets up a contrast between Armenians and non-Armenians. So far, the distinctions that Armenians make between themselves have been set only within the context of the Armenian community itself. But as was indicated earlier, many of the contrasts at the heart of these distinctions reflect evaluations of the position of Armenians *vis-à-vis* non Armenians. Cypriot Armenians are too Anglicised; militancy is undesirable because of the possible negative reactions of non-Armenians; the LACCC eliminates its opposition by reporting them to the Home Office as subversives; and so on. Most of the comparisons that Armenians make between the London community and Armenian communities elsewhere relate not only to the internal differentiation within the community, but to the position of that community within the host society.

The internal boundaries within the Armenian community are clearly, therefore, not an aspect of the organisation of this community which can be kept separate from the social boundary maintained between Armenians and non-Armenians. Many of the distinctions that Armenians make between themselves are reflections of differences of perception and judgement in the accounts taken of the influence, responses, and attitudes of non-Armenians. What Armenians are saying about the ways in which they should organise their relationships with one another is, therefore, fundamentally and dynamically related to their differing views about how they should organise their relationships with non-Armenians. In seeking to work through their differences to define codes of Armenianness, Armenians are, in the process, setting forth their respective views on the way in which Armenians should operate as a collectivity in the larger world not only of London or Britain, but of the Armenian diaspora as a whole. We must, therefore, now turn to look more closely at the way in which Armenians operate within that wider context.

Chapter 3

Armenians and non-Armenians

Almost every Armenian I met in London asked me the same question about my fieldwork: 'Why do you want to study Armenians? Most people don't know anything about us.' Armenians have an overwhelming impression of their social anonymity as a group in Britain. Non-Armenians in London according to my experiences and those of my Armenian respondents very rarely appear to be aware that there is an active Armenian community in their midst, and much more commonly are unable to put the label 'Armenian' into any kind of historical or social context. In other words, they rarely know where Armenians come from, what language they use, what religion they practise; in short, who the Armenians are. In this chapter I will attempt to explore some of the factors involved in the development and maintenance of this anonymity, the advantages which Armenians attempt to exploit, and the disadvantages which are at the heart of many of the fears of Armenians about their future as an ethnic group in London.

Circumscription

To be an Armenian in London is not a full-time affair. As I shall attempt to show in the following pages, Armenians, for the most part, live and work alongside non-Armenians. Within the spheres of their neighbourhoods of residence and at their workplace, their Armenian identity is at best secondary and in some ways irrelevant. These spheres are compartmentalised both one from the other and from that sphere in which Armenians interact with other Armenians. That is to say, Armenians often work beside one set of people, live beside another, and spend their leisure time with another set of Armenians. The Armenian 'community', therefore, is far from all embracing, and to be involved in it as an active member requires a conscious effort at communicating and making time to be with Armenians.

Armenians are residentially dispersed throughout almost every borough of

Greater London, with the exception perhaps of those in East London. There are more Armenians in Acton, Ealing, Chiswick, Wembley, and Muswell Hill, i.e. the affluent residential suburbs of West and Northwest London. In no area, however, do the Armenians form a dense and therefore visible concentration, with shops, restaurants and schools catering to the ethnic population. If one considers that the maximum figure ever quoted for the size of the Armenian population in Greater London is 15,000 (usually more frequently between 10,000 and 12,000) and that this is scattered over a city with a population of 9 million, even a relatively greater presence of Armenians in several boroughs does not by any means connote a concentration sufficient to leave a visible ethnic stamp on any one residential area.

The majority of Armenians whom I met in London were living in owner-occupied properties. In forty-seven Armenian households about which I have reliable information in respect to status of residential accommodation, thirty were owner occupiers and seventeen were tenants. Of the seventeen who were living in leasehold accommodation eleven were composed of members all under the age of thirty-five; ten households were those of unmarried tenants; seven had household heads who were full-time students; and two more had household heads who were part-time students as well as being engaged in gainful employment.[1]

I have very little direct evidence on the development of home ownership, but the few cases I do have indicate that the purchase of a home followed very closely upon arrival in Britain, and for those arriving first with the intention of pursuing their education, very closely upon completion of studies. On a number of occasions I met Armenians who were willing to undergo quite serious financial strains in order to purchase their own home. Ms GT, a divorcee, was residing in rented accommodation but with a net salary of only £80 per week she none the less committed herself to the purchase of a flat. Mr BJ was single, unemployed, and deeply in debt, but carried on paying the mortgage on his home. Ms M had sold her suburban house but before she could purchase a new home was made redundant. None the less, with no immediately foreseeable prospects of employment, she went ahead with the purchase of a new house with a large mortgage. More indirectly, we should remember that migration of Armenians to London in any sizeable numbers began in the late 1950s and early 1960s, and that many Armenians in London have been resident in this city for much less than the twenty years or so experienced by this wave of migrants. As an indication of this, out of seventy-five adult respondents (i.e. aged over fifteen) about whom I have reliable information regarding length of residence in Britain, only some one-third was either resident in Britain for twenty years or more, or were born in Britain. Thus, the apparently high proportion of Armenian home owners in 1981–2 within a recently arrived immigrant population suggests a tendency towards rapid acquisition of residential property.

Table 1: Length of residence in Britain; adult Armenian sample

Status	Number
5 years or less	20
6–11 years	19
12–19 years	11
20 years or more	12
British-born	13
Total	75

On the other hand, I have never witnessed reports from Armenians who are tenants about difficulties as a consequence of their Armenian identity in acquiring leased accommodation, and a number of Armenian tenants indeed have non-Armenian landlords. Complaints about finding housing usually relate to the expense, quality, location, etc. of the accommodation. A number of Armenians have, in the past or in the present, rented accommodation from Armenian landlords. Armenians who were seeking rented housing during the time I was in London did make enquiries through Armenian friends and acquaintances. I know of one Armenian landlady who advertised the future availability of housing units under her ownership through word of mouth among Armenians. In spite of this, preferential treatment is not necessarily accorded to Armenians in the final allocation of property. I know of two occasions where an Armenian was refused accommodation by an Armenian landlord and the property let to a non-Armenian. In another reported instance, an Armenian tenant was threatened with eviction by an Armenian landlord for non-payment of rent. In this case, the Armenian tenants reta-liated against threat of eviction and in another reported instance against high rents by threatening to take the matter to the local rent tribunal. In the latter case, the tenant was reported to be a kinsman of his Armenian landlady. On the other hand, I have known of Armenians who have moved out of accom-modation let by Armenian landlords or refused the offer of accommodation from such people because the housing in question was considered to be unsuitable in some respect. In any case, even where Armenians do let property from Armenian landlords, the number involved are so small (in terms of the property I know to be let by Armenian landlords, I estimate no more than two dozen, although there certainly may be other housing units of which I am not aware) and the property offered for let generally involves single, small buildings subdivided into a number of furnished flats or bedsitters and scattered over a number of different boroughs in London, that no sizeable concentrations of Armenians result.

One could speculate that the ability of many Armenians to purchase their own home and the apparent absence of any open discrimination against prospective Armenian tenants by non-Armenian landlords has widened the choice of residential location and enhanced dispersal. On the other hand, as we saw in the relationship between Armenian tenants and landlords, no overriding priority appears to be attached to the establishment and maintenance of relationships between Armenians through proximity of residence.[2] This pattern is not only specific to Armenian tenancy but on the few occasions when I did witness Armenians making plans for the purchase of a new home and deliberating about its possible location, only one woman, Ms M, made any mention of proximity to Armenians as a factor in her search. In the event she did not purchase a home in Ealing where she had first searched 'because there are more Armenians around' but in North London. What is particularly interesting about this case is that Ms M first made the move to London from Surrey so her mother could be closer to her Armenian family and friends. The permanent location she chose was relatively distant from both. When Mrs CW decided to sell her large house and move to a smaller flat, she was advised by an acquaintance not to make her purchase in the same area although this would have allowed her close proximity to the two churches and the Armenian House. 'The area has really deteriorated', she was advised, 'I would look a little farther away.' No mention was made by either Mrs CW or her adviser about seeking residential proximity to the community institutions or to Armenian populations.

What is particularly interesting about the lack of prominence given to this subject in specific discussions of residential location is that the dispersal of Armenians is a subject which comes up in more general discussions, particularly in comparisons drawn between the London community and the community of origin. There is a perception that the dispersion of Armenians in London has created difficulties in maintaining contacts between them, and a perception as well that Armenian communities in the Middle East were more concentrated and segregated from the host population. Two also complained that a new formality had entered the visiting between private homes, with people no longer dropping in unannounced but waiting to be invited or for arrangements to be made in advance. Thus, Armenians appear to be aware that a shift in settlement patterns has occurred with migration to Britain from the Middle East which may have affected relations between Armenians, but they do not use this awareness to necessarily argue for an effort to be made towards greater residential proximity.

In other words, although there may be external factors such as income and accessibility to a wide range of accommodation which facilitate the residential dispersal of Armenia, there are grounds for believing that this pattern is not entirely coincidental. The more dispersed Armenians are the more invisible socially they are within Greater London; and the more invisible they are the greater their freedom of movement within the non-Armenian host society. Armenians do not, for the most part, need other Armenians in order to acquire accommodation but neither, I believe, do they want to need other Armenians in this respect. Such a pattern of choices can also be found in other spheres such as employment and education.

But before I go on to discuss these, it should be pointed out that if Armenians are not giving prominence to residential location in the establishment and maintenance of relations with their ethnic cohorts, neither do those participating in community activities appear to be giving much prominence to this factor in the establishment of anything but narrowly bounded relations with non-Armenians. When forty-three respondents were questioned about the manner in which they had established friendships upon first arrival and/or after a period of settlement in London, only nine replied that they had made friends in their residential neighbourhood. Of these nine, two were non-Armenian, British-born spouses of Armenians and two, a married couple, had established such relationships through their management of a local sweet shop. In short, while Armenians may not be living beside their Armenian friends neither are they necessarily making friends of those they do live beside. By friends, I mean, and the Armenians I interviewed meant, a relationship that goes beyond casual and brief encounters on the street.

If Armenians are not congregating residentially, are they doing so through their place of employment? Since separate information is not available on Armenians in the British National Census Records and I did not have the resources to conduct a census myself, I have no comprehensive statistical records on the distribution of occupation and workplace for Armenians in London. However, from my observations, I can say with reasonable certainty that no one workplace provides employment for more than a handful of Armenians at any one time. If there is a workplace employing tens or even hundreds of Armenians, Armenians whom I met do not appear to know about it, nor to view it as a prospective source of employment. Furthermore, Armenians often do not live near their workplace so that their workmates are not necessarily their neighbours.

The dispersal of Armenians through a myriad of places of employment may be related to the kinds of occupations in which Armenians appear to be commonly employed. They appear to be concentrated in skilled white-collar work (architectural draughtsmen, electronic technicians, etc.) the professions (architects, engineers, journalists, lawyers, etc.), or in self-employment. The occupational breakdown for sixty-one gainfully employed Armenians about whom I have reliable information in respect to occupation (I exclude in this calculation women managing their domestic households full time, retired men and women, and full-time students) is shown in Table 2. It should be pointed out that several of the men listed in the category of self-employed ran family businesses and were assisted by their wives in this. Also it needs to be pointed out that two of the three included under the category of blue-collar work (i.e. occupations requiring manual labour) were skilled workers – one a

Table 2:   Employment among the Armenian sample

Occupational class	Men	Women	Total
Self-employed	14	3	17
Salaried professionals	14	4	18
Skilled white collar	9	4	13
Semi-skilled white collar (i.e. typists, clerks, secretaries, beauticians, etc.)	–	10	10
Blue collar	3	–	3
Total			61

metalworker for an antique restoration firm, and the other a welder on construction sites.

Educational levels appear to be high. Out of eighty-one adult Armenians about whom I have reasonably reliable information concerning educational background, fifty-four had received some kind of post-secondary education. However, educational levels appear to be comparatively lower for women (see Table 3). It should be pointed out that thirteen of the fifteen women who had received some vocational training held secretarial, beautician, or hairdressing diplomas. Although this sample is not claimed to be representative, some of the factors which may have contributed to such a high proportion of those receiving post-secondary education should be noted. In the first place, the numbers may have been distorted by the inclusion of a number of students presently enrolled in programmes of education at colleges or universities who came to Britain expressly to further their education. Nevertheless I have included these individuals even though not all of them will necessarily settle permanently in Britain because all are active participants in association-sponsored gatherings in the London Armenian community. Furthermore, many of these students have family members (brothers, sisters, aunts, uncles, cousins, if not parents) who are settled in London. Also, in the past, it has been very common for Armenians arriving in Britain with the

Table 3:   Educational attainment, Armenian sample

Level of education	Men	Women	Total
Post-secondary academic	31	15	46
Post-secondary/non-diploma course	5	3	8
Post-secondary vocational training	2	15	17
Secondary education only	2	5	7
Incomplete secondary	2	1	3
Total			81

original purpose of furthering their education to settle in the country subsequently. This not only indicates the possibility that at least some of these students may eventually settle permanently but also has no doubt contributed to the high levels of education among Armenian adults in London. That is to say that for a sizeable proportion of Armenian immigrants, Britain was preselected for its educational facilities and not surprisingly, therefore, many of those now settled in London have attained relatively high educational levels. Women, on the other hand, were sometimes sent to Britain to increase their proficiency in the English language or to attain secretarial diplomas in order to improve their employment opportunities in their country of origin. However, some of these subsequently remained and settled. Other women accompanied family and husbands. It is perhaps not surprising then to find women more likely to be engaged in semi-skilled white-collar work. However, this trend may be changing as more women are enrolling in post-secondary academic programmes rather than vocational training programmes.

It must also be pointed out that this level of educational attainment does not appear to be unique to the London Armenian community. In Lebanon, by 1975, the Armenians, although forming only 8 per cent of the total population, made up 10 per cent of the engineers, 6 per cent of the physicians, 23 per cent of the pharmacists, and 25 per cent of the dentists. The Lebanese Armenian community appears to have been, on the whole, a wealthy one, contributing by 1975, 15 per cent to the national income and operating 25 per cent of the Beirut gold market (Der-Karabetian, 1981, p. 212).

The point I wish to stress is that, considering what appear to be the generally high levels of education among Armenians and the kinds of skilled employment they appear to be seeking, the ability of adult Armenians, particularly males, to concentrate in any one industry or workplace on the basis of ethnicity is constrained by the need for appropriate vocational skills or educational qualifications. As prospective employees of Armenians, Armenian businesses tend to be small family-run retail enterprises which require only a small work-force of salaried employees, and sometimes none at all. Those enterprises with a larger work force, such as garment manufacturers, tend to require manual labour and/or specialised skills; there appears to be little demand for the first among Armenians, and the latter constrains the ability of Armenian employers to hire workers solely on the basis of ethnic identity. In one of two of the larger concerns Armenians had non-Armenian partners which, again, may have worked to limit the employment of Armenians.

If Armenian businesses appear to be limited in their ability to absorb Armenian employees, they also appear not to attach a high priority to cultivating an Armenian clientele. At larger Armenian-association-sponsored gatherings such as dinner dances or concerts the programmes are often a compilation of advertisements for Armenian businesses and notices from well-wishers. However, Mrs W, who was responsible for the organisation of one of these programmes, reported considerable difficulty in persuading Armenian businessmen to take out such advertisements:

> We always call people and for example I had to sell adverts for the book. It's only £30 but people refused. This bothers me, especially when I know they can afford it. Some of these people are very wealthy. I don't mind if they don't buy an advert. Let them buy a ticket or give £20, even £5 or let them help, but when you call, they say, 'I don't know' or 'I have to think about it', 'maybe'. I don't just leave it. I call them back if I know they can afford it, until they agree.

Even Mrs W did not expect the businessmen to be particularly interested in the potential audience of new clients they might be reaching through these advertisements but she stressed the idea of the purchases as contributions to the fund-raising efforts of the association. In the event, out of thirty-nine advertisements, thirteen either made no reference to the businesses of the persons involved, mentioning only their personal names, or gave no indication of the nature of the businesses mentioned, and a fourteenth was a notice placed by the trustees of St Sarkis's Church.

There are several possible contributing factors to the limited ethnic entrepreneurism among the London Armenian population. In the first place, the population as a whole is small and therefore would be unlikely to be capable of profitably supporting extensive ethnic entrepreneurism. Secondly, the population is dispersed. Retail and service outlets such as groceries, restaurants, jewellers, hairdressers, etc. which rely on regular, multiple small purchases cannot address themselves to a localised Armenian population. Armenians who wish to frequent Armenian commercial outlets would be required to travel long distances in order to purchase similar items or services which are available in non-Armenian shops nearer their home or work. Few Armenians appear interested in doing this. Thus, one Armenian-owned hairdressing shop which I frequently visited did, in fact, have several Armenian female clients, but these appeared to be drawn for the most part from the same or nearby boroughs and overall formed a minority of the clientele, which was largely non-Armenian. A sizeable proportion of Armenian businesses in London are either wholly or partially engaged in import and/or export, a service which may be unlikely to draw prinicipally on a private London clientele of any sort. Several provide specialised services such as the manufacture of plastic components, the distribution of motor components, or the sale of expensive Oriental carpets which would appeal to a rather selective clientele.

The corollary of this last point is that few Armenian merchants appear to make any special effort to provide a specialised service for the specific needs of Armenians in London. There appear to be a few Armenian grocers or restauranteurs which carry a wide range of items of Armenian cuisine. On the other hand, the cuisine popular among Armenians is generally of

Levantine, Mediterranean, or Iranian origin and is available at non-Armenian grocers and restaurants as well. Armenian grocers and restaurateurs sometimes identify themselves as provisioners of Middle Eastern cuisine or food items rather than specifically Armenian. Armenian businesses, as a whole, often have Anglicised or neutral titles which give little hint of Armenian ownership. Thus, even if a prospective Armenian clientele existed which actively sought to frequent Armenian-owned commercial outlets, they would be hard put to to identify the range of services on offer or their location, scattered as they are throughout London and the suburbs.

Armenians, then, are likely to be working with non-Armenian workmates and/or dealing with non-Armenian customers, and are unlikely to be forming the bulk of their contacts with other Armenians, if any, through their workplace. However, for that population of Armenians participating in association-sponsored gatherings in London, contacts established at work with non-Armenians often do not appear to form any sizeable proportion of extra-work relationships. Out of twenty-five respondents gainfully employed who were specifically queried about this aspect of work relationships, fifteen replied that they had met friends in Britain at the workplace, but eighteen of the twenty-five reported that more than half of all of their friends were Armenian, and four replied that all of their friends were Armenian. Only three replied that half or less than half of all of their friends were Armenian. Armenians, then, do not appear to be carrying over in any substantial way relationships established in one setting into another setting. Their workmates are unlikely to be their immediate neighbours and neither group appears to be people with whom many of the adult Armenians I studied spend any significant proportion of their leisure time.

We have seen so far that Armenians do not appear to congregate through residential location or workplace, nor through educational establishments. There are no Armenian full-time educational establishments in London. The only London Armenian educational establishment of any sort is the Sunday School, which meets for four hours weekly and on Sundays only. All Armenians who have received some part of their education in Britain have attended a non-Armenian school where Armenian language, history, arts, or religion form no part of the curriculum. The residential dispersal of Armenians constrains any concentration of Armenian children in particular non-Armenian primary or secondary schools. Even where greater selection or mobility is present, such as in the attendance at private schools, colleges, or universities, there does not appear to be a much greater concentration of Armenian students in particular educational establishments. Clearly, the fact that Armenians do not control the system of admissions in fee-paying establishments or the scale of fees and the variation in individual requirements in terms of educational programmes limits the trend towards particular institutions. Concern about the consequences of this last form of dispersal is widespread, and the absence of an Armenian primary or secondary day school in London is often contrasted with the situation in other Armenian communities. But there appears to be little confidence in or expectation of the eventual establishment of an Armenian day school. The implications of this for education in the Armenian language are of major concern among Armenians and will be dealt with later on in this chapter. For the moment it remains to be said where and when Armenians do in fact, congregate and interact with one another in London.

Most sustained and regular contacts between Armenians occur within their leisure time, in the exchange of visits between private homes and through participation in association-sponsored gatherings. Leisure time, of course, can mean different things to different people. Not all Armenians attend school or are employed outside the home. Some are retired; a few are unemployed. Women may be engaged fulltime in the management of the household. But the fact that other women and other Armenians more generally are occupied in work or school commitments outside the home and with structured workhours means that more often than not meetings have to be arranged outside normal work and school hours. With the exception of the Anahid monthly meetings almost all association-sponsored gatherings take place in the evening or during weekends. Association-sponsored gatherings are often held in a variety of halls leased for the purpose in the West End of London as well as in the institutions. Most Armenians do not live in the West End or necessarily in close proximity to their Armenian friends. Consequently they often have to travel long distances in order to be with other Armenians.

Communication is also affected by dispersal. If individual Armenians residing in London lose contact with one another, it can sometimes take months or even years before the contact is re-established. Ms C and Ms SU were both enrolled in an English-language course. When the course was completed the two women moved on to other commitments, shifted their residential location, and, although both remained in London (apart from a brief stay abroad by Ms SU), it was four years before they met again at a song and dance recital sponsored by an Armenian association. This, in spite of the fact that Ms SU at one point did make a concerted effort to locate Ms C, searching for her at earlier association-sponsored gatherings, making enquiries through other Armenians, etc. As we saw earlier, Christmas and Easter gatherings at the two Armenian Apostolic churches provide an opportunity for Armenians to renew their acquaintances with former schoolmates, neighbours, friends, etc. from their country of origin whom they either rarely meet during the course of the year, or who may be residing in London unbeknown to them.

Similarly, keeping up with the round of association-sponsored gatherings can often prove difficult. The limited number of venues where such meetings can be advertised and the varied locations of such meetings often mean that Armenians learn about them after the fact, perhaps when it is too late for them to arrange their schedules accordingly, or, if an entrance fee is charged, when the tickets available have already been sold out. Tickets sold in advance are usually available from private vendors who may have to be approached at their place of residence or work, which can entail travel over long distances, not only to the gathering itself but also to the location of the vendor.

In short, for most Armenians interaction with their ethnic cohorts forms a limited and narrowly bounded section of their weekly or annual round. This circumscription in turn, has serious implications for the efficiency of communication between Armenians in London, which can hamper and further limit interactions between them. It is hard work to be an active member of the Armenian community in London, requiring careful planning and a constant vigil for relevant information.

Integration versus segregation

Armenians are aware of these difficulties. Assimilation is viewed by many Armenians as a real and ever-present danger, and for some as an inevitable consequence of migration to Western countries. Assimilation, it was explained, was not a problem in the Middle East, where the host population was distinguished from Armenians by religious differences, i.e. the Muslim/Christian divide. As Mr and Mrs F explained it:

Mrs F: In Middle East, in Iran, we have not much fear, because there are Mohammadans . . . But in the Middle East, there is a wall between the Mohammadans and us.
Mrs F: They want to marry each other and the Armenians want to marry each other.
Mr F: There are never any marriage between us or very rare.
Mrs F: One in a million.
Mr F: But here, everything is free. I think I don't have to go to an Armenian church. I can go to this Protestant church here or it's the same thing with the christening, is that how you say it? Yes, christening. A man up in Scotland thinks: I don't have to go all the way here, I can have the christening in a church near me.

I know of one Ethiopian Armenian woman who although raised in the Armenian Apostolic Church now attends a Baptist church in England. Another occasionally asks an Armenian friend to light a candle for her in the Roman Catholic church near the latter's home. Two Armenian women attended Christmas midnight mass in a Catholic church. But by and large, Armenians do not appear to be shifting their church allegiances. They simply do not go to church.

According to Mr S, a deacon of the church, Armenians were more devout in the Middle East because their host societies were also more devout, but the secular nature of Western societies has unavoidably influenced a trend towards secularisation among Armenians residing within them. Only two women explicitly expressed consternation over this trend, comparing it to the much higher rate of church attendance in their community of origin. By and large, Armenians do refer to this secularisation but usually treat it as a bare fact, requiring no further reflection or introspection. Nevertheless, when introducing their community to an outsider like myself, Armenians who were the most casual of church-goers referred to the Church as its heart. As Mrs Y explained it:

> In every community we have a church. I don't know why. It's a, yes, basis for the community. For us, it's not just religion. It's the core for the community. They have many activists. The sports activities and things like that. We are not like any other church. We have many things from before Christianity which they have absorbed into Christianity. Like our songs. Our songs are not like other continental churches where you hear the same thing in this country and that country. Ours is not like that.

The Armenian Apostolic Church, as its title implies, is a national church. As we saw earlier, the bishop of the Church in London plays a role in the community outside the church and can be approached for assistance by Armenians who are neither church-goers or even members of the Apostolic Church. These secular, in some cases even openly atheistic, Armenians still marry in the Church, even where the spouse is non-Armenian. Similarly, Armenians will visit the Church without actually attending the service inside it and at Christmas and Easter, particularly, the gatherings which take place in and around the churches attract Armenians who might otherwise never visit the institution. The Apostolic Church, as an institution distinctive to Armenians is, I would suggest, like their language, an important symbol of Armenian ethnicity and its continuity. However, as we shall see shortly, unlike their attitude to the decline in proficiency in the Armenian language, there does not appear to be any widespread concern about the decline in church attendance.

I would speculate that unlike a language, which must be used regularly to survive in practice, the Church can continue in spite of a sharply reduced congregation. So long as there is a building in London designated as the Armenian Apostolic Church and a resident priest, the Church as an institution is seen to go on, ever ready and available in reserve for weddings, christenings, deaths, or on important religious and social occasions such as Christmas and Easter. It should be kept in mind that both Armenian Apostolic churches are supported by trust funds and therefore do not require regular monetary contributions in order to continue operating. It is much harder to keep a language in reserve to be taken out and brushed up on suitable occasions. Thus, although Armenians are aware of their secularisation, no one specifically speculated about a time when there would no longer be an Armenian church of any kind in London. The same cannot be said for speculations over the fate of the Armenian language in London.

The issue of exogamous marriages, alluded to by Mr and Mrs F, is, however, a recognisable issue of common concern. According to Mr O, half of the marriages registered on the London Apostolic Armenian Church rolls were between Armenians and non-Armenians. These records were unfortunately not open to me. Several Armenians recollected that in the Middle East, the price for such exogamous marriages would have been complete ostracism from the Armenian community and according to Mr L, an Iranian Armenian, actual physical danger to the individuals involved. But in London, according to Ms M, who is married to an Englishman, there is no concerted opposition to marriages contracted with Christian Europeans:

> Because there has always been this thing about Europeans being superior but not a Muslim Arab: that's considered marrying down ... if a girl married an Englishman, people say that probably she couldn't find an Armenian, that's why she married an Englishman. If a girl isn't pretty, they say, 'Oh, she'll probably marry an Englishman because she won't be able to find an Armenian.'

Three other Armenians also talked about this attitude towards Muslims. Both Mr AJ and Mr L, young Iranian Armenian male adults, claimed that Armenians in Iran thought they were superior to the majority Iranian Muslim population or, as Mr AJ put it, 'they think they're more civilised than the rest of the population'. According to Mr QH, a Syrian Armenian, the Armenians were a 'civilising vanguard' to the Arabs because they looked to Europe.[3]

Vahe Oshagan, in his analysis of the self-image of Armenians as presented in literature emanating from Turkish Armenians at the turn of the century, also discusses their orientation to European culture:

> To be an Armenian in 1900 was still to be very much an imitator, at best, a follower of foreign ways and literature, especially French. [Oshagan, 1981, p. 207]

But in this orientation was also apparently a 'crushing sense of inferiority *vis-à-vis* the Western cultures' (*ibid.*, 214). In the first decades after the massacres, this Western-oriented image of the Armenians continued to be perpetuated, although it was accompanied by the image of the 'exile' as well. Aghop Der-Karabetian, who conducted several psychological surveys in Lebanon, reports a belief by Armenians in that country in their 'high cultural taste and artistic talent' (Der-Karabetian, 1981, p. 246). When the same surveys were conducted in Los Angeles with young native-born American Armenians, Der-Karabetian reported that in comparison with the Lebanese Armenian respondents:

the U.S. respondents expressed stronger belief in the devotion of mothers and the comparative value of Armenian literature, and weaker belief in the more hard-working nature of Armenians and in the superiority of Armenian upbringing. [*ibid.*, p. 248]

Jack Antreassian, discussing the self-image of Armenians in America, suggests a feeling of the inadequacy of community life and a collective sense of parochialism and inferiority (Antreassian, 1981, p. 254). All of this together may be taken to suggest that if Armenians did not necessarily feel superior to Muslims or other Middle-Eastern populations, they did not feel inferior to them, whereas there were elements of this sense of inferiority and inadequacy in relation to European or more generally Western cultures. This may have contributed to the relative acceptance of marriages contracted with Europeans.

With the exception of those referred to above, most other Armenians, although adamant that in the Middle East marriages between Muslims and Armenians were rare in the extreme, were more reticent about discussing the reasons behind this pattern, attributing it to the differences in religion which did not equally exist between most Europeans and Armenians. (The fact that most Armenians knew that at the time I was married to a man of Muslim derivation may have contributed to this reticence.) Mr O, on the other hand, claimed that marriage with Arabs of any religion, even Christians, would have been almost unthinkable in the Middle East, in contrast to the frequency of marriages between Christian Europeans and Armenians.

I personally know of some twenty households in London whose heads are either themselves offspring of exogamous marriages or spouses of non-Armenians. I know of three other exogamous marriages whose Armenian member has close friends or family members domiciled in London but who are themselves presently residing in other parts of Britain. Another Armenian, who is the product of an exogamous marriage, was domiciled in London until shortly before my fieldwork but is now completing his studies in another British city. I include this man in this discussion because he regularly visits London and participates in community events, not least because he is courting a half-Armenian girl domiciled in the city. The marriage in this last case and those of five of the twenty London households are reliably known to have been contracted outside Britain, but only four of these were contracted in the Middle East. They were initiated in:

Iraq, with Arab spouse, religion unknown;
Cyprus, with Christian Greek-Cypriot spouse;
Iran, with Christian-Assyrian spouse;
East Jerusalem, with Christian-Arab spouse;
Ethopia, with Christian-Scottish spouse (the couple shortly afterwards settling in Britain);
France, with Christian-French spouse.

One other household in London consists of an Armenian wedded to an Iranian spouse, but whether the marriage was contracted in London and the religion of the non-Armenian spouse are not known to me. All of this perhaps indicates that marriages between Armenians and non-Armenians, at least Christian non-Armenians, were not as uncommon in the Middle East as all my informants suggested. This is also suggested by Der-Karabetian's finding in Lebanon that, by 1974, 11.1 per cent of the marriages of Armenian Apostolic males were contracted outside the community. Intermarriages appear to have been most common between Armenians and Christian Arabs in Lebanon (Der-Karabetian, 1981, p. 243). However, it must be pointed out that Lebanon was a fairly unusual case in comparison with other Armenian communities in the Middle East in that it had a large and fairly Westernised Christian non-Armenian population. Those London Armenians who most strongly asserted the rarity of exogamous marriages in the Middle East were, with one exception, from Syria, Iraq, and Iran, where most of the population were Muslim.

Whatever the actual rate of Armenian out-marriage in the Middle East, it is clear that Armenians feel that such marriages are more accepted in Britain and, hence, are more likly to occur. Armenians in London certainly do not appear to consider such exogamous marriages unusual or a cause for opprobrium, although in general terms certainly a cause for concern. Once such a marriage is a *fait accompli*, there appear to be no visible barriers to the full participation of the Armenian spouse in London Armenian community life. Many of the Armenian partners of the exogamous marriages I personally recorded were regular participants in association-sponsored gatherings and, in several cases, their non-Armenian spouses also regularly participated in such meetings, while both were involved in visiting private Armenian households. In fact, the major concern expressed about the high rate of exogamy is that it will lead to a decline in community involvement of the adult Armenians concerned and, more importantly of the offspring of these marriages. As Ms V, herself the product of a marriage between an Iranian-Armenian man and a Scottish woman put it:

> If I see an Armenian boy with an English girl, I don't want to talk to her because I think: why should he be with an English girl? There are plenty of Armenian girls around. I can see what happened with Mum speaking English and now we can't speak Armenian.

Nevertheless, Ms V and her brothers participate in Armenian community life as do other offspring of exogamous marriages. More significantly, Ms V is presently involved in a relationship with another half-Armenian, which is considered likely to lead to marriage. Her brother is courting an Armenian girl. Similarly, Mr KD, the offspring of a marriage between an English woman and an Armenian man, is himself married to an Armenian spouse. In short, such marriages do not inevitably lead to the assimilation into non-Armenian society of either the Armenian spouse or the half-Armenian off-spring.

The linguistic problem to which Ms V alluded is not specific to the concern over the consequences of exogamous marriages. The effects of circumscribed Armenian ethnicity are most noticeable to Armenians themselves in respect of the decline in proficiency in the Armenian language among their children. Armenian children who were either born in or mainly raised in Britain do tend to converse for the most part in English. Even when addressed in Armenian they will reply in English. Their literacy in Armenian is usually limited to what they have managed to pick up in the four hours of the Armenian Sunday School, that is for those who attend the school.

> When I look at my daughter, I think how much more difficult it is for her than it was for me because for me, really we thought everybody was Armenian but with my daughter, I think you have to start with the language. The language is not the only thing that makes you Armenian. The important thing is your attitude but language is the key, I think. When they're small, it's one thing but then they start to go to school and the only thing you can do for them is the language and to mix with Armenians.

Parents like Mrs W often feel that they are fighting a losing battle to counteract the engulfing non-Armenian culture transmitted to their children through British schools, friends, etc. Mrs W and Ms M claimed to have been pressured by an English teacher, and an English doctor, respectively, to communicate with their children in English only, thereby relinquishing the Armenian language altogether. Similarly Mr VW, a college student, complained that he had been reprimanded by a teacher for speaking to an Armenian schoolmate in Armenian and not in English. On a more general level, British-born Armenians are often pointed out as the least likely to attend association-sponsored gatherings, as well as the least likely to be proficient in the Armenian language.

Although I have only a few relevant cases, there also appears to be the feeling that youngsters are more likely to be exposed to dangerous and corrupt influences in non-Armenian circles and that it is the duty of responsible Armenians to prevent the penetration of such influences into Armenian circles. In a speech addressed at the end of a concert to commemorate Vartanan, the bishop counselled the audience not to be influenced by what goes on around them: 'by the people with blue and green hair'. The head of the Armenian Scouts Association, when confronted with three Armenian youthful members sporting just such luridly coloured hair, took steps towards their expulsion, in spite of opposition from other members. 'I had to worry about the other kids, especially the younger ones', he explained. Mr and Mrs P were becoming increasingly concerned about their adolescent daughter's involvement with a set of English and Irish friends. They attempted to persuade her to attend association-sponsored gatherings for Armenian youth. Their concern appears to have been directed not only towards the distance of their daughter from the Armenian community but also to what was seen to be the unsavoury and possibly even dangerous location of her meetings with her non-Armenian friends – a pub. 'Does this look like a pub girl to you?', cried her mother in despair.

But lest it appear that Armenians are seeking to jump lemming-like into an abyss of non-Armenian society, which is unambiguously viewed as a harbinger of assimilation and even corruption, I shall attempt to show that there are important advantages to Armenians in their social anonymity as a collectivity. Armenians, I suggest, appear to be juggling several potential personas in their dealings, particularly with non-Armenians, choosing that which appears to be of optimum benefit in each situation. Their ability to do so rests on the relative anonymity of Armenianness in itself. In some dealings with non-Armenians, as we shall see, Armenians attempt to mute their Armenian identity, but in other cases they may emphasise this aspect of their background from other perhaps more socially disadvantageous categorisations.

A young Armenian man primarily raised in Britain who claimed that he sometimes felt closer to British people than to Armenians described a section of the Armenian community in Los Angeles as follows:

> In Hollywood there are signs saying 'No Dogs or Armenians'. There are a lot of Armenians in Hollywood. There's one street there that looks like something out of Armenia. The Armenians in Hollywood don't have a good reputation. Basically, they're using the system in the best way they can. They're all on welfare. They're Armenians from the Soviet Union who couldn't make it there. They're the misfits. In the 1950s, a lot of Armenians emigrated to Soviet Armenia. The ones that couldn't make it there emigrated to the United States and of course the Americans let them in. They'll take anybody if they think they're against the Reds. The old Armenians are very upset about the newcomers because the Armenians used to have a good name in California *like they have here.*

There are several important strands in this account: first, that the Soviet Armenian emigrants form a very visible community in Hollywood; secondly, that they are unusual in that they are indigent; thirdly, that their indigency in combination with their visibility has adversely affected the reputation of all Armenians in California; and fourthly, that the Armenians in London have a good reputation. Before going on to consider the last of these points, it should be pointed out that the analysis made by the London respondent is not necessarily exclusive to London Armenian perceptions.

Jack Antreassian, an American Armenian, writes that Armenians in the USA take pride in their view that 'Armenians are always self-reliant and law-abiding, rarely recorded on welfare rolls and police blotters' (Antreassian, 1981, p. 253). But perhaps even more relevant is Antreassian's view that there is no image of Armenians in America:

since there is no general consciousness in the United States of the existence of the
Armenians, as there is, for example, of the blacks, the Jews, and the Irish. And
lacking that, of course, there can be no image. [*ibid.*, 251][4]

This perception is particularly interesting since it is very similar to the image
of Armenians in Britain but, unlike the fairly small Armenian population in
Britain the Armenian population of North America is estimated at over half a
million people (Lang and Walker, 1978). But although there are relatively
large clusters of Armenians in California and New York and in Watertown,
Massachusetts, the North American Armenian population is dispersed over
communities from the east to the west coast, from Canada in the north to Los
Angeles in the south-west. And it is dispersed over a much larger population
than in Britain as a whole. However, another of Jack Antreassian's comments
is illuminating as he contrasts this blurred or non-existent image with the
impact that Armenians have made in the Middle East, particularly in Lebanon (Antreassian, 1978).

In 1966, the main diaspora communities were listed in the Erevan periodical *Hayreniki Dzayn* as the USA (and Canada) with 450,000, Iran with
200,000, Lebanon with 180,000, and Syria with 150,000 (referred to in Lang
and Walker, 1978, p. 11). Although the overall figures for the Middle-Eastern
communities are not vastly greater than for the North American population,
they make up in their respective countries a larger ratio of the total population. One might also attribute the difference in visibility to the Muslim
affiliation of the host populations distinguishing them from the Christian
Armenians by religion, but this would not explain their impact in Lebanon
where there is, as was pointed out earlier, a proportionately large Christian-
Arab population. But there is another aspect of these different Middle-Eastern countries which may go some way towards explaining the differences
between the position of Armenian communities situated within them and an
Armenian community such as that found in London. Most of the countries
from which London Armenians originate are polyethnic systems in which
ethnicity is highly charged, both politically and economically. One can only
speculate on this point but it seems reasonable to suggest that in countries
where inter-ethnic relations are based on multiple sectional divisions, relations which are often tense and which not infrequently erupt in violence,
identification with one or the other of the constituent ethnic sections would
not resolve a minority's wish for security and acceptance. Blending in with
these settings, however, would not necessarily be served by the muting of that
minority's ethnic identity. Where ethnicity penetrates into a number of public
demands, blending in might require the overt expression of ethnic group
membership in order to achieve recognition and participation. The presentation of a separate and distinctive Armenian identity in such circumstances
might also serve as a means of asserting neutrality in the enmities and

hostilities which feature in the relationships between other co-resident ethnic groups (as Armenians tried to do in Lebanon at the outbreak of civil war). Add to this suggestion the indication in the reports of the respondents and Armenian writers referred to earlier that Armenians in the Middle East did not view their difference from these perhaps more dominant ethnic populations as embodying an inferior status but as a mark of equal status (or perhaps in some cases even of superiority) and we have a possible explanation for the greater social visibility of Armenians as a collectivity within the countries of the Middle East. If 'not being different' in Britain means muting one's ethnic identity when seeking acceptance into economic, residential, and educational domains; in the Middle East 'not being different' may have required drawing attention to that collective ethnic identity in a bid to establish its parity with, and independence of, the respective ethnic groups found in these different countries of origin. In Britain, Armenians may also have been influenced by the stigmatisation that is often associated with visible ethnic and racial difference, i.e. Armenians do not want to stand out in a way that is perceived to be associated with inferior status. If Armenians in North America do not want to be recorded on welfare rolls and police blotters, neither do the London Armenians.

But, while allowing for flexibility, this social anonymity of London Armenians has not in their view made their ethnic identity less problematic, because less immediately relevant to many of the spheres in which they operate, but more problematic than the situation in their countries of origin, where it was clearly and visibly demarcated. The disadvantage of the success-ful integration of Armenians within the British socio-economic system is that it is seen as having made the perpetuation of their ethnic identity more difficult and, therefore, more doubtful.

But what of our London-Armenian respondents' assertions that Armenians in London have a 'good' reputation. For Armenians in London, I would suggest, do not have a 'good' reputation. For most Londoners, una-ware of the presence and nature of the Armenian community, it, like the American Armenians described by Antreassian, has *no* reputation at all. It is clear that 'reputation' is here being treated not as the presence of certain identifiable features attributed by the majority population to the Armenians, but as the absence of such externally attributable features. That is to say, a 'good' reputation is defined in terms of the absence of negative features which can be attributed by non-Armenians. Although adopting different strategies of boundary management, London Armenians may not necessarily be seek-ing a position radically different from the position Armenians were perceived to have in the Middle East. But their understanding of what constitutes inferior status *vis-à-vis* the host population may have shifted. In neither case do they define their reputation directly in terms of its characterisation by non-Armenians, but in terms of their own perceptions of what features of their reputation afford the best possible status *vis-à-vis* these non-Armenians. The reputation of Armenians in London is 'good' because its virtual non-existence does not act to limit the opportunities of Armenians in education, housing, and employment. It is 'good' because its blankness affords Armenians flexibility in their dealings with non-Armenians.

When discussing the social anonymity of Armenians in London, account must be taken of the small size of this ethnic population in a large and densely populated metropolis. A few thousand Armenians can easily be swallowed up in such a setting without making any impact on the awareness of the non-Armenian population. For reasons beyond my control, I was not able to follow many Armenians into their work or school environment, and so my analysis of the way in which Armenians interact with non-Armenians must inevitably be partly speculative. There are, however, indications in the attitudes and reactions that I was able to observe that the social anonymity of Armenians is due not only to their small numbers but also to the fact that some Armenians at least seek to maintain a low profile.

First of all, it should be made clear that it is possible to do this partly because Armenians are not easily distinguishable in terms of their appearance. There are many Armenians with dark hair and dark-coloured eyes, but there are also many others with fair complexions and light-coloured eyes. Many Armenian women dye their hair various shades of blonde or auburn. Both men and women dress in European fashion.

Armenians are very often highly capable linguistically. It is not at all uncommon to find Armenians who speak five or more languages, and the majority of first-generation immigrants speak at least three languages fluently. Most first-generation and second-generation Armenians in London speak English with relative ease and many had a prior knowledge of the language before arriving.

These attributes, together with the fact that Armenians, although in the majority belong to the independent Armenian Apostolic Church, are none the less Christians make it all the more possible for Armenians to be unobtrusive within the London context.

Armenians also, however, appear to adapt their self-labelling to enhance this tendency. It has already been noted that a sizeable proportion of Armenian commercial enterprises bear titles which give no indication of their Armenian ownership. The Armenian House, which is part of a row of terraced houses situated in a side street in the West End of London, bears only a small barely distinguishable plaque with the words Armenian House. St Sarkis's Church, which is situated in an even more secluded garden square, bears a somewhat larger plaque indicating its identity as an Armenian church. But St Peter's Church, which is housed in a building leased from the Church of England which was originally used as an Anglican church, is situated on a major thoroughfare and has no external indication of its Armenian character.

In the summer of 1981 it did bear such a sign but shortly afterwards this was removed and not replaced during the remaining ten months of my stay in London. Thus, it would be virtually impossible for a passer-by to identify it from its external appearance as anything other than the Anglican church it appears.

Individual Armenians will sometimes adapt their personal labels where these are possibly obtrusive. Almost all Armenians have retained an Armenian surname distinguishable usually by its ending '-ian'. I know of only four cases where Armenian surnames were shortened or altered. However, first names are often European in form. Armenian women, in particular, were very often given European names such as Caroline, Rita, Mary, Jenny, Diana, Isabel, Eva, Alice, etc. in their countries of origin. Men are more likely to have distinctively non-European names such as Aram, Nerses, or Hovhannes. Both men and women may use European versions of their first names, so that Andranik becomes Andre, Harotune becomes Harry, Mihran becomes Michael, Krikor is translated to Gregory, Hasmik to Jasmine, and so on. In one case, an Armenian woman uses the unconnected European name of her shop as her personal name when dealing with some of her customers and her original, non-European personal name in other circumstances. Women who have married non-Armenian men take on their husband's surname so that they may be functioning with a name which gives no indication of non-European origins, such as Mary Porter, the first name having been changed from Mirena to Mary. I must point out, however, that although I do know of a number of such cases as recounted above, since I was usually introduced to Armenians in an Armenian context I do not know how widespread this practice is within non-Armenian settings. The case of Mrs BY, however, gives an interesting indication of what can happen if an Armenian name begins to appear problematic when dealing with non-Armenians. Mrs BY used to wear a name tag in her work as a shop assistant but:

> I had so much trouble, I took it off. People would look at the name and they would say: 'what's that?'; 'where do you come from?'; 'Armenian, what's that?' It really bothered me that people didn't know about Armenians. Only educated people know about Armenians.

Her decision to take off her name tag was clinched when a customer of Turkish origin, seeing her badge and recognising the name as Armenian, warned her to tell her husband 'that the Armenians had better stop killing Turks or else they'll be sorry'. 'After that, I went to my boss and I told him: "I can't wear this badge anymore, it's making too much trouble for me." '

As this case indicates, Armenian names, in themselves, need not necessarily identify Armenians to non-Armenians, but they do identify the person as not of Anglo-Saxon origin, as an immigrant. As immigrants, Armenians may potentially be placed, at least by outsiders, in a dual ethnic category, i.e. on the basis of their country of origin. In other words, Armenians could be identified as Lebanese, Iraqi, Egyptian, Iranian, etc. I think it highly probable that Armenians play off these categories one against the other.

Several Armenians have been able to use attributes or skills deriving from their country of origin to good effect in London. There are four Armenians I know of working on Arabic or Middle-Eastern affairs journals, three as journalists and one as a researcher. Their knowledge of Arabic in all four cases was extremely helpful, as was their knowledge of current affairs in the Middle East. In another case, an Iraqi-Armenian woman worked as an Arabic–English translator for a group of doctors. In another case, a recently settled Lebanese Armenian was employed by a Lebanese architectural firm. Ms PY, an Irianian-Armenian woman, was granted entry into Britain upon the request of her prospective employers, a joint Anglo-Armenian-Persian concern. Her knowledge of both Persian and Armenian, she feels, was instrumental in the acquisition of her job. Mrs P, a Cypriot Armenian, has besides her English customers some Greek-Cypriot and Armenian customers. With the second group of these she speaks in Greek and with the third in Armenian. Ms C, an Iranian Armenian, was offered a business partnership by an acquaintance of Persian origin, and so on.

However, when thirty-nine first-generation Armenians were questioned about their friendships, twenty-nine replied that they had no non-Armenian friends in London from their country or even from the same general region of origin. Only ten replied that they had some non-Armenian friends, but by no means many, from their country or region of origin. In two of these ten cases, the friends involved were not specifically from the same country of origin but were Arabs from the Middle East. Thus, although Armenians in their inter-action with non-Armenians may identify themselves by their country of origin, and even derive important benefits thereby, there does not appear to be a widespread effort among the population studied to establish rela-tionships of intimacy with non-Armenians from the same country of origin. In other words, there do not appear to be many Armenians who are achive members of two ethnic groups in London, the Armenian community as well as one based exclusively on country of origin.

More significantly, I suspect that Armenians may sometimes use their Armenian identity to disassociate themselves from any potentially negative connotations which may be associated by non-Armenians with the country of origin. When attending a displomatic party, Ms M, a Lebanese-Armenian woman, was involved in a conversation with an Englishman who criticised the imputed vulgarity of Lebanese women. Ms M pointed out to this man that the reason she was different was that, although she was from Lebanon, she was an Armenian. Similarly, Mrs G, also a Lebanese Armenian, boasted about how when on holiday she had been able to make it difficult for non-Armenians to work out her nationality. She had confounded them when thinking about the Middle East, they assumed she was either Arabic or Jewish. Within the same conversation, Mrs G also referred to the supposed vulgarity of Lebanese women unlike German and French women, presumably excluding herself, as an Armenian, from this appraisal.

Within an Armenian context, however, country of origin again becomes emphasised to distinguish between groups of Armenians. I suggest that Armenians can alternatively mute their foreignness or characterise themselves as Middle-Easterners, or as Armenians, or Lebanese, or Iranians, etc. depending on the situation in which they find themselves and the person being addressed. Armenians are, of course, at one and the same time all these things and this should not be taken to mean that they are actively trying to hide aspects of their background that may not be convenient. I suspect that it would be very rare among the group of Armenians I studied to find individuals who, whatever the situation, would deliberately prevaricate about their Armenian ethnicity, or their country of origin, or their migrant status. But what does appear to be happening is that a particular aspect may be emphasised over others to suit different circumstances. It must also be stressed that different Armenians will stress different aspects, so that the variety of emphasis shifts not only between situations but also between people. Armenianness itself has no clear-cut unambiguous meaning, as we have seen already in the musings of Armenians about themselves. However, the important advantage that Armenians have as an ethnic group in London is that their relative social anonymity means that most non-Armenians have no pre-set image of Armenianness. Therefore, an Armenian can present his or her ethnic identity to a non-Armenian and yet stress particular aspects of it, such as Lebanese origin or distinctiveness from other Lebanese, which may seem relevant to that situation, or his or her overall perceptions of that identity, without fear of challenge. Thus, when Ms M and her mother, Mrs LX, were trying to emphasise the unique nation status of their ethnicity to a young British woman of mixed-European origins, they stressed that although originating from Lebanon, they were not Arabs. To make the point, Ms M said that 'Lebanon is not my home', and Mrs LX said 'Very few people [Armenians] picked up any Arabic customs.' Had Mrs LX said this in an Armenian gathering, particularly where Iranian Armenians were present, there would no doubt have been heated disagreement, for many first-generation Armenians agree that they have been influenced by the cultures of the different countries in which they resided. On many other occasions, Mrs LX herself has referred to Lebanon as 'my country' and pointed out the Arabic culinary dishes she has learnt to prepare there. But the picture these women were painting of the relationship of Armenians to Lebanon was not challenged by their non-Armenian listener because she had never heard of Armenians before.

In my own relationship with Armenians, on several occasions my

Armenian interlocutors tried to verify first what I had been told by other Armenians or what books I had read about Armenians before making their own statements. In some respects this variation in self-presentation is not unlike the patterns described by Eidheim (1969) for one group of Norwegian Lapps. The Lapps in question also mute their ethnicity in interaction with non-Lapps, but the distinction between self-presentation in the two spheres, public and private, is far more sharply drawn than in the London-Armenian case. This difference between the two cases may be due to the fact that the Lapps appear to adapt their public (i.e. when interacting with non-Lapps) styles of presentation to an already given social stigma attached to their ethnic identity, while the Armenians are, in some senses, trying to avoid the development of stigmatisation. Armenianness has, therefore, retained a more ambiguous character than the Lappish ethnic identity, not least for non-Armenians but also for Armenians as well. What is particularly important for the development of Armenian ethnicity in London, as I shall attempt to show later on in this chapter, is that the ambiguity of Armenianness is used to introduce elements into the concept which can be transmitted as authentically Armenian to second-generation Armenians with as little challenge as that issued by non-Armenians. But it remains to be said what Armenians think about non-Armenians in London.

Many Armenians complained that the British were cold and that they had experienced considerable difficulty in establishing relationships of intimacy with individuals among them. Yet, for the most part, this reserve was not viewed as directed specifically towards Armenians but as a characteristic of the British themselves, i.e. 'that is how the British are'; not, 'that is how the British are towards us'. In fact, only one Armenian complained about racism and even here the complaint was not referred to the particular experiences of Armenians but to a general feature of British society. When it was pointed out to an Iranian-Armenian man who had claimed that he had never experienced racism in Britain that Blacks in England had experienced this, the retort was that since the Blacks had rioted and burned (a reference to the summer riots of 1981) they could expect nothing else. In short, he felt that the racism that Blacks had experienced 'was their own fault'. Armenians did not, with one exception, identify their situation in Britain with that of other ethnic groups in the country, such as those numbered amongst the West Indian or Asian populations. Far from that, two women complained that Britain was being spoilt 'by all these foreigners', foreigners here clearly excluding the Armenians themselves and referring to West Indians or Asians. One of these women had only been domiciled in England for five years at the time she made the statement. Another woman who leases out flats and bed-sitters avoids open advertisement of vacancies in the fear that Blacks or Irish might apply 'because they make trouble'; this in a residential area where there is a high proportion of West Indians, Asians, and Irish. Still another felt that 'the coloured people always start fights'. On the other hand, six Armenians reported having one or more Asian or West Indians among their non-Armenian friends, and two reported Irish friends. But in spite of this, Armenians rarely identify their situation in Britian, in terms of similarities, with the situations of these other ethnic miniorities. An important exception to this is the Jews.

Seven individuals compared the Armenians to the Jews, expressing variously admiration for their hard-working nature, their organisational abilities, their internal solidarity ('like us'), or their concern for traditions ('like us'). Three of these, in particular, expressed admiration that the Jews got what they wanted, 'they went out to get it', i.e. a state, whereas the Armenians were still without their 'lands'.

The identification of Armenians with Jews is not new. Christopher Walker writes of the myth of the 'Armenian Jew' which has sprung out of the historical stereotype of the Armenians as good businessmen (Walker, 1980, p. 12). Ronald Suny, in his discussion of the image of Armenians in the Russian Tsarist Empire, describes the increasingly common theme in nineteenth-century Russian conservative writings of the Armenians as 'foreign, Asiatic elements' which was used to link Armenians with Jews. Armenians came to be referred to as *inorodtsy* (aliens), 'a term usually reserved for Jews, nomads, and a few Siberian tribes' (Suny, 1981, p. 125). But whereas these indentifications of Armenians with Jews sprang from the perceptions of outsiders and usually involved some extension of the stigmatisation of Jews to Armenians, in London some Armenians themselves suggest this identification and appear to consider the comparison a positive one. It may be that this is due to the relative improvement in the status of the Jews, but for one Armenian at least the comparison was still distasteful for she was concerned to emphasise that the Armenian national movement which she supported should not on any grounds be compared with the Jewish Zionist movement but rather with the Palestinian movement for national self-determination. The identification of Armenians with the Palestinians 'who have a cause like us' is especially prevalent among the more militant Armenians, particularly ASALA supporters or Dashnaks. But this identification is not oriented towards the position of Armenians as an ethnic group in London but rather in terms of a movement considered to be of relevance to Armenians throughout the world and especially in the diaspora communities.

It is not surprising to find Armenians failing to identify with stigmatised ethnic groups in London since they clearly have not as yet suffered the same kind of negative role models set by outsiders. However, there is a fear among some Armenians, as we saw earlier, that they may eventually suffer a similar fate because of the actions of some groups among them. The way in which Armenians respond to this perceived threat and the identification of their more militant members with the Palestinians is related to the manner in which they interpret the historical development of Armenianness, most importantly the massacres of 1915 and the consequent dispersal of Armenians. But a proper account of the ideology that has developed around perceptions of national history requires its own analysis and will be dealt with in Chapter 4.

However, it should be pointed out here that even those Armenians who are troubled at the public militancy of some of their colleagues do not necessarily want Armenians to be unknown as a group. In spite of their puzzlement and surprise at my choice of subject for study, Armenians regularly expressed delight and approval at the efforts of an outsider to reach an understanding of Armenian culture. When Christopher Walker published an analysis of a period of Armenian history, the LACCC sponsored a celebration of its launching. Quite a number of Armenians have purchased the book as they have historical and linguistic analyses of Armenian subjects by other authors. In particular, they are interested in, and encouraging of, the work of non-Armenian authors. Copies of an M.A. thesis by Rachel Sabbagh on the development of library resources for London Armenians were to be found in the possession of several individuals in London. I was repeatedly asked for a copy of my own thesis when completed. However, scholarly historical, linguistic, and even anthropological writings are unlikely to reach the attention of more than a handful of non-Armenians, most likely what the Armenians themselves call 'educated people'. Their approval of these kinds of expositions reflect the desire of some Armenians, and I suspect many more than I know of personally, to ensure that the 'right' kind of image is painted of Armenians. The specific constituting elements of that image are not necessarily as important as the fact that they do not create difficulties in the relationships between Armenians and the non-Armenians around them. Mr BY wanted the Armenians to be known for a contribution to a charitable organisation, such as the Spastic Society of Britain, or for their excellence in sports. Others were keen to point out particular Armenians who are internationally renowned for their commercial, or musical abilities, or for their generosity. In short, there is a desire that Armenians, if they are to be known, should be known in a positive light. If the option was to be known for deeds that would be interpreted negatively then Mr BY preferred that Armenians not be known at all. In fact, Mr BY went one step further and suggested that if Armenians were going to behave in such a way as to earn the contempt and enmity of non-Armenians, by killing Turkish diplomats for instance, then he could foresee a day when he would no longer want to be an Armenian. Contributions to the Spastic Society are unlikely to win headlines in the newspaper dailies; violence and militancy are much more likely to find a place there. Concern about this kind of media coverage is indicated by the formation of a special public relations committee of the LACCC which was entrusted with ensuring that reports in the media were accurate and favourable to the Armenians. If publicity and visibility mean being known in such a negative light then the alternative of inconspicuousness, although perhaps wounding to your pride, may seem far more positive by comparison. In other words, a 'good' reputation is one which will allow an individual to be an Armenian without creating difficulties and antagonisms in his dealings with non-Armenians. 'Good' in this context may end up being no more than a blank reputation for all but a small proportion of non-Armenians in London, but the point that must be stressed here is that this is not necessarily the only way most Armenians want to be thought of. Quite the opposite; the ignorance of non-Armenians about the ethnic identity of Armenians is very often very distressing for Armenians. But anonymity may be for all practical intents and purposes, the only way in which Armenians, at the moment, can have a 'good name' in London, at least 'good' as it is defined above.

Role conflicts

For every option created, another may become limited. Small population size, dispersal, and anonymity have facilitated the manoeuvrability of Armenians within London, but it has also facilitated exogamy, decline in church attendance, and a decline in proficiency of the Armenian language, while it has limited communication and interaction between Armenians. Anonymity has allowed Armenians to effectively emphasise, in turn, personas suited to multiple dealings with non-Armenians, enhancing their ability to take on occupational and neighbourhood roles within non-Armenian settings. But every commitment an Armenian takes on, in which his ethnic identity is successfully secondary or irrelevant, influences the workings of commitment to participation in the London Armenian community.

Apathy is a byword in London Armenian circles. It is invoked in such phrases as 'they don't care' or 'nobody wants to help' when individuals are unwilling to take on managerial roles in associations; when there is a low turn-out at association-sponsored gatherings; when parents fail to enrol their children at the school or in the Scouts; when there is reluctance to make contributions to fund-raising campaigns, and so on. During the 1982 'elections' to the Anahid association, approximately thirty-five women attended out of some 200 registered members. After a sometimes heated discussion of past and future programmes, volunteers were called for the formation of the coming year's running committee. A long and drawn-out process followed. Nominations were proposed and declined by the nominees. Women attempted to cajole each other into volunteering. Intermittently one or the other of the women gave an loud, impassioned plea for volunteers. I was myself asked twice to volunteer. Slowly and painfully, names of 'volunteers' were added on to the blackboard at the front of the room, until finally, when patience was almost exhausted, the magical number of nine was reached and the meeting broke up. Clearly what was billed as an election involved no selection of one candidate over another since the competition was mainly about who could leave the meeting free of committee responsibilities. As Ms JM, one of the women chairing the meeting, explained:

> It's always the same. Whenever we have elections, they stay away because they're afraid they might be asked to be on the committee . . . I think it must be that, because we have over 200 members and only 35 women are here. And to choose 9 people from 35 is very difficult because some of the people are ineligible because they've already served two years on the committee [referring to the association's constitutional rule that after two years of service a committee member must step down and remain off the committee for at least one year] and then there are people like me. I'm already so busy at the school, I don't feel I can take on another commitment and then there are people who just don't want to. I don't know; they're afraid because there is a lot of work to do.

The committee is supposed to meet once a month. Ms JM, herself, did not volunteer for the committee. She was already involved in supervising the small Sunday School library and felt she could not take the time for yet another managerial role within the community. Overwhelmingly, the women who refused to sit on the committee claimed they could not spare the time to do so, although not all of these were involved in other association activities. Some women may have failed to attend the elections for fear of pressure to join the committee, as Ms JM claimed, but there are certainly others who find it difficult to attend any Anahid meeting because it conflicts with their work hours or domestic obligations.

Conflicts such as this are an ever-present factor weighing in the balance when Armenians make decisions about the range of their involvement in community activities. Ms PY could not attend the Christmas service at the church because it fell on a working day and she was reluctant to sacrifice one of the fourteen days available to her every year for her holidays. One of her employers is Armenian himself. Ms C could not bring her young son for a special Lent service (in which the washing of the apostles' feet by Christ is re-enacted using children for the roles of the disciples) because it conflicted with her work hours. On a more regular basis, Ms C resents the hours she spends at the Sunday School every weekend accompanying her son who is enrolled as a pupil at the school. Although a school bus is provided to bring the children to the school, Ms C is worried about the supervision of children to and from the vehicle:

> There is no one who will take the responsibility and look after the children. You see the bus is outside. If there was someone I wouldn't come. Sunday is my only free day and I have a lot of things I want to do, but there is no one and I have to come and just sit all day, all day and do nothing . . . I am wasting my time bringing him here. He's not learning anything. He knows everything but he won't speak.

But because as a result of this Ms C was present at the school most Sundays, she was asked to assist in the administration of the school facilities for the following year. Mr BY, a Catholic Armenian, cannot send his sons to the Sunday School because it conflicts with the hours of the Catholic Sunday School they attend:

> You see what bothers me about these schools is that they always make them at a time that's convenient to the teachers and not to the people . . . Sunday is the only day that the whole family has to be together. Other days, I work different hours from my wife, but on Sunday we can all be together. If we go to the Sunday School, by the time you get back, you've lost the Sunday dinner. Look at [W] (one of the members of the school committee). She doesn't come back until 2.30 p.m. on Sundays.

Mrs W, herself, resigned not soon after from the committee on which she had served for nearly four years. 'It's time other people got involved', she explained. Maintaining a full administrative and teaching staff at the school is not always easy, as teachers and parents relinquish their positions to devote more time to other spheres or even leave London altogether.

Mr and Mrs F find it difficult to send their son regularly to the Scouts Association meetings on Saturdays because there is no transportation provided to take him from his home in South London to the venue in West London. Both the Fs work full time during the week. Mrs F sings in the church choir on Sundays and serves on one of the Armenian House committees. Mr F is active in the activities organised by the Armenian National Committee. Saturday is their day to rest and carry out domestic odd jobs at home.

Mrs Y is both a teacher at the Sunday School and a member of the Ararat Choir, which meets for rehearsals on Sunday afternoons at the Armenian House, several miles away from the school. She would not be able to do the latter, she explained, if a friend did not drive her from the school to the Armenian House on Sundays. Young people, of whom according to Mrs Y, there is a shortage in the choir, could not, she felt, be reasonably expected to give up their free Sundays for choir practice. Ms DA and her mother, Mrs D, are a teacher at the Sunday School and a member of one of the two church choirs, respectively. Both women pointed out how, as a result, Sundays, their day of rest, was extremely busy, rushing from one activity to another.

Mr HM, an officer of the Tekeyan association, claimed that the association's activities took up so much of his time that he was unable to attend very many of the other association-sponsored activities. Mr O, once one of the community's more active members, now rarely participates in association-sponsored gatherings since he started an import – export business which takes up much of his time. 'And if you go to one, then you have to go to all of them so I don't go to any of them.' Mr KD works at night and therefore can only attend association-sponsored gatherings taking place during the weekend. Mr and Mrs NM found they had to drastically curtail their participation in such gatherings after their baby was born and demanded much of their time. When Mrs G gave up her small business she was besieged, she said, by requests from numerous associations to sit on their running committees: 'They all say, now that you're a woman of leisure, can you join the committee. And I told them I have to think about it.' As this statement indicates, women often have to bear the brunt of much of the organisational work of the community's associations since they are more likely to be engaged full time in the domestic household and to be able, or to be assumed to be able, to restructure their commitments in order to accommodate these responsibilities. Organisations like the Tekeyan, AGBU, LACCC, and the Armenian House all have ladies committees which are active in organising their dinner dances, selling tickets for these and other events, and so on. But the top posts in the central running committees of those associations tend to be occupied by men. However, time conflicts such as those listed above occur frequently for both men and women.

Armenians also sometimes complain about the cost of attending such association-sponsored gatherings as dinner dances which charge hefty admission prices of between £15 and £22. Even less lavish events often involve an admission price. 'There are other things I would prefer to spend my money on', explained Mrs PB. On the other hand, fund-raisers find their efforts to solicit participation in such events or independent contributions frustrating and time-consuming. 'They don't like to put their hands in their pockets', complained Mr Z, who is interested in setting up a new community centre if the funds can be raised. Of course, the same person can be at one time a patron and on another occasion a fund-raiser. Thus, Mrs W complained to me about the lack of support given to some of the school's fund-raising efforts but on another occasion she complained about the quality of the food served at a Scouts fund-raising garden party which, according to her, was not worth the amount of money she had spent.

Such conflicts are exacerbated for Armenians who have built up a network of non-Armenian friends with whom they wish to spend their leisure time. Such Armenians are more likely to be those primarily raised in Britain, whether as offspring of exogamous marriages or where both parents are Armenian. These individuals may resent what they see as pressure from other Armenians to associate only with Armenians; pressure to be Armenian. Ms AT, a nineteen-year-old who was born and raised in Britain, is coming under increasing pressure from her parents and Armenian friends to limit her association with non-Armenian friends but she feels more comfortable with her British friends and is an active member of a British sports club. Similarly, one of two young brothers who were born in Cyprus but had spent half of their childhood in Britain explained that: 'sometimes I can look at the Armenians as an outsider. Basically because I feel very much at home in England.' His brother added that: 'I have more in common with English people than I do with Armenians in Paris but we're supposed to be

Armenians.' Ms U, the offspring of an Armenian Father and a French mother, who was born and raised in France, understandably resented the emphasis she perceived among Armenians on endogamous marriages. Most of her friends were non-Armenians of various national origins and she was particularly agitated when criticised by an Armenian friend for spending too much time with Palestinians at the expense of Armenian movements. Mr TL, the offspring of a Scottish mother and an Armenian father, who was born and raised in Britain, never participates in Armenian community activities. The community, he felt, was backward looking, 'clinging together, just for the sake of clinging together'. Britain was his country and retained his prior loyalty. The few Armenian friends he has he has met by chance through school or work. Even Ms GT, an Ethiopian Armenian, who arrived in Britain as an adult, resented what she called the 'nationalism' of Armenians and the pressure on her to spend her leisure time only with Armenians. Most of Ms GT's friends are non-Armenians and she attends a Baptist church rather than the Armenian Apostolic church.

Most Armenians who have some contact with the community and its organisations at some point or another come under pressure to commit more of their time to association with other Armenians; pressure which comes both from their elders and their peers. Those who are particularly active in the community sometimes feel that they are shouldering an unfair burden of this commitment. Other may resent the imputation that they are not devoting enough of their time when they feel that they have been as active as they could be. And still others, as we have seen, resent the pressure altogether, preferring to spend at least a sizeable proportion of their leisure time with non-Armenians. This latter group, particularly those among them that are the next generation of Armenians, the truly British Armenians, form the heart of the concern shared by many over the future of Armenian ethnicity in Britain. The problem is how do you raise a child to be an Armenian when for the most part he or she is unavoidably surrounded by non-Armenians? Part of the response appears to have been an emphasis on the development of cultural means with which to be an Armenian.

Compensations

In essence, the problem is what makes a person an Armenian? On one level, the answer is very simple. A person is an Armenian if he/or she can trace some line of descent from Armenians. In practice, this usually means s/he has at least one Armenian parent, although some Armenians were willing to push this one or more generations further back. But if this ascribes to a person a place in the category of Armenians, it does not say anything about whether he or she will choose to act upon this placement. For that, Armenians agree they have to have the right attitude. They have to want to be Armenian. But even if they have this attitude they must have access to means with which to act out that commitment. Armenians then are concerned to pass on to their British-born or raised children the means with which to act out their identity. In their attempts to do so they have emphasised some old criteria and appropriated new ones. These include naming, language, visible customs, and nationalism.

As was pointed out earlier, few Armenians, other than those women who have married non-Armenians and taken on their surnames, alter their Armenian surnames. On the other hand, Armenian parents do not seem in any hurry to endow their British-born children with Anglicised first names. This may be significant in that Armenian first-generation women in particular were often, as I said earlier, given European names in their country of origin, and as we saw earlier some Armenians seem willing to adapt their first names, if not actually legally change them. None the less, out of thirty-two Armenians born in Britain, both children and adults, eighteen were given names that are not easily recognisable as Western European. Of the thirteen who were given Anglicised or generally European first names, eleven were the offspring of exogamous marriages, indicating quite understandably some influence in selection of names by non-Armenian spouses. It is difficult to say how deliberate and conscious this pattern of naming is since no Armenians discussed this or made reference to it as part of their overall strategy for rearing their children as Armenians.

Armenians are, however, quite conscious of and explicit in their stress on language, although they are not always sure how they propose to ensure the continuing use of the Armenian language. There appears to be little faith in the Sunday School's sole influence. Quite a number of parents pointed out their efforts to communicate in Armenian with their children at home, but there was a mood of pessimism about the eventual success of these attempts. Parents either slipped into English or children obstinately continued to reply in English. Parents were encouraged to make a greater effort to communicate with their children in Armenian during a speech by one of the LACCC officers at a recital given to commemorate the end of the Sunday School session. It was suggested – somewhat to the amusement of several of those present – that they adopt a penalty system in their homes whereby a fine was paid every time a family member spoke in English. To accede to this proposal or to less extreme suggestions by other Armenians is particularly difficult for parents with non-Armenian spouses. Non-Armenian spouses do sometimes them-selves attempt to gain proficiency in the Armenian language, but the efforts are usually short-lived and sporadic. Hence, the only shared language for communication at home may be English. Children themselves may be reluc-tant to attend the Sunday School as well as to communicate in Armenian at home. Not all parents, it would seem, are equally willing to press their reluctant offspring on these points. The Saturday activities of the Armenian

Scouts Association are also conducted for the most part in Armenian, or so its leaders claimed, but far fewer children are members of this association. Whatever the difficulties, successes, or failures, there remains a widespread feeling that where it comes to language, a fundamental of Armenian culture is at stake and the effort to maintain it is worth while and should be made.

There is also an attempt to hand on Armenian 'customs'. These for the most part relate to cuisine, the arts, and literature. It is questionable, particularly in the first of these three categories, whether these 'customs' are truly distinctively Armenian in origin. The culinary dishes which Armenians sometimes characterise as 'authentically Armenian' are on the one hand common features of the non-Armenian cuisine in many Arabic countries as well as in Cyprus and Greece and, on the other, popular throughout Iran. Adult first-generation Armenians will sometimes admit this point themselves. As Mr QY, an Iraqi Armenian, put it:

> It's not so important that it is really Armenian food. If you look closely, you might find that the origins are Persian or Turkish. The important thing is that people think it's Armenian; that it's something they can remember their mother or grandmother making; they can pass it from generation to generation; that they can show their children this is the way my mother made this. It provides some continuity.

First-generation Armenians who have experienced the general popularity of these dishes in their country of origin are unlikely to be deceived about their unique Armenian character, but Armenians born or primarily raised in Britain, who have only experienced the presentation of this cuisine within an Armenian context are unlikely to be aware of this background. Thus, Ms V, a British-born Armenian of part Iranian-Armenian parentage, recounted to me the kinds of Armenian dishes she liked and her preference for them over British cuisine. The dishes she listed were all Persian in origin. When I pointed this out to her, she replied that having been introduced to this cuisine only by Iranian Armenians, she had had no way of knowing that it was popular among Persians as well. As few first-generation immigrants appear to have any or many non-Armenian friends from their country of origin, their children will not necessarily receive immediate exposure to the background of this cuisine through interaction in London with Arabs, Persians, Cypriots, etc.

When talk is of 'Armenian dances', the reference is to folk-dances executed in groups. Not many either first-generation or second-generation Armenians appear to be comfortably familiar with the steps of such dances, and some not at all. Young adults or adolescents are more likely to be knowledgeable in this regard, but they appear to have been taught at least some of these dances, if not all, in London, at such venues as the Armenian Scouts disco. How many of these dances are uniquely Armenian in origin is difficult to say. However, Ms KV, who is active in teaching such dances to young Armenians and in leading these dances at parties, told me that she had learnt many of them through her participation in an Israeli dance troupe. Several Western-Armenian speakers attributed these dances to Iranian Armenians. However, whether this is because such agencies as the Armenian Scouts Association, where these dances are taught, are dominated by Iranian Armenians, or whether these dances were truly widespread in Armenian communities in Iran is difficult to clarify. Certainly, many Iranian Armenians, particularly those middle- aged, though gaily joining in these group dances, continue to execute only one or two basic steps, whatever the music being played, or the steps being performed by their fellows. In short, a group dance at an Armenian dinner party is often a very varied performance with much improvisation alongside surer and more intricate execution. The point is that, whatever the origin, these dances are seen as part of an Armenian tradition but a part which is being chiefly exercised and spread by Armenian youth. Thus, in this case, it is the youth who are 'passing on' these customs both to their elders and to other Armenian youngsters.

The Armenian songs that are sung at recitals and played on tapes at home have, without doubt, lyrics written by Armenians, although some of the melodies may be shared with other Caucasian nationalities. These songs may originate from songwriters in Soviet Armenia, although others were penned by their counterparts in diaspora communities. In London such songs are performed publicly by the Ararat choir, a few amateur soloists, at least two local Armenian musical bands that I know of, and the occasional visiting Armenian singer from other countries. The songs and their performers can become important symbols of Armenianness. In the first place, they make up an important component of many of the recitals put on by such associations at the Tekeyan or the LACCC. The large, lavish and formal dinner parties which Armenian associations are so fond of organising to the best of my knowledge always feature an Armenian band or singer. Very often, they feature two bands, one a European band, i.e. non-Armenians singing non-Armenian songs; and the other an Armenian band, i.e. Armenians singing largely Armenian songs but possibly some non-Armenian songs as well. According to Mrs W, who participated in organising one of these dinner dances:

> We could have managed very well with just Mirage [the European band] but we thought it's an Armenian function so we should have an Armenian band as well.

These dinner dances are held in large luxury London hotels. The food which is served is prepared and served by the hotel caterers and normally features British or French dishes. The Armenian guests arrive in the latest Western fashions in evening dress. The Armenian band and the presence of the bishop are thus the only formal indicators of the Armenian character of the function.

Soviet Armenia is an important source not only for such music, but also for continuing input into the Armenian arts in London in other ways. Films produced in Soviet Armenia as well as magazines and books are imported into London. A Soviet Armenian dance and song ensemble visiting Britain put on a concert specifically for the benefit of the London Armenian community. Visiting scholars and other notables from the republic will meet with the community. Finally, groups of London Armenians regularly visit Soviet Armenia every year.

There is input from other diaspora communities as well. Newspapers and leaflets are imported from France, the USA, the Middle East, etc. Armenian theatrical groups from Lebanon and Canada have visited the London community. An Armenian dance company from Paris visited the community as well.

Within London itself, the Tekeyan has twice sponsored art exhibitions of the work of Armenian artists residing in Britain. The Theatre Club, sponsored an amateur production of an Armenian play every year, although these were not taken from original scripts.

To sum up, an eclectic repertoire of diacritical features has been built up to signify and provide a vehicle for Armenian distinctiveness. The repertoire is not static. Not only are cultural influences that affected Armenians in their various countries of origin channelled into it but also attributes which were distinctive to Armenians both in their countries of origin as well as in London, such as certain types of surnames and language, continue to be of significance and to spark off discussions and introspection about the means of their maintenance in respect of the prevailing conditions. Nor is it only the old of whatever source that is being adapted for use in London, for fresh input continues to be channelled into the repertoire from Soviet Armenia, the heartland of Armenian settlement; other communities in the diaspora; and from the inventiveness of London Armenians. What all of these things do together is to provide a way to be an Armenian in London and the means to socialise a new generation into Armenianness. That is not to say that the youth are necessarily attracted by these features. But when Ms AT, British-born of Cypriot-Armenian parentage, rejected the songs and dances featured at the Scouts disco, dinner parties, and so on, she rejected them as 'Armenian songs and dances'. For her mother, these were the group dances that 'the Iranians are crazy for'. For Ms AT, the relevant contrast was between the Armenians and the British. For her mother, the relevant contrast was between the Iranians and the Cypriots.

In other words, first-generation Armenians are, I suggest, much more likely to be cognisant of, and therefore possibly critical of, the shifts and developments in Armenianness that have been associated with settlement in London, than second-generation Armenians. Almost all Armenians in London, whether born and raised in Britain or outside of it, are at least one generation's remove from the troubles in Turkey in 1915. It is these events which have provided more than the songs, dances, theatres, or food; a cultural legacy for Armenians, a legacy which has taken on a new vitality and immediacy with migration from the Middle East to the West and, in so doing, threatens to become increasingly problematic. Chapter 4 will be devoted to this legacy of the 'wandering and displaced Armenian'.

Conclusion

As an ethnic group, Armenians are socially anonymous in London. This characteristic has been enhanced by the tendency of Armenians to disperse residentially and occupationally. Anonymity, or rather the absence of stigmatisation as yet, has in turn promoted the integration of Armenians into British society within these occupational, residential, and educational spheres, but has also in turn enhanced their anonymity. Armenians clearly derive important benefits from this blank reputation, benefits which many are unwilling to jeopardise. However, their dispersal has also meant the increasing circumscription of their ethnicity, with consequent difficulties created in the communication and interaction between London Armenians, as well as conflicts between the roles played in non-Armenian spheres and those played in the Armenian community. Armenians themselves are concerned that their largely successful integration into British society will eventually produce their complete assimilation into it, and the disappearance of Armenians as an ethnic group in London. But the very difficulties created by dispersal have meant, for these people at least, self-consciousness about what it means to be an Armenian in London. To paraphrase Mrs W's comment: in Syria, I wasn't even aware that there were non-Armenians around but for my daughter, to be an Armenian in London will not be so effortless. To be an active Armenian in London; a member of the Armenian community requires effort, commitment of time and money and careful planning.

Most Armenians must constantly evaluate the extent and manner of this commitment as domestic, work, and school pressures are brought to bear on them. Armenians are also conscious of the need for and difficulties of, socialising their children into what they hope will be a meaningful and vital ethnic identity. Thus, there occurs what is sometimes a conscious attempt at building a tradition of Armenianness and a framework for its realisation. The Armenian community in London has no territorial component. It exists in the mind of Armenians and manifests itself in the commitment of individuals to be Armenian; to organise and participate in gatherings of Armenians; to establish and maintain communication between Armenians; to develop and pass on a tradition of Armenianness. It is this commitment which Armenians refer to when they say 'they don't care', 'nobody wants to help'; 'they don't want to put their hands in their pockets'. It is this commitment which they are afraid of losing. It is the loss of this commitment which would spell assimilation, rather than dispersal, circumscription of ethnicity, or exogamous marriages *per se*.

Among London Armenians the management of social boundaries exhibits two major trends which might appear, at first glance, contradictory. This is a group of migrants who individually and as a collectivity have cloaked their common ethnic identity as Armenians in a variety of representations. They have been able to handle their baggage of identities selectively to emphasise those aspects most appropriate to the different situations which they encounter in London, and thereby constrain the development of potentially disadvantageous categorical characterisations of them by non-Armenians. This flexible representation of self and community in combination with the initial fairly widespread ignorance of non-Armenian Londoners about this collectivity, have meant that Armenians have so far been able to participate, with relatively few constraints, in the economic, residential, or education settings to which their respective and varied skills and aspirations direct them. For a large part of their round of activities within London, Armenians are regularly interacting with non-Armenians. Their ethnicity has become, for practical purposes, a part-time ethnicity, restricted largely to the domain of leisure. Among themselves, the way in which Armenians seek to act out their ethnic identity seems open to a variety of sometimes conflicting interpretations. But just when one might come to the conclusion that 'Armenian' may be no more than a label rather than a meaningful identity, another trend which belies such a conclusion manifests itself. For Armenians are also making a concerted and creative effort not only towards participation in this part-time community but also towards developing and maintaining a tradition of Armenianness which will ensure the continued vitality and meaningfulness of Armenian identity for succeeding as well as first-generation London Armenians. In short, we have, on the one hand, a trend towards the dismantling or weakening of social boundaries in a number of domains, while at the same time, in respect to the same group of people, an ongoing trend towards the construction and assertion of boundaries in another domain. But these are not such contradictory tendencies as they might appear, for it is precisely because Armenians are aware of the former of these trends that they seek to assert and develop the latter, i.e. it is important for Armenians to define and develop the boundaries of their community precisely because they feel that the success of their integration into other spheres threatens their assimilation as a collectivity. As some Armenians themselves have pointed out, it is a more self-conscious effort at maintaining these social boundaries than their management of such boundaries in the Middle East where they were more visible as a distinguishable ethnic collectivity, because in London these boundaries cannot as easily be taken for granted.

As was indicated in the introductory chapter, the case of the London

Armenians provides a rather different perspective on the management of group boundaries from that which so often seems to be implied in the literature on ethnicity. It suggests that the sense of commitment felt by and the efforts invested by the members of an ethnic group (but this can pertain to other forms of social groupings as well) in the symbolic delineation of the social boundaries of this group will be most significant and self-conscious not when such symbolic constructions serve to signify and validate visible and clearly demarcated group differences in terms of economic factors or value-orientations, but rather when such differences are not clear, discrete, or highly visible. It is at the point when groups of people are incorporated into shared political economic and social systems; when they are thrown into intensive contact with each other; when the cultural differences between them seem to be gradually reduced that we see social boundaries being thrown up to accentuate and demarcate the lines that were becoming ever more blurred. It is this paradoxical assertion of social boundaries just when they seem least tangible and instrumental that has sometimes been viewed as 'false consciousness' (Watson, 1977, p. 12). But to so label it would be to ignore the self-consciousness which has appeared in the management of these boundaries by London Armenians. It would be to overlook the complex and often painful process in which the London Armenians themselves question the meaning and significance of maintaining the social boundaries between themselves and others. In seeking none the less to assert such boundaries, Armenians are not denying the crucial significance of their associations with non-Armenians. On the contrary, their participation in the Armenian community and their attempts to define and articulate its perimeters are gauged in terms of the type and degree of that association, and the kinds of commitments and interests which they have vested outside the community.

Notes

1 None of these tenants is living in council accommodation, although I know of two who applied unsuccessfully for council tenancy.
2 However, one woman pointed out that the fact that most of her neighbours in the building of bed-sitters in which she was a tenant, were Armenian was a strong attraction and was one of the reasons why she preferred not to move near to her work.
3 Mr AJ and Mr QH were actually encountered in Manchester rather than London, although Mr QH had formerly resided in London and continued to maintain contacts with the community there. I have included their statements here because they pertain to a subject which is not specific to the London Armenians.
4 Similarly, David Lang characterises the Armenian image in literature as 'nebulous, variable and rather hard to define' although he does not specify to which literature he is referring (Lang, 1981, p. 148).

Chapter 4

The historical legacy

So far in this exposition the manner in which Armenians organise themselves in London as a group, their perceptions of the divisions between them, the manner in which they relate to non-Armenians in London, and the means they have developed and reinforced to express and act out their ethnic identity have been discussed. But Armenians also have ideas about why it is important to be an Armenian. Fundamental to these ideas is a perception of the historical legacy of Armenians everywhere, in particular the massacres and expulsions which occurred in Eastern Turkey in the late nineteenth and early twentieth centuries. Much of the ideology that has developed around these perceptions is essentially nationalist; it does not relate specifically to the Armenian community in London but is shared by Armenians throughout the world. But this nationalist ideology shapes the ethnic identity of, and its definition by, Armenians in London. It provides, so to speak, the 'why' of being an Armenian, whereas language, associations, church, music, dancing, songs, food, etc. form the 'how' of being an Armenian in London. In this chapter, I will attempt to show how an ideology whose basic premises are accepted by almost all Armenians has become problematic by its very resurgence and the conclusions that have been drawn from this renewal for its fulfilment through direct action. But before it is possible to discuss this ideology properly, the selected elements on which it is based need to be examined.

The texts of the legacy

Central to the perception of historical legacy among the Armenians is the concept of the Armenian homeland. Three factors make it difficult to precisely delineate this concept in historical terms. The first is the mystery surrounding the origins of the Armenians as a people. Armenians are first mentioned in references to 'Armina' and 'Armenians' in Persian and Greek sources between 550 and 500 BC (Lang and Walker, 1977, P. p. 6; Walker, 1980, p. 20; Nansen, 1928, p. 232; Burney, 1982, p. 79). But these references do not confirm whether Armenians arrived in the highlands of Eastern Anatolia and Transcaucasia at this time or earlier, or from whence they had arrived, although it is known that their language falls into the Indo-European group of languages, along with Farsi.

Lang, an historian, suggests that 'the modern Armenian nation is in fact the product of a process of ethnic mingling which has been going on for thousands of years in Transcaucasia and the mountains and valleys of the Ararat-Vannic region' (Lang, 1980, p. 37). Lang, in spite of the doubts of some scholars to which he alludes, identifies the ancient 'Hayasa' mentioned in Hittite annals with the term 'Hayastan', by which Armenians refer to their country; he also identifies King Arame, the founder of the Urartian kingdom (which flourished in this region between the ninth century and the beginning of the sixth century BC) with the legendary Armenian King Ara, and Urartu itself with the name of Mount Ararat. Burney, an archaeologist and specialist in Urartu, cautions against the insistence on similarities between proper names and geographical names, rejects any direct relationship between the Urartians and the Armenians and suggests that the Armenians may have been one of a number of groups who, taking advantage of the weakness of the Urartian kingdom during its final years in decline and eventual collapse, migrated into its territories and established themselves there. For Burney, there is no question but that the Armenians were newcomers to the Urartian regions (Burney, 1982).

The second factor is the geographical position of the territories identified by the Armenians as their homeland. Eastern Anatolia and Transcaucasia have been a constant scene of battles between competing empires. Thus the first direct reference to the Armenians occurs in the inscriptions at Behisitun (Iran) in which Darius describes them as one of the countries to come under his control and pay tribute to him (Garsoian, 1981, pp. 29–30). Darius was not the only conqueror of these territories. Successively, they were to come under the suzerainty of the Achaemenid, Hellenist, Seleucid, Roman, Parthian, Sassanid, Byzantine, Saracen, Seljuk Turkish, Mongol, Ottoman and Russian Tsarist Empires. As Nalbandian points out: 'only in one period of Armenian history has the whole region been a united kingdom under a single ruler in the first century B.C. under Tigranes the Great' (Nalbandian, 1963, p. 2). Tigranes II, an Armenian king, after considerable conquests and expansions, was himself forced to submit to the Romans in 66 BC and completed his reign as a vassal of this empire until his death in 55 BC (Walker, 1980, p. 23; Lang, 1980, pp. 130–6; Nansen, 1928 pp. 247–8). Not only was this area the scene of competing interests between successive empires but of competing interests between the members of the indigenous Armenian ruling class. Walker quotes Cyril Toumanoff's description of this 'class of dynastic princes':

> [They] were older than kingship which derived from them. Their principalities were self-sufficient and self-determined, being territorialized tribes and clans of old. And their rights over these states were fully sovereign, including executive, judiciary, legislative and fiscal independence, control of their own armed forces, and, from the princes' point of view at least, the right to negotiate with foreign powers. [Quoted in Walker, 1980, pp. 22–3]

Thus it was not uncommon to find noble families in the course of their intrigues against each other, aligning themselves with different imperial powers (ibid., p. 29). As empire succeeded empire, the power of these dynastic princes and the territories governed by them waned and then flourished again, expanded and contracted; the area was partitioned between competing powers with regions being recaptured and lost again. Thus the general descriptions of authors like Nalbandian and Hovannisian of the territorial boundaries of Armenia, or maps like those of Walker which define one boundary for 'Armenia in Ancient and Medieval Times', do not clearly distinguish for the reader which period among such historic upheaval is being referred to or what criteria are being used to define the boundaries of this entity. The problem is not resolved by reference to contemporary international boundaries, since these, for reasons which will be dealt with later on in this chapter, are not accepted by the Armenians. Thus when Armenians refer to their 'lands' it is clear that the reference is to the vicinity of Eastern Anatolia and Transcaucasia but the precise territorial parameters of this reference remain often ambiguous. It may include, as Nalbandian does, contemporary north-western Iran, or it may extend to Cilicia as it is outlined by Hovannisian, or it may also include the presently autonomous Soviet regions of Nakhchivan and Karabag, parts of the republics of Georgia and Soviet Azerbaijan, or it may not (Nalbandian, 1963, p. 2; Hovannisian, 1981: 'Map of Historic Armenia and surrounding Lands, p. 6; Lang and Walker, 1978, map, p. 13).

The third factor to complicate the discussion of historic 'homeland' are the numerous population movements which, not surprisingly, occurred in the process of the conflicts over this region. Some examples of such population movements include the migration of Armenians, with increasing pressure from Seljuk Turkish invasions, to Cilicia in the tenth century. By 1080, Prince Rupen (Ruben I) had established an independent Armenian principality in Cilicia (Walker, 1980, p. 32; Dedeyan and Thierry, 1982, pp. 297–8) which was to align itself with the Crusaders as well as with the Mongol Court (Walker, 1980, p. 2). Armenian Cilicia lasted until 1375 when Sis fell to the Mamelukes, but Armenian communities continued to reside in this area until 1915.

At this juncture it should be pointed out that Christianity had been adopted by the Armenians as a national religion in 301 AD, although estimates vary between 286 and 314 AD (Walker, 1980, p. 24). St Gregory the Illuminator is credited with the introduction of this religion through his conversion of the Armenian ruler, Tiridates III. The Armenian church developed independently of both the Greek and Roman Churches (Lang and Walker, 1978, p. 4).

Another movement of an Armenian populace was initiated by Shah Abbas, at the turn of the seventeenth century, when he transferred the community of Julfa on the Araxes River to the Persian city of Isfahan where the Armenian suburb of New Julfa was established. The Armenians of Julfa attracted the attention of Shah Abbas through their talents as master stone-cutters and more importantly by the skill of their merchants in trade. The displaced traders were given the monopoly of the Persian silk trade and eventually developed an international trade network which brought both them and the Persian monarch considerable prosperity (Carswell, 1981, pp. 88–9). Although this was not the only movement of Armenians into Iran, it formed an important nucleus of the development of the modern Iranian Armenian population. The Treaty of Turkmen-chai between the Persians and Russians in 1928 facilitated a renewed migration of Armenians back into Transcaucasia, where at that time there was a Tartar majority in the Khanates of Yerevan and Nakhichevan, a migration which formed the nucleus of the modern Armenian populace in Transcaucasia, although greatly swelled, in the period following the massacres of 1915, by Armenian refugees from Turkey (Walker, 1980, pp. 47, 55).

Armenians also moved beyond these regions altogether, either through forced deportations, or through a search for better economic and social opportunities, into the various regions of the Byzantine empire to such areas as modern-day Cyprus and Bulgaria and then into the Crimea, Russia, Romania and Poland (Lang, 1980, pp. 172, 173, 184; Lang and Walker, 1978, p. 4). From Persia, the Armenians migrated into India, Singapore and Java (Lang and Walker, 1978, p. 5).

The Armenians were not the only ones to be involved in these population movements. As was pointed out earlier, Burney considers that the original migration of Armenians into Eastern Anatolia and Transcaucasia was as one of a number of groups also participating in this movement. Less speculatively, the defeats suffered by the Byzantines in the eleventh century at the hands of the Seljuk Turks led to their loss of control over 'Armenia' and the increase of migration of Kurds to Eastern Anatolia, a process which was stepped up after the conquests of the Ottomans in the sixteenth century. Krikorian lists the presence of Turks, Kurds, Nestorian and Chaldean Syrians, Greeks, Circassians, Kizilbash and other groups in Eastern Anatolia by the nineteenth century. During this period Armenians were a minority of the overall population in this region, although in some provinces they formed the largest single ethnic group within this heterogenous population (Krikorian, 1977; Lang and Walker, 1978).

It is the events of this period, especially the second half of the nineteenth century and the first quarter of the twentieth century, which are of particular relevance to the contemporary conceptualisation of historical legacy among London Armenians. During this period, Armenians were not only a minority in much of their 'historic homeland' but this territory was partitioned between two major powers: Ottoman and Tsarist Russian. Under the Treaty of Turkmen-chai (February 1828) control of the khanates of Yerevan and Nakhichevan passed from the Persians to the Russians (Walker, 1980, p. 47). Shortly afterwards, military conflict began between Russia and Turkey which ended in the Treaty of Adrianople (1829), setting a frontier between the two which is similar to the border presently between the Soviet Union and Turkey (Nalbandian 1963, p. 25; Walker, 1980, p. 54). It is from this partition, i.e. the frontier between Transcaucasia and Eastern Anatolia, which was first delineated between the Persians and Ottomans, that the distinction between 'Eastern Armenian' and 'Western Armenian' and that between Eastern or 'Russian Armenia' and Western or 'Turkish Armenia' derives (Walker, 1980, p. 37; Hovannisian, 1981, p. 7).

Within the Ottoman Empire, Armenians, like other non-Muslim subject peoples, had the status of a millet (religious community) which was headed by the Armenian Patriarch of Istanbul, who after 1860 was elected by a General Armenian Council which included both laymen and clergy (Krikorian, 1978, p. 3). The millets were internally largely self-governing (Walker, 1980, p. 85). But non-Muslims had special liabilities within the Ottoman legal system, most important of which was the inadmissability of their evidence in the Muslim religious courts. Thus in conflict with a Muslim, an Armenian was at a considerable disadvantage as the former could apply to have his case heard in a religious court, thereby excluding the latter from presenting his own case (Walker, 1980, p. 87). Christians did not perform military service, in exemption of which a special tax was levied on them. They were not allowed to bear arms, unlike their Muslim neighbours (Bardakjian, 1981, p. 146). The Armenians alone had the obligation of providing free winter quarters to the nomadic Kurds, which could amount to considerable expense for the reluctant hosts in the provision of food for both the Kurds and their animals (Walker, 1980, p. 89). Nevertheless, until the latter half of the nineteenth century, the Armenian population was regarded as the 'loyal millet' by the Ottoman government (Krikorian, 1978, pp. 107–8). During the latter half of the nineteenth century and the first quarter of the twentieth, the relations between the Armenians and the Turks were to change considerably.

This period saw a general weakening of the Ottoman Empire both territorially and economically. The government became increasingly dependent on European bank loans. The Ottoman Empire's indebtedness increased to the point that in 1881 it was forced to cede the revenues from its salt and tobacco monopolies; stamp, spirits and fish taxes and silk tithes: 'A

"Public Debt Administration" (PDA) was set up, with a board of seven men, six of whom were representatives of the European bond-holders. Turkey was thereafter reduced to a state of economic vassalage' (Walker, 1980, p. 94). The corollary to this new economic dependence was that the European powers which had considerable investments at stake in the Ottoman Empire became committed to its preservation, while the Ottoman rulers became increasingly hostile to and defensive about European interference in the internal affairs of the Empire.

In 1875, the Christian peasants of Bosnia and Herzegovina rebelled and this was followed by an uprising in Bulgaria in 1876 which was brutally put down. In 1878 the Balkans were granted liberty from Ottoman rule in the Treaty of Berlin (Walker, 1980, pp. 106–7, 112–17; Nalbandian, 1963, pp. 28–9; Lang, 1980, p. 286). The Armenians, who had sent a delegation to the Conference petitioning for some form of local self-government (but not independence), found their hopes disappointed with the promise of reforms only but with no provisions made for their enforcement.

These events had two important effects on Ottoman perceptions of the Armenians and the development of Armenian movements for autonomy, respectively. It increased the Sublime Porte's suspicion and distrust of the Armenians, who had turned to the European Christian powers, in particular Russia, with their demands for self-government and reform, attitudes which were exacerbated no doubt by Turkey's loss of administrative control over the Balkan territories. On the other hand, it encouraged the development of nationalist movements among the Armenians, who inspired by the Balkan example, increasingly adopted policies of direct action to achieve reforms in Eastern Anatolia particularly. These, in turn, increased the tension between the Sublime Porte and the Armenians. This tension reached its peak under Sultan Abdul Hamid in 1895–6.

Shortly after the Treaty of Berlin, Abdul Hamid reorganised the internal boundaries of the provinces of 'Turkish Armenia' redividing them from the three provinces of Erzerum, Sivas, and Diyarbekir to 'six vilayets' (provinces) which included Erzerum, Van, Bitlis, Sivas, Diyarbekir, and Mamuret el-Azis (Walker, 1980, p. 122). But the reforms which had been listed in the Treaty of Berlin for the government and administration of these provinces were not carried out. The newly organised Armenian political parties began to develop a campaign of resistance, the intention of which appears to have been as much to arouse the attention of the European powers to the situation of the Armenians under Ottoman rule as actually to confront the Ottoman bureaucratic and military machine. Placards urging revolt on the Muslims of Central and Western Anatolia appeared; confrontations sprang up in Sasun which ended in the massacre of hundreds of Armenians; and demonstrations in Constantinople, such as the Kum Kapu and Bab Ali both of which ended in bloody violence and deaths (Walker, 1980). All this was as nothing compared with what was to follow. A series of organised massacres swept the Armenian communities carried out by armed brigands but apparently assisted by the police and the hamidye cavalry and which resulted in a total Armenian death toll estimated at between 100,000 and 300,000 (Nansen, 1928, pp. 288–9; Walker, 1980; Lang, 1980; p. 287; Arlen, 1976, pp. 173–7). These were followed in August 1896 by the capture of the Ottoman Bank in Constantinople by Dashnakstitiun revoluntaries who demanded the enactment of reforms in the Eastern provinces. Eventually, with the intercession of a Russian diplomat, the captors managed to escape but a terrible massacre of Armenians in Constantinople followed (Krikorian, 1977, p. 109; Walker, 1980, pp. 164–70; Nansen, 1928, p. 290).

Armenian revolutionaries continued to operate in the East, organising themselves into small armed bands based in the inaccessible mountains, and mounted several expeditions against local Kurds and Turks (Walker, 1980, p. 177; Nansen, 1928, p. 292; Atamian, 1955, pp. 108–9). But Armenians were not the only forces mounted in opposition to Abdul Hamid's region. Groups of exiled intellectuals in Paris, including members from the various peoples of the Ottoman Empire, began to organise opposition to the Sultan's rule (movement of the 'young Turks'). Included amongst these were the Armenian Dashnaks (Walker, 1980, p. 181). In 1908 an uprising of discontented army officers in Macedonia provided the opportunity to put the revolution into effect. Abdul Hamid remained on the throne but the 1876 constitution was restored, and alongside Turks, Arabs, Albanians, Greeks, Armenians, Slavs, and Jews were also represented in Parliament (Walker, 1980, pp. 181–2). It soon became clear, however, that real authority was vested in the 'Committee of Union and Progress' (CUP) of the 'Young Turk' party of 'Union and Progress'. In April 1909 Abdul Hamid staged a counter-coup which was short lived and led to his deposition, but during this period of renewed upheaval fighting broke out between Turks and Armenians in Adana which resulted in the massacre of thousands of Armenians (Walker, 1980, pp. 182–8).

Although the Dashnaks signed an agreement of co-operation with the 'Young Turks' after the failed counter-coup of Abdul Hamid, the CUP was to become increasingly dominated by men of ultra-nationalist thinking who subscribed to a Pan-Turkish ideology (Walker, 1980, p. 189; Nansen, 1928, p. 296; Atamian, 1955, p. 182). This ideology envisaged first the 'Turki-sation' of the minority groups in the Empire, then the absorption of the Azerbaijanis of Russia and Persia and finally the unification of all the Turanian people of Asia (Walker, 1980, p. 100). The Russian Empire, more specifically its Transcaucasian Armenian districts of Kars and Yerevan, stood in the way of such an expansion (*ibid.*)

When the First World War broke out in 1914, Turkey was aligned with the Axis powers and Russia was aligned with the Allies. Before this the

Dashnakstitiun leaders were requested by the CUP leaders to organise an uprising of Armenians in Transcaucasia against Russia but they refused. The Dashnaks counselled against Turkish involvement in this 'European conflagration' but assured the 'Young Turks' representatives that Armenians would do their duty as Ottoman subjects should war break out (Walker, 1980, pp. 197–8; Nansen, 1928, p. 298; Atamian, 1955, p. 186; statement from Roupen, a refugee of Sassoun, in Bryce, 1916, p. 21). When war finally broke out Eastern Armenians formed volunteer corps fighting alongside the Russians, while Turkish Armenians were enlisted in the Ottoman Army. According to the reports of eye-witnesses compiled in a volume edited by Viscount Bryce and Arnold Toynbee, Armenia was quiet during the first months of the war until Ottoman armies on the Russian front began to suffer defeats, most spectacular of which was at the Battle of Sarikamish. Much was made by Ottoman officials of the presence of Armenian volunteer legions in the ranks of the Russian Army. Armenian soldiers in the Ottoman ranks were subsequently disarmed and formed into special labour batallions.

Resistance by Van Armenians to forcible enlistment and a far less successful resistance by Zeitun Armenians was decreed a revolt by the 'Young Turk' government and an example of the general treachery and disloyalty which could be expected from the Armenians. A plan was put into effect for the deportation of the entire Armenian population from Eastern Anatolia and Cilicia. In the course of what was to follow some two-thirds of the Armenian population of these regions were to lose their lives.

Successive Turkish governments as well as Turkish historians, have denied that these deaths were intended as part of the plan of the 'Young Turk' central government, putting the blame on uncontrolled attacks by Kurdish villagers and brigands. However, the reports of the eye-witnesses, among them not only Armenians, but German, American, and Danish missionaries, foreign residents, European and American consular officials (compiled in the volume presented in the British Parliament by Viscount Bryce in 1916 and a subsequent addition to this Blue Book published by the British foreign office in 1917); the reports of German diplomats whose country was an ally of Turkey in the war; the further published accounts of eye-witnesses like the Bedouin, Faiz El-Ghusain; the detailed self-accounts of Armenians who survived the deportations, like that of Kerop Bedoukian, leave little doubt that the massacres of Armenians were part of an organised and coherent plan devised at the highest levels of officialdom (Bryce, 1916; Foreign Office, 1917; El-Ghusein, 1917; Walker, 1980; Bedoukian, 1978).

In most Armenian communities, after the general deportation had started the adult men were summarily executed and the convoys of deported women and children were forced to march across vast distances with few or no provisions of food and water, subject to the attacks of brigands on the road as well as the gendarmerie appointed to guard them. The majority died of hunger, exhaustion, or of outright killings by their predators before they reached their ultimate destination, the Syrian desert. Those who did survive eventually passed through Aleppo, from where some were sent southwards on to Damascus but many others were sent to open-air camps along the Euphrates, notorious among them Deir-el-Zor, Ras ul-Ain, and others, where in the burning heat of the desert, bereft of food and water, they slowly died.

Estimates of how many Armenians died through the massacres and deportations vary, but the figure of 1 million suggested by Dr Lepsius is commonly accepted (Walker, 1980, p. 230; Sarkisian and Sahakian, 1965, p. 31; Nansen, 1928, p. 305). With the exception of the Constantinople community, little remained of the Armenian population in Turkey. The survivors dispersed throughout the Middle East, to Iraq, Syria, Lebanon, Egypt, some to America and Europe, and others joined the swollen stream of refugees in Transcaucasia. Although many fine words were spoken in Europe and America about the necessity of finding a solution to the 'Armenian Question', dispersion was allowed to become the *de facto* solution. Armenians had moved beyond 'historic Armenia', before but it is the events of 1915 and 1916 which account for much of the contemporary dispersion of Armenians today. It must be pointed out, however, that the majority of Iranian Armenians owe their presence in Iran not to the massacres but to previous population movements. Today, the only portion of the 'historic homeland' internationally recognised as such is Soviet Armenia, but Armenians have not given up their claims to other territories, in particular the 'six vilayets' of Eastern Anatolia. Those communities outside Soviet Armenia are viewed by Armenians as part of the 'Armenian diaspora' in exile.

In view of these events, it is not surprising that in answer to the question: 'What is an Armenian?', a London Armenian would be unlikely to confine his or her answer to the contemporary composition and nature of the London community. Rather, this community would form but one instance of a general phenomenon spanning not only the contemporary international structure of the settlement of the Armenian population as a whole but an interpretation of the historical factors which led to the formation of this structure and frequently also an interpretation of what form this settlement should take in the future. In other words, it would encompass not only where Armenians are today, but where they were yesterday, and where they should be tomorrow. The following are two replies to this question with somewhat different emphases offered by two London Western-Armenian women to non-Armenians:

> There is a republic of Armenia in the Soviet Union. But also there was another part of Armenia in Eastern Turkey. In 1915, the Turks massacred a million and a half Armenians and the rest they deported. That's why today, we are scattered all over the world. I am second-generation Armenian born abroad . . . [in answer to question from the listener as to whether Armenians wanted to go back to Eastern

Turkey] Yes, we do. We have Armenia but we want our lands back.

Because the other day I met a woman in the tube station and she really hurt me. She said: 'Where are you from?', and I said: 'I'm Armenian'. She said: 'Armenia, where's that?' I explained to her that there was an Armenia but there isn't any more, it's under Russia and that maybe one day there will be again, God knows. She said: 'Oh, why do you need to make it so complicated, why don't you just say, you're English?'. I said: 'I'm British but I'm not English.' I said: 'If Germany invaded your country and took over and you had to speak German, you wouldn't want to speak German all the time, you would want to speak your language and we want to keep our language'. But the British, they don't understand because they have never been without a country . . . We Armenians, we feel foreigners wherever we are so it doesn't matter to us where we are.

A difference between these two statements which should be borne in mind is that between the fairly emphatic 'we want our lands back' and the much vaguer and less certain 'maybe one day there will be again, God knows'.

In spite of the difference in emphasis, few of the Armenians with whom I came into contact would be likely to disagree with the formula of either of these two explanations on a general level, but the difference in emphasis does become important in expanded discussions of specific elements. One can divide the content of this discussion for the purposes of analysis into five major components: origins and formations of the Armenian people; the massacres; the national struggle; the displaced and homeless Armenian; and Soviet Armenia.

It is clear that any such analysis must keep in view the fact that developments in the interpretation of Armenian collective identity in terms of historical legacy did not originate in London and are not specific to it. However, the major aim of the following analysis is to examine the manifestations of these developments as they appear in the London Armenian community and not as they appear amongst the Armenian population world-wide or some of its perhaps more influential centres of planning and organisation. Hence, for example, although the statements issued by and the actions carried out by ASALA itself have an important influence both on the activities of their supporters as well as their opponents in London, my primary concern is not with the former *per se* but the manner in which their words and deeds are interpreted by the latter. Similarly for the Dashnakstitiun supporters, who are influenced by the decisions made in the headquarters of their party in Beirut; or for Armenians, both militant and not who may support particular theories originated in Soviet Armenia or in other parts of the diaspora about the origins and formation of the Armenian people. When, therefore, general statements are made about 'Armenians', the term, unless otherwise indicated, refers to the London Armenians with whom I came into contact and not necessarily to Armenians elsewhere.

Origins and formation of the Armenian people

It is perhaps not surprising that Armenians are concerned with and passionate about their more recent history, i.e. the events of 1915 and the consequent dispersion. But it may at first glance, be surprising to find that no mean number of Armenians are interested in seemingly more distant and esoteric aspects of their history. During the course of my fieldwork, the LACCC sponsored a lecture by a visiting American linguist on 'Armenian Early History as Determined by Linguistic Means', which was attended by an audience of some fifty people. The speaker explained that Armenians did not surface historically until 525 BC when they were mentioned by Darius in an inscription (Behisitun); that before this time there is no concrete material, i.e. no archaeological evidence, relating to the presence of Armenians nor to the formation of this group of people. There was, however, linguistic evidence which provided clues to the origins and formation of the Armenian people. In the light of this evidence he proposed what he presented as a standard academic view: that between 3,500 BC and 2,500 BC a people who were to later become on the one hand, the Armenians and on the other, the Greeks, were present in the Balkan region. Some of these people went south and west to Greece and others went south and east to become 'proto-Armenians'. This claim was made on the basis of certain linguistic correspondence between Greek and Armenian at their earliest levels, more so than with either Persian, Slavic, or Sanskrit at their earliest levels. Some loan words could be found in Armenian from the Hittite and Hurrian languages as later words were also borrowed from the Persian language. He categorically affirmed the absence of any generic relationship between the Urartian, Hurrian, and Armenian languages, although he suggested that there may have been intermarriages between Urartians and Armenians. The thesis suggested by this linguist is certainly no radical departure as since Herodotus's suggestion that Armenians originated from Phrygia, the origins of the Armenians have been looked for in the west and in more contemporary writings archaeologists like Burney appear to share the theory of westward origins. But the Armenian audience had not arrived unprepared with theories to challenge such a claim.

Three members of the audience, in turn, queried the speaker about theories advanced by Soviet Armenian scholars that Armenians were indigenous to Eastern Anatolia, which would imply that the Indo-European movement originated in Eastern Anatolia. Each, in turn, received the reply that this was an 'appalling theory'; 'nonsense'; that no scholars in the West would accept such a theory; that the majority of scholars in the USSR would not accept such a theory; that the monograph promoting such theories had been entirely condemned in the academic world, etc., and yet each persisted. Another participant queried the speaker about X's notion of the origins of the Armenians in Mesopotamia, which was also greeted with derision and the words: 'X sometimes wrote things that were more patriotic than accurate'. Another listener was upset at what she took to be the suggestion that Armenians had borrowed words from the Greek language: 'Maybe the Greeks took the words from the Armenians?', she asked. When the speaker explained that the issue was not one of loans from either one but of common origin, his reply was greeted with choruses of 'good!' from several other women in the audience. 'I'll never accept that!', said one to her neighbour, referring to the misconstrued suggestion that Armenians could have borrowed words from the Greeks. Another member of the audience asked about the relationship between Persian and Armenian, and was apparently surprised when the speaker explained the process by which Armenians borrowed words from the Persian language. 'You mean to say that the Armenians borrowed it from Persian?', he asked, although it is commonly accepted by Iranian Armenians that they have, over time, incorporated Persian words into their language. Another member of the audience wanted to know what the speaker thought about the notion 'current' in Soviet Armenia that Urartians were proto-Armenians, which would again imply that Armenians were indigenous to Eastern Antolia. This notion too was quickly squashed. Another four questions were concerned with the reasons for migration by the Armenians, the source of their 'elasticity', the etymology of the word 'Hai', and so on.

Three members of the audience afterwards expressed in private distaste for the nationalism with which, they felt, the tone of some of the questions had been imbued. But such passion and concern over events which occurred several thousand years ago is by no means unique to the audience gathered at this lecture. In an article published in one of the London Armenian papers, Mr DV, one of two brothers domiciled in Britain who have exhibited particular concern with linguistic-based theories of the origins and formation of the Armenian people (but neither of whom is a linguist and neither of whom were present in the lecture described above), argued that the Semitic languages 'should be re-catalogued as families of Indo-European dialects'. Employing dubious philological comparisons, he proposed that the Hyksos, Hittites, Jews, and Greeks were all 'Armenian tribes'. Yahweh, Noah, and Eve were all derivatives of Armenian names and mythical figures. Furthermore, the myth of Noah:

> indicates the geographical source of their origination, the Jews were obviously the lowland Armenians (like the Western Armenians of the diaspora), and went appropriately further down (looked at it from above the Armenian highlands), 'lower' into Egypt and then Israel, while the Greeks are the Caucasian Highland Armenians (like the Eastern Armenians of Soviet Armenia today) who went up to Greece.

Here again, we find the notion that the Armenians were indigenous to Eastern Anatolia and Transcaucasia, but in this case also that Greeks, Hyksos,

Hittites, and Jews were, in fact, Armenian tribes who migrated from this place of origin. No mention is made at all of any theory that Armenians originated outside Eastern Anatolia and Transcaucasia. The appropriation of biblical figures further brings 'historic Armenia' even closer to a position of 'original source', a quasi- 'cradle of mankind'. Orally, one of these brothers advanced the notion that Urartu was a stage in Armenian history, rather than the predecessors of the Armenians in Eastern Anatolia, that there was definite proof 'that the Armenian language was developed 5,000 years ago, then it makes sense that the culture had also begun to develop then'. In an article published in another London Armenian journal, Armenian is made synonymous with the ancient 'Hayasa' and there is no hestitation in stating that:

> Southeast of the Hittite settlements as early as 1800 BC. the name Armenians is historically given to the entire nation which gradually arose from the intermixing, politically and culturally, of Armen and Hayasa peoples.

In a display of folk costumes from different periods of Armenian history modelled at a Mother's Day lunch sponsored by the Anahid Ladies Association the first of the costumes to be exhibited was Urartian, which the mistress of ceremonies announced 'were the geographical, historical and cultural ancestors of the Armenians'. Hasan Talai, whose speciality is the archaeology of Northwest Iran and Transcaucasia during the period of the Urartian kingdom, was asked on a few occasions to affirm the direct link between Urartu and the Armenians. Little credence or attention was paid to his attempts to explain the problems created in the history of this area by gaps in the archaeological record. 'Urartu and Armenians are one and the same', declaimed Mr PR. 'The linguists are filling in the gaps', asserted Mr DV.

The importance in popular Armenian perceptions of their history, of asserting ancient origins in 'historic Armenia' long pre-dating any reference to, or evidence of, the presence of Armenians in the historical and archaeological records should be clear by now. Although not all Armenians are equally interested in this phase of their history, the issue can arouse passions in laymen who have no formal connection with the worlds of philology, history, linguistics, or archaeology. An Armenian respondent ventured an explanation of this concern which seems as reasonable as any:

> Armenians tend to be worried about any suggestion that the Armenians were migrants. Because if they were migrants, the Turks were also migrants then they also have a right to be on the lands of Eastern Anatolia.

In other words, concern with early origins is at least partially an extension of contemporary assertions of a historical claim to the territories of Eastern Anatolia and Transcaucasia as the 'Armenian homeland'. It is not enough to recount that Armenians lived in this region for hundreds of years. Since, as was described earlier, for centuries they were intermingled with other populations which also came to be domiciled in this area, it becomes important to assert the primacy of the Armenian claim over all others. One way to do this is progressively to pre-date the claim. Ultimately, this can become a rejection of any migration, no matter how early its date. As the American linguist told his Armenian audience:

> I can see how you would find it flattering, to think that you were the indigenous people, that you were the American Indians of Asia Minor and every one else were newcomers . . .

The historical record can then become akin to a mythology of ultimate origins even encompassing the biblical Genesis story, a mythology which is born out of the contemporary ideological needs of Armenians thousands of miles and thousands of years away from the place and time of origins they now claim. It is, in fact, because of this distance, I believe, that ultimate origins assume a particular importance. Physical distance and contemporary dispersions become expiated by a renewal and extension of the historical affiliation between the Armenian and his 'lands'. If many Armenians are now far from 'home', it becomes especially important to view this state of affairs as but a brief passage in a long, unbroken link between the Armenian people and a particular territory.

But antiquity and continuity in history are also significant elements in their own right in self-definitions of Armenian collective identity. Other ancient nations, like the Hittites and the Assyrians, the Medes and the Babylonians, may have waxed and waned, declined into but a shadow of their former greatness, or entirely disappeared but the Armenians have 'survived the ravages of history to the present day . . .', begins the London-Armenian writer in his 'perspective' on Armenian history, a conclusion which also appears in an Armenian history book for children (bought for the five-year-old child of one of my respondents) (Mekhitarist Fathers, 1978). But this concept of continuity refers not only to the people themselves but to their culture. 'Other nations like the Assyrians or like the Kurds, there are a lot of them but they have lost their culture', explained Mr VJ. And since one of the major elements of that culture is perceived to be its language, the distress, described earlier in the account of the linguistic lecture, at what were interpreted as suggestions that the Armenians had borrowed words from other languages becomes more readily comprehensible. Antiquity and continuity of people and culture not only become significant elements in the historical legacy of the Armenians they also mark that historical legacy as unique and distinctive in relation to other peoples.

When this particular interpretation was made by one Iranian Armenian and countered with the example of the Persians who, also an ancient nation, had survived as an intact cultural and social entity, the forthcoming reply was that, 'they didn't have a genocide'. Thus, the scene is set for a further deepening of the special character of historical continuity and antiquity as also a heroic endurance against all odds. And that heroic endurance of the past becomes also a prescription for future survivial. According to Mr O, a Western Armenian,

> The Armenians won't disappear. If we were going to disappear we would have disappeared a long time ago, at the Arab invasion, the Ottoman invasion, the massacres.

But the other side of the face of heroic endurance is the concept of the Armenian as victim. And this too is seen as not only an aspect of the past but also, if not inevitably of the future, certainly of the present:

> Our country has always been between two great powers, like the Romans who wanted the country to be able to attack the Persians and the Persians who wanted Armenia as a stronghold against the Romans. Always there have been great powers fighting in Armenia. Unfortunately it continues till today.

As we shall see later, this concept of Armenians caught between two great powers, in contemporary terms the USSR and the USA, is invoked to explain the difficulty Armenians have in altering the present disposition of Eastern Anatolia. But the notion of the Armenian as victim is pervasive, being used in relation to other contemporary issues as well as on a more general level.

It is echoed in the analysis made by Mrs G of the invasion of Lebanon by Israel in 1982. Mrs G was born in Lebanon and her mother was still residing in West Beirut at the time of the invasion and the seige of West Beirut by the Israeli Army. In the account Palestinians, Jews, and Turks become almost interchangeable, at least in relation to the hapless Armenian:

> And the Palestinians, what will they do? I never liked the Palestinians. We wanted them to go out but we never wanted to exterminate them. Even Pierre Gemayal [then leader of the Christian Phalange in Lebanon] said: 'We didn't want this. We didn't want them killed this way, we just wanted them to go out.' I was never one who wanted the Jews exterminated, never, but why do they do this? That's why I never liked the Jews. The Jew, either he crawls, you don't even know he is there or he wants all the power, he can't take the middle ground, never. *We have been through this before.* I hate the Turkish, nobody hates the Turkish like I do but even I never said we should exterminate the Turks. We just want our lands. You can say we are the most fanatic family there is but we always try to teach our children: we have to remember it was a long time ago; they were very ignorant; there was a lot of propaganda. That is the problem the Armenians have always had: we can't be aggressive enough. In this world, you can't succeed like that. My son [who was five years old at the time] said to me: 'Mother, if we don't kill them, they will kill us', that's what he said to me and he is absolutely right.

We were joined by Mrs JD shortly after the close of this statement. Mrs JD agreed with Mrs G that Armenians:

> are very straightforward. But sometimes I think that it would be better for our nation if we were more political, more hypocrite.

Similarly, on an earlier occasion, Ms HZ, an Armenian historian, explained that the Turks had always been excellent in diplomacy, this being the reason for their ability always to take advantage of the Armenians. In a separate conversation, Mrs CW felt that the frequent divisions within the Armenian nation, 'old but divided', was 'why other nations have been able to take advantage of us'. The cumulative picture is one of the Armenian as the perpetual man in the middle, the eternal vicitim of international conflicts which he had no part in shaping and over which he has little or no influence; a 'lamb' who was too naive, too straightforward, too peaceful to be able to defend himself against the unscrupulous machinations of malevolent external forces.

The legacy of Armenian history as a whole, therefore, crystallises in popular conceptions around three major strands through which continuity is the major linking theme: the lands, heroic survival, and victimisation. The implication for the present is that if Armenians have survived for so long and against such odds, they must continue to do so without ever forgetting their homeland.

But to examine fully the relationship of contemporary Armenians to their collective past, it is necessary to look more closely at their perceptions of that period which has more than any other prompted the interpretation of history along these lines: the massacres. Before doing so, however, one final strand of more ancient history must be dealt with.

Jack Antreassian, an American Armenian writing about the self-image of Armenians in the USA, reports:

> Three things leap out of a jumble of virtues we customarily flaunt, intended, I suppose as principal features of our image as we would like others to see it. Armenians are the first Christian nation; Armenians were massacred by the Turks; and Armenians are always reliant and self-abiding, rarely recorded on welfare rolls and police blotters. [Antreassian, 1981, p. 253)

The last two of these features appear also in the London-Armenian community. However, the Armenians as the 'first Christian nation' does not appear to be treated with the same importance as Antreassian reports for American Armenians. London Armenians, as we have seen, do place some importance on their common Christianity with the majority of the British population. The perception of the Church as a national symbol of Armenianness and, hence, a vital part of the community, in spite of falling attendance, is also prevalent. However, few people made a point of stressing the precedence in antiquity of the Armenian Apostolic faith. A few were rather concerned to stress the continuity between the Apostolic faith and the 'pagan' religions which preceded it. Continuity between the periods of Armenian history appears as important, therefore, or perhaps even more important than the pioneering precedence set by the adoption of Christianity as a national religion.

The massacres

After reading a number of history books covering the period of the massacres, I came to my fieldwork prepared to hear this subject crop up frequently in discussions with Armenians. The subject did crop up but not in quite the way I had expected. Although a number of life histories of Western Armenians and one Iranian Armenian included references to the migrations of parents from Turkey, I heard only two detailed accounts of the personal sufferings and travails suffered by parents or grandparents during the massacres of 1915 or 1896. References to the massacres, although recurrent, were often curt, matter of fact, almost a kind of ritual expression of collective sorrow. References to the Turks rather than specific references to the massacres also occurred and were often antagonistic, even at times expressing hatred such as that of Mr FS:

> You see, we suffered hardships from the Turks, you may know that. And anyone who praises the Turks or is in their favour, is unacceptable to us. Maybe this is chauvinist but that is the way it is.

But Mr FS's statement was delivered in a flat, calm voice. In a casual conversation (i.e. outside of formal lectures on the subject) the massacres were rarely discussed in detail and while the content of the statements may have included passionate words, these were rarely matched by a similar passion of delivery. Discussion of the massacres is more detailed in public addresses, journals and other publications. But a significant portion of this form of commemoration and remembrance has been formalised and regularised; 24 April has been designated a national day of mourning for the massacres.

Two important milestones, I was told, in the development of these features of national mourning were 1965, the fiftieth anniversary of the massacres; and 1975, the sixtieth anniversary of the massacres. In 1965, Vazgen I, 'Catholicos of all Armenians', issued an encyclical, published in a London Armenian journal 'instructing solemn observance in 1965 of the fiftieth anniversary of the mass martyrdom of the Armenian population in Turkey, during the years of World War I'. The Catholicos declared 1965 a year of national mourning for the Armenian population and made four more specific provisions for the realisation of this commemoration:

> That in all Armenian churches on April 24th there take place special religious ceremonies and memorial services to pray for the peace and enlightenment of the souls of our myriads of martyrs.

> That there be placed in all Armenian churches before the holy altar a lamp of perpetual light dedicated to the memory of the Armenian martyrs . . .

> That in all Armenian communities and colonies, under the auspices of the Armenian church, through the cordial cooperation of all Armenian associations, without exception, there be organized solemn gatherings of national observance,

lectures and literary functions of Armenian and non-Armenian audiences, devoted to the April massacre.

That the Armenian ecclesiastical authorities, national organizations, historic, literary and cultural foundations, and the Armenian Press consider their paramount duty to revive, in words and deeds, the sacred memory of the Armenians, of the clergy and prominent writers and national workers martyred during the years of the Great Massacre, by publishing the historic evidence, documents, studies, memoirs, literary and artistic works of Armenian and non-Armenian authors. [*Agregak*, April 1965]

I saw no special lamp before the altar but all three other provisions continue to be carried out in London and have been improved upon. The London Armenian associations do publish articles in their journals on subjects related to the massacres although more so in the journal of the Armenian National Committee, and there is general encouragement of, and attention paid to, publications dealing with the massacres or the period of the massacres. In April a special memorial service for those killed in the massacres continues to be conducted in the churches.

In 1975 the Armenian Secret Army for the Liberation of Armenia (ASALA) was formally launched. In 1975, as well, in Armenian communities throughout the word, special co-operative committees composed of representatives of the various associations and parties were set up to organise the commemoration of 24 April. In London this committee continues to operate, albeit in a somewhat less than wholly inclusive form. On 24 April 1982 two protest marches were conducted through the streets of the West End of London. One was sponsored by the Armenian National Committee and set forth at 10 a.m. in the morning. Another was sponsored jointly by the Popular Movement, the Committee in Defence of Armenian Political Prisoners, and the British Armenian Community Association and set forth two hours later. This, I was told by the participants, was the first time that the demonstration was not held in unison. The Dashnak supporters accused the other associations of causing the split and supporters of the rival triad accused the Dashnaks of the same. Estimates of the attendance at both demonstrations combined ranged from 300 to 600. Both sets of demonstrators marched down the streets waving placards, shouting slogans until many were hoarse, and handing out leaflets to passers-by.

On 25 April the Armenian National United Committee for the 24 April Commemoration sponsored a gathering held in a West End hall, whose programme consisted of a speech from a visiting American Armenian, a song sung by a soloist, a poetry recital, and several songs sung by the Ararat Choir. Eight associations were listed on the announcement of the event as represented in the sponsoring committee. None of the associations responsible for organising the marches of the day before was included on this list, and the other two major affiliates of the Dashnakstitiun were also absent from it.

Members of all of these associations were, however, in attendance as members of the audience on this occasion. Whether these associations were excluded from official representation through their own choice or that of the participating associations, I do not know, although it is likely that elements of both were operating. Both of the demonstrations stated their purpose as being not only the commemoration of the massacred dead but also a public demand for Armenian self-determination. As mentioned earlier, in the month preceding 24 April a series of lectures, films, and a photographic exhibition were sponsored by these politicised associations and focused on the 'national liberation struggle'.

Commemoration of the massacres has, therefore, acquired in London two distinct public manifestations. In the more public and militant forms, the massacres have become synonymous with the 'Armenian Cause'. In the rival manifestation, according to Ms M, a member of the BACA, the massacres had come to be represented as having emparted a duty to the survivors to continue 'being Armenian'. This duty consisted of teaching the Armenian language, keeping the traditions but 'irrespective of going back to our lands'. The memory of the massacres, in other words, was being used to perpetuate the Armenian diaspora. People who oppose the militancy of the BACA and its fellow associations would be likely to phrase their approach somewhat differently. According to one of these, Mr O, what activated and perpetuated the diaspora communities was their desire for justice to be done:

> A small nation burns for justice. It won't disappear because it is determined to get justice but when it finally achieves its aim, the people lose that purpose. But that's natural.

The sense of purpose instilled by the massacres and the deportations is, therefore, conceded to be a diaspora phenomenon and relevant only while the diaspora continues in its present form; but the ultimate aim remains the restoration of Armenians to their 'homeland'. Most Armenians would agree, although for the majority this ultimate goal is seen as being dimly distant, just short of the unattainable.

For those who oppose this perception of Armenian destiny, the massacres in fact assume their greatest importance and immediacy for their work is seen to be continuing. According to Mr F, the Armenians were now being subjected to a 'white genocide', a gradual loss of their customs, language, and identity as Armenians. Other Dashnak supporters as well as ASALA supporters view assimilation as imminent, perhaps a generation or two away at the most. They frequently cite the example of the Armenian community in Poland, which thrived in the fifteenth and sixteenth centuries but which after 300 years assimilated into the majority Polish population. If the Armenians assimilate then the aims of those who instigated the massacres will have been achieved. Nowhere is that aim seen as being closer to its objective than in the

Armenian communities in the Western world. In migrating to the West, Armenians are not only exposing themselves to the irresistible attractions of European and North American culture as discussed earlier, they are also furthering themselves geographically and spiritually from the 'lands'. There-fore, for these people, 'return to the lands' cannot be allowed to remain a distant goal. If the 'genocide' is not to be completed, Armenians must actively work towards their imminent restoration to their 'homeland' and its indepen-dence. The time for mourning, according to Mr F, is over. It is the time for waking up.

Perhaps not surprisingly after sixty-eight years, the impact of the massacres has changed. Remembrance has become regularised and formalised, but in this process has become no less an important feature of Armenian culture. If the massacres for most Armenians are no longer a memory of personal sorrow and loss, they more than any other feature have become the official definition of the modern diaspora Armenian. Who is the Armenian? He is the descendant of those who were murdered and displaced from their 'lands' and it is as such that he can be found in Britain. As we shall see, the massacres have been appropriated as their own even by those Armenians whose ancestors were not involved in them. But there are diverging opinions as to how this legacy should be interpreted in relation to the contemporary situation of Armenians in London. Or are they as divergent as they appear?

The national struggle

On the face of it, the supporters of militancy and armed struggle are people with a belief in their ability to affect their own social circumstances. They view this movement, if not themselves personally, as revolutionary, and as part of an 'international movement' of kindred oppressed groups similarly seeking justice and 'national liberation'. Most frequently they identify with the Palestinian movement for national self-liberation, which is seen as the movement of a displaced people to win their rightful home. They are keen to dispel any notions that like the Zionist movement the fulfilment of the Armenian objectives for national self-determination would be the cause of future displacement for the peoples presently residing in Eastern Turkey. ASALA supporters none the less accuse the Dashnaks of affinity to the Zionist model and of the intention of displacement. But neither the Dashnaks nor the ASALA supporters propose any clear model of projected relations between 'returning' Armenians and resident Turks and Kurds in Eastern Turkey. The thrust of their argument is to stress the position of the Armenians as a displaced people like other displaced peoples, rather than to draw a projected image of the Armenians as potential rulers in a future Armenian state to which they supposedly will have been restored. But for them, the Armenians need no longer be the perennial victims. They have the capacity to determine their future. Many Armenians do not share this certainty. Perhaps the most common criticism of the ASALA and like organisations made by these latter Armenians is that whatever the ethical considerations concerning a campaign of assassinations, these actions are doomed to failure. This criticism sometimes occurs in the form of a back-handed compliment, such as that made by Mrs PB, a young Iranian Armenian:

> I don't think it will do any good. Unless the world situation changes a great deal or one of the superpowers, either United States or Russia become interested in the Armenian cause, I don't think anything will happen for the Armenians. Sometimes I am very grateful to them because at least they are doing something, but unless the situation in the world is going to change, I don't think it will do any good. United States is not going to do anything because of their ties with Turkey and I don't think Russia is very interested because if it was, it would have done something a long time ago, after the second world war. I think of the Palestinians. They have the Arab countries behind them and they have a very good organization but every day, their situation gets worse and worse.

Similarly Ms PY, who has close friends both among the Dashnaks and the ASALA supporters, cited the Palestinian example:

> Look at the Armenian Question. They want to have armed struggle but these people are in warm houses, they have jobs . . . For me, the only people that are important are the Armenians in Turkey. Otherwise, are you going to bring people from Europe and the United States to fight in Turkey? The Palestinians, they are on their lands, they are with their guns on their lands and look where they are. They want to fight for their lands because they are in a terrible situation; they are in refugee camps. Armed struggle in Europe? I just don't see it. When you ask these people about it, they say we are forming contacts with the Kurds. But the Kurds are religious fanatics. They are illiterate and uneducated and only a small minority said they will collaborate with the Armenians. What about the others? You don't even have the support of your own community. They say, maybe we will succeed in thirty-five years. You can't expect the world to stay still for thirty-five years while you *slowly, slowly* try to achieve your ideals. I don't believe that people here will give up what they have for their country.

Similar criticisms have been made to me by other Armenians which can be roughly grouped thematically into two main points. The first, as in Mrs PB's criticism, is that Armenians will not be able to influence the framework of international decision-making, or, more specifically, as in the case of Mr O, that assassinations will not have this influence. According to Mr O, a campaign of propaganda and even bribery was necessary in order to attract the all-vital interest of a powerful government. The second most common criticism, like that voiced by Ms PY, is that the Secret Army appear to have no coherent strategy as to how they hope to achieve their objectives. They are, according to Mr EJ, striking haphazardly and randomly:

> Just ask them what they want from Turkey. That could make a Ph.D. in itself. 'We want to liberate our lands, I think but I'm not sure.' They never actually say what

they want. Oh, we'll kill off some ambassadors. The English go after foxes. The Armenians go after ambassadors.

The response to these criticisms by those who support the movement is rather vague. Ms M replying to Ms PY claimed that it was not possible to develop a long-term strategy. It was necessary to deal with one stage at a time. For the time being, the Secret Army's policy of pressuring the Turks abroad was the right one. Similarly, Mr F, a Dashnak supporter, responded with something less than certainty when I questioned him about the time scale for achieving a return to the 'homeland':

> I can't say that. Its impossible to look into the future. We don't know how we will get back our lands but I can tell you that all Armenians are living by hope.

So in what way has the return of the 'lands' been made more immediate a possibility than it appears to many other Armenians? Supporters of armed militancy cite as the major success of these operations the attention which it has brought to the Armenian case, most importantly in Turkey itself. They claim that Turks are for the first time admitting that there is a problem, albeit still denying the extent of, or government culpability for, the massacres. Whether or not this interpretation of the situation in Turkey is apt, there is little concrete discussion as to how such interest is to be translated into 'liberation of the Armenian lands', for that matter what constitutes this territorial liberation. What will be the nature of the political unit aspired for in Eastern Turkey, its relationship to Soviet Armenia, and the extent of the territories being claimed? Those are questions which are not readily accounted for in any plans published by or discussed by the politicised London associations and their supporters.

'The battlefield of our struggle is the diaspora of our people and any position where our enemies or its sponsors exist' reads the seventh point in the outline of the political program of the ASALA, published and distributed in London by the Popular Movement. The diaspora-based operations of the ASALA, Justice Commandos, and other such organisations may or may not have had an influence on the disposition of Eastern Turkey, but they have had an influence on the internal workings of the Armenian communities in the diaspora. They have provided a focus for the organisation of young Armenians in particular. According to Ms M, they have been the catalyst for the revitalisation of Armenian ethnicity and have brought back into the fold of the community youngsters who were drifting away. Indeed, I myself witnessed two such conversions of two young Western-Armenian women who previously had had limited involvement in community affairs and who stepped up that involvement considerably when they began to participate in the activities organised by ASALA supporters. What is illuminating about the nature of their involvement is that whatever the level of their commitment to the ideology of the ASALA and its supporter organisations, they were undoubtedly attracted by the opportunities afforded by these latter to socialise with young Armenian men and women, one of these women acquiring a boyfriend thereby. Mr L, another ASALA supporter, goes even further than Mr M. The 'cause' according to him is the only acceptable reason for remaining an Armenian. Without it, Armenianness becomes imbued with nationalist and racist sentiments, i.e. separatism for separatism's sake. Without it, a London Armenian has no meaningful justification for resisting assimilation. According to Mr L, only an Armenian who actively works for the 'cause' has that justification. The belief in the cause then, in this view, has invigorated the Armenian legacy and modernised it. Similar sentiments to those of Mr L and Ms M can also be had from Dashnak supporters.

If we look more closely at the timing of the development of the ASALA, some factors which may have been involved in attracting interest among certain sections of Armenian communities to the cause it espouses become clearer. The ASALA was established in 1975, in Beirut, Lebanon, when the civil war there prompted a renewed migration of Armenians to the West. This instance of westward migration was preceded several years earlier by similar movements from Cyprus, Iraq, Egypt, and succeeded by movements from Iran. In communities like that of London where these Armenians settled there is little separation from the majority population according to religion; the Church, although an important symbol, does not have a primary role in the organisation and maintenance of the community; there are no full-time Armenian schools; and 'homeland' and the massacres are distanced both in time and space. In short, both the traditional institutions of Church and school, and the ideology of 'homeland' are seen to have become or are in threat of becoming increasingly marginal and, hence, less able to play a central role in maintaining the Armenian community. One reaction to this has been to condemn emigration from the Middle East, ironically sometimes by Armenians presently residing in London. But clearly this reaction cannot provide any significant message for the majority of Armenians who have left the Middle East and settled permanently in the West, although some students in London maintain that their intention remains to return to the Middle East. Another reaction, I believe, has been the re-invigoration of the concept of 'the lands'.

I venture to suggest that how and when restoration to the 'lands' is achieved through the strategy of armed militancy is of less moment to its supporters in London – if not to its organisers and executors outside of London – than that it has provided a new rationale and means for being an Armenian. You are 'keeping Armenian' not for its sake only or for some distant, dimly felt aim, but because you are actively working towards your restoration to and liberation of your 'homeland', and you act out that commitment by participating in demonstrations, publishing and distributing circulars and magazines promulgating the 'cause', attending lectures and debates on this subject, and organising petitions and raising funds in support of Armenian political prisoners. Whether or not these activities will result in the materialisation of their formally stated objectives is less important than that you are 'doing something'. 'Doing something' implicitly evokes a contrast with a particular kind of inaction. This particular kind of inaction is defined in respect to the non-politicised association who are described as 'not doing anything' or 'just talking'. Therefore, the actions of the militants and the campaign which they support are set in an aggressive style deliberately intended to contrast with the unobrustive nature of much of London Armenian community activities *vis-à-vis* the non-Armenian population of the city. It is less important that the 'homeland' has been brought materially closer than that you should believe in the immediacy of the issue in such a way as to lend meaning and vitality to your life as an Armenian in the diaspora.

In this respect, therefore, the contrast between the interpretations made by people like Mr O, on the one hand, and people like Mr L on the other, of the legacy of the massacres and deportations is more apparent than real. Both share the premise that the events of 1915 have imparted a legacy for Armenian survivial whose ultimate fulfilment will be the restoration of the 'lands'. But whereas many Armenians, both in the public and private aspects of their participation in the community, operate on a day-to-day basis outside that ultimate aim, reaching back to it for renewed commitment only periodically, supporters of the ASALA and the Dashnak activists seek to make it the central organising principle of Armenian ethnicity. Because these two modes of operation share a central ideological premise, the development of the latter has produced an ambivalent response even among some of its detractors. There are people like Mrs PB who, although sceptical about the chances of success for the ASALA operations, none the less says she 'adores their courage'; at least 'they're doing something'. Or there is Mr VW who feels that 'killing doesn't solve anything' and that these operations are damaging the reputation of Armenians in London, but who also feels that 'they have some ideas'; 'they are doing something'. Or the reaction might be somewhat defensive like that of Mrs CW who doesn't participate in demonstrations on 24 April because they might 'incite the Turks' against the Armenians still in Turkey, but who hastens to add that 'its not that I don't love my nation'. Or there is Ms GT who points out that 'it's not that I don't feel strongly about the genocide, about what happened to my people' but feels that it is not good to look for 'revenge'. But there are also as yet few, but none the less significant, indicators that the attempts at reasserting the centrality of this shared premise has achieved the opposite effect for some Armenians, raising doubts in their minds about the premise of the commitment to 'the lands' as a whole.

What is threatening for many Armenians about the activities surrounding this renewal is not only that they seek to influence the manner in which Armenians organise themselves in relation to one another, but more importantly that they have a potential for disrupting the relationships between non-Armenians and Armenians. In an ethnicity as circumscribed as that of the Armenians in London, a potential development such as this would signify a major departure. The whole point of the assassinations and bombings carried out by the ASALA and its ilk, and the non-violent activities of their supporters is to draw attention to the Armenian case. But Armenians in London, and according to Jack Antreassian in other communities in the Western World as well, have accrued important advantages through their social anonymity (Antreassian, 1981). The recent publicity which has come to the Armenians has been, to say the least, ambiguous and more often than not condemning in its treatment of the campaign of assassinations, painting a picture of extremist terrorists seeking revenge. If that publicity grows and is seen to foretell group stigmatisation, then some London Armenians who are involved in the community may begin to ask themselves whether the 'lands' are really more important than their own status and that of their community in their adopted country. Some have already started asking themselves these questions. Most of these still refer doubts about the commitment to a generalised 'other'. 'These people here', or 'they', or as we saw earlier 'the rich' don't want to go back to Eastern Anatolia. Two half-Armenians were the exceptions, explicitly rejecting any personal commitment to Eastern Turkey as their homeland but only one of these was a regular participant in community activities. But rejection of 'the lands' is to reject a concept that has meant much to many more Armenians than the minority who support 'armed struggle'. If Eastern Anatolia is not the homeland then what place is? And what is to be the nature of the link between Armenians scattered worldwide?

The displaced and homeless Armenian

Like Mrs FH three other Western Armenians claimed that they had no special attachment to any particular place or country since, as they had no country of their own, they were equally foreigners wherever they went. More commonly, few first-generation Armenians expressed any strong attachment to Britain. This is perhaps not surprising since these people were not only born and raised outside Britain but in many cases have resided in this country for, as yet, a relatively small proportion of their lives. Among these are also Armenians who do not intend, or who are unable, to make Britain their permanent place of residence. However, only two Western Armenians, one from Cyprus and the other from Lebanon, expressed any attachment or longing for their country of origin. Iranian Armenians, on the other hand, commonly expressed strong sentiments of attachment to Iran, and a perception of a deep and abiding link with the country. Mrs Y, who had left Iran after the 1979 revolution there, found the departure very painful:

> I love Iran and I am very sad now because I lost it. It's my country after all. I was born there and raised there.'

Even more in contrast to the Western Armenians who rarely appear to entertain any serious notion of returning to their country of origin, several Iranian Armenians held this possibility in reserve. For most this was conditional upon a change in the present political climate of Iran and on their circumstances in Britain. 'If things get better in Iran, maybe I will go back there', or 'If I can't stay here, then I think I will go back to Iran.' But for a few students, return to Iran was not viewed as a vague possibility but as likely: 'There is no other country like it for me', explained one of these students. 'For me, Iran is a priority', claimed another.

Iranian Armenians explain their attachment to Iran in terms of the long history of the Armenian community in Iran over some three centuries. In contrast, Western-Armenian families have often undergone several successive migrations since their original deportation from Turkey, and have experienced little more than one generation's link with any one particular country. But significantly, in view of the differences in the personal backgrounds of Western and Iranian Armenians, Iranian Armenians in London do not appear to attach any less importance to the massacres and the deportations than do their more directly affected compatriots. The massacres for them are not something that happened to other Armenians but to all Armenians. Furthermore, only once did I hear a Western Armenian claim the massacres as the exlusive legacy of those Armenians who can trace their origin to Turkey and deny its relevance to Iranian Armenians. Iranian Armenians not only claim the massacres but also the concept of 'the lands'. In fact, the politicised associations which direct their attention to the national self-determination of the Armenians and the 'liberation of their lands' (i.e. Eastern Anatolia in particular) are dominated by Iranian Armenians. Those Iranian-Armenian students who were the most adamant about returning to Iran were for the most part active in these politicised associations. But for these, return to Iran was not only related to an attachment to the country of origin but to a perception of Iran, and the Middle East more generally, as a 'revolutionary centre' or as a 'centre for our revolution'. In the case of a woman whose husband was a part-time student, return to Iran was bound up with the superior facilities of the larger Armenian communities there which, she felt, would help her to bring up her son as an Armenian.

Hence, return to Iran may be related at least for those most certain of it, to the perception discussed earlier, that emigration to the West embodies a loss of the 'attributes of being an Armenian', a move away from the 'roots' and 'national objectives' of the Armenians (editorial in *Momentum*, a London Armenian magazine published by the Dashnakstitiun affiliate, the Armenian National Committee). Thus, what is an apparent contradiction between an attachment to a homeland from which migration to Iran began over three centuries ago and an attachment to Iran because of this enduring link becomes neatly resolved. Return to Iran is not only a return to the country of origin but a return to a location nearer to the 'historic homeland', nearer to the centres of planning for the 'liberation of the lands', nearer to the centres of other revolutionary movements with which this Armenian movement seeks to identify itself and a place where Armenians have a better chance of preserving their ethnic identity.

Thus, in London the concept of 'the lands' and the legacy of the massacres ideologically joins together in a shared heritage and self-definition groups of Armenians whose historical backgrounds are divergent. But beyond London it is seen as linking them with Armenians in communities scattered over different countries and continents. The dispersion that resulted from the massacres of 1915 impinges on the life of every Armenian in the London community; today also for Iranian Armenians who now also are far from family and friends. Although some Armenians, in particular Cypriot Armenians, may have more of their family and childhood friends with them in London, there is hardly one who had not experienced some kind of separation from close intimates. Thus, Mr G, a Lebanese Armenian, has a brother in Beirut, another in the USA, and his mother moves between three continents, visting now one son and then another elsewhere. Nor is this a particularly unusual case. Nor does the pattern of dispersion appear to be becoming stable in the near future. The superficiality of attachment felt by many London Armenians for their successive adopted countries (and, according to Jack Antreassian, at least to some degree in the USA as well) appears to have encouraged a propensity for recurrent migration in response to political and economic crises affecting the host societies. But the communities which these migrants then form are not bound only in their perception of a common heritage of suffering and displacement. They are also bound by a network of associations and institutions which function internationally; by imported publications and local magazines and journals which publish reports of events in Armenian communities elsewhere; by visits back and forth between friends and family and perhaps, most importantly, Soviet Armenia.

Soviet Armenia

During the height of the cold war in the 1950s Soviet Armenia was the source of much internal tension within Armenian communities, particularly in the USA (Atamian, 1955). But today it is rare to find an Armenian in London who does not speak with some pride of the achievements of Soviet Armenia, whatever his or her political persuasions and opinions of the communist regime there. Some of the ways in which continuing contact is maintained between the London community and Soviet Armenia have already been described in the previous chapter. But it is important to stress here that Soviet Armenia forms the nexus of much of the contemporary Armenian national identity. If the aspects which have already been described appear at times bordering on the macabre (being preoccupied with past suffering and deaths, and with the Armenian as victim) Soviet Armenia provides the happy side of the nationalist coin, a source of joy and pride.

For most London Armenians, their presence outside this centre of Armenian achievement and development does not appear to be problematic or guilt-ridden. The role of the diaspora Armenian implicitly appears to be viewed as one of support and encouragement for the republic, and in return the dialogue that is thus maintained nurtures and renews the Armenian communities outside it. But for those who seek to revitalise the centrality of the 'homeland', Soviet Armenia may become problematic, not because it is central to the political platforms of either of the two major groupings (although the Dashnakstitiun affiliates maintain their right to criticise the regime in the republic and its relationship with the Soviet system) but because, as I have witnessed on a few occasions, it can be used to place them on the defensive.

In one of the series of lectures sponsored by the Armenian National Committee in the run-up to 24 April the visiting Armenian speaker commented that because of Soviet influence Armenian parties, with the exception of the Dashnaks, had accepted Soviet Armenia as a solution to the 'Armenian Question', and he included the Secret Army. This statement, perhaps in conjunction with the memory of the Dashnakstitiun's previous vociferous opposition to Soviet Armenia, prompted several defensive questions from the audience, both from young and old Armenians. From one elderly gentleman came the comment:

> Many of us have been to Armenia, having been back to our motherland, we have felt refreshed. It may not be exactly as we like but nevertheless our churches and culture operates there. Is it right for Armenians to use America and 'Voice of America' against Soviet Armenia? [From a member of the audience came a shout of 'hear, hear!']

'Yes', replied the speaker, 'they have relative freedom but objectively they don't have everything. We have a responsibility to say so but we don't want "Voice of America" to be used. We don't want any other government to interfere.' From another member of the audience came the comment:

> Armenians can never agree about anything. They need to be governed [referring to the dependence of the republic on the central state apparatus of the USSR]. Armenia as it is now is closest to my soul, closer than Britain or America.

and he went on to mention several Armenians of note and their accomplishments. Again the speaker claimed that it was not his desire to 'fight against the Soviet Union or my people in the Soviet Union but I have a responsibility to say there are problems'. Another member of the audience felt that the speaker had given a misleading interpretation of the nature of the commemoration of the massacre appearing in Soviet Armenia. He felt that the speaker had underrated it, as there were, in fact, a memorial built to it, and literature, novels, and films on the subject.

If Dashnaks, because of their past, are particularly vulnerable to suspicions that they still harbour ill will to Soviet Armenia, ASALA supporters on the other hand are vulnerable to criticism that they are too supportive of the Soviet system as a whole. In one argument, an ASALA supporter who had been defending the USSR's record of achievements was met with the response:

> You're a fine one to talk. You wouldn't go to Armenia. All the Armenians who went to Soviet Armenia [recent migrants] are coming back and you should hear the stories they tell.

But perhaps most difficult to answer for all the 'national liberation' activists is the following criticism:

> After all, we have a country. Okay, its under the Soviet umbrella, but its ours, its called Armenia, its our place, we don't have to displace anybody to live there. I told [M]: 'If you feel so strongly about it, why don't you go to live there?' She said: 'There's not enough room there for all the Armenians from the diaspora so we need the lands in Anatolia for all the Armenians to go and live there', all the Armenians here who'll never go and live there.

Ms M's quoted reply to Ms U's criticism is a common explanation volunteered by these activists, even when no such questions are put to them. Thus, unlike many other Armenians, they do appear to be somewhat defensive about their presence outside Soviet Armenia.

The existence of Soviet Armenia can put activists in a double bind. On the one hand, they cannot be seen as too critical of Soviet Armenia, since the state has such a special significance for so many of their compatriots and for themselves as well. On the other hand, there is no question that the existence of Soviet Armenia as a tangible, contemporary 'motherland' makes it that much harder to work up a sense of urgency about that other 'homeland', where Armenians no longer live. In a practical sense, the diaspora has already become the diaspora to Soviet Armenia, but in an ideological sense Soviet Armenia is but the most visible part of the 'motherland' to which the diaspora is related. But Soviet Armenia is potentially an important ideological let-out for those Armenians who do not wish to give up the concept of 'motherland' but who are concerned about the possible consequences of the campaign to reassert the centrality of the entire 'motherland'. However, this let-out can produce its own conflicts with the host society in which Armenians are participating, particularly in Western countries, which are antagonistic to the USSR and particularly if Cold War tensions again arise.

The polarisation of East and West is complicated further for Armenians by an underlying ambivalence about the Western powers, irrespective of their anatagonism to the USSR of which Soviet Armenia is a part. The Western countries, and perhaps especially Britain and the USA, are seen as having failed the Armenians in their time of greatest need: for example, by failing to induce the Ottoman government to introduce reforms in Eastern Turkey in the late nineteenth century or to induce conquered Turkey to provide compensation and restitution for the deported Armenians after the cessation of First World War hostilities. And the indifference of the Western powers is seen as continuing in respect of their present strategic alliance with Turkey. But many London Armenians disapprove of the communist regime in the USSR in spite of their pride of the accomplishments of Soviet Armenia within it, and in spite of the absence of suggestions that the republic should in the near future disengage from the USSR. Hence, the loyalties of London Armenians to Soviet Armenia are caught between their ambivalence about the role of their adopted country *vis à vis* both the republic and that other larger 'motherland', and the ambivalence of many about the economic and political structure of which the contemporary 'homeland' is a part.[1]

Possible consequences of an interpretation of exile and lands

So far this chapter has focused on the way in which London Armenians interpret their history in relation to their present and future. But, as has also been pointed out, the London community is part of a network of Armenian diaspora communities. Its members have both informal ties with members of Armenian communities elsewhere and through their associations also formal ties with these communities. The charter used by London Armenians to give their activities as a group meaning has equal application to Armenians world-wide. The manner in which members of these other communities interpret the legacy has not only a direct effect on Armenians in London through their relationships with these other Armenians but also can have an effect on London Armenians through their impact on non-Armenian Londoners. Those Armenians who are concerned about the impact of the activities of their more militant counterparts on their integration may try to contain the effects of individuals and associations in London, but ultimately they have little control over the movement which these support since it is neither conceived in nor directed from London. Equally, they have little control over the impact that the activities of members of this movement outside London have on the consciousness of non-Armenian Londoners in terms of the kind of British media and governmental attention paid to them. Nor do they have much control over the manner in which less militant Armenians outside London choose to respond to the movement. If, through the activities and statements of Armenians outside London, Armenians in London become more visible to their neighbours, their previous anonymity may work against rather than for them. There will be no previously established yardstick to balance against or context in which to place this militancy. Armenians in London are aware of this and their primary concern over this militancy relates to it:

They don't know anything about Armenians. They will think we are all terrorists

is a worry which recurs in one form or another.

If Armenians as an ethnic category become more visible in London and in a negative manner, then they may find that their ability to adapt their representation of themselves as Armenians to different situations of interaction with non-Armenians and to their different interpretations of that identity is hampered by the expectations of non-Armenians. Some may choose then to understate even further their identity as Armenians in their dealings with non-Armenians; alternatively others may choose to try and change the basis of the visibility of Armenians as a category. How they do so will no doubt be influenced as much by the reactions of their compatriots outside London as by those inside it. But it is unlikely that even if more London Armenians adopt a higher profile for their associations or themselves individually that they will do so with one voice. The impact of heightened visibility would then not only influence the relationships of Armenians with non-Armenians but also their relationships with each other. It would mean taking to a non-Armenian forum a complex debate between Armenians themselves about the place of the Armenians as a collectivity among non-Armenians; about the domains in which Armenians should operate as Armenians and the form and content in which that identity should be acted out in relation to Armenians as well as to non-Armenians; about which organising principles should motivate the Armenians as an ethnic group *vis à vis* the total gamut of the different commitments and involvements of Armenians in London. In short, there would be a complex debate about what should be included and what should be excluded from the construction of relationships between Armenians as Armenians; a debate which has not yet received full public and formal expression within the London community let alone outside it. To formalise this debate through the perceived necessity of representing it to non-Armenians could hamper the fluidity of the negotiations between Armenians and further encourage the tendency to try and locate individual Armenians along the ends of a continuum of approaches to this negotiation rather than along it. It could make it harder to be 'neutral', not only between sections of Armenians but also in respect of the domain in which individual Armenians are willing to tolerate pressure to act as an Armenian and the domains in which they do not wish to be subjected to this constraint.

Thus, even if Armenians become more visible as a category, whether or not particular associations or individuals then take an active role in trying to shape the consequent image of Armenians will depend not only on how they perceive their relationships with non-Armenians to be affected by it but also on their perception of its possible effect on the relationships between Armenians.

Conclusion

For many years Armenians have operated with a general view of history in which the past was set and the future would be best set in a place other than their present location. And yet the stress in Armenian interpretations of their own history is on continuity; continuity of a people and a culture as well as continuity of that people's link to a particular territory. If that view is taken to its logical conclusion then what occurs in the present, in what the Armenians call the diaspora, would have to be seen not in terms of its own intrinsic worth but as a means of ensuring the passage between two defined points. But most Armenians in London are not governed by this view. They are first and foremost concerned, quite understandably, with personal aspirations which are fully contextualised within the diaspora: for jobs, education, and homes for themselves and for their children if not always in London then elsewhere in Europe, or in North America, or perhaps Australia (but for most not in the Middle East, let alone Eastern Turkey). A schism exists between personal aspirations and the aspirations considered appropriate to the collectivity. But for the most part, this schism is not problematic, since each aspect of it is appropriate to distinct spheres of identification and social interaction. While aspirations of the collectivity may lend meaning and purpose to the efforts of London Armenians to remain, and to educate their children to remain, Armenian, they have little import for their attempts to operate just as success-fully in spheres where their Armenian identity is at best secondary: at work, at school, perhaps in the residential neighbourhood as well. But around support for a campaign of violent militancy, a political movement has developed in the Armenian community which seeks to define a mode of conduct which has implications beyond the contemporary sphere in which a person's identity and role as an Armenian is primary. In a sense it asks that the view of history as defined above be taken to its logical and extreme conclusion. It is perhaps not surprising then that its greatest appeal is to the young who have fewer long-term investments in other spheres. But the public militancy of the activists and their support for a campaign of violence elsewhere is perceived by others as at best a nuisance and at worst as endangering the relationships between Armenians and non-Armenians.

As yet the danger is seen as potential and not as immediate. Thus, the most pervasive public response, as we saw in Chapter 2, has been to contain this movement as much as possible both by limiting its institutional access and, more importantly, by refusing to debate it. On a private level, the movement may be represented by its critics as futile and ineffective. Such responses do not however reject the importance of the 'historic motherland'. But a few Armenians, whether critical or supportive of the movement, also have come to question the commitment of Armenians generally to a 'historic homeland'. All of these responses, whatever the implications for ideological commitment to the lands, have reasserted the priority of the position of Armenians linked to and dependent on larger populations of non-Armenians. They have in a sense reasserted the centrality of the diaspora in response to the pressure to reassert the centrality of the 'lands'. But in so doing they have also emphasised the position of Armenians in London as locked into not only a larger social structure within Britain but also an international framework, which includes the Armenian communities of the diaspora as a whole and the only visible contemporary manifestation of the motherland: Soviet Armenia. The manner in which London Armenians continue to negotiate their roles regarding each other and non-Armenians depends therefore on a complex series of factors over which they have only limited control. It will depend as much on what those Armenians outside Britain do as on what those within Britain do; as much on how non-Armenians outside Britain react to the activities of the Armenians in their midst as on how non-Armenians inside Britain respond. The link of London Armenians to Soviet Armenia will inevitably be influenced by the degree of antagonism between the larger geopolitical entities in which they are respectively placed. All of these factors interact but this is not to imply that London Armenians are helpless and passive by-standers to the consequences of the interplay between these currents. In shaping the form of their relationships with one another, London Armenians will however, have to respond not only to the differences between them but also to the effects which developments in a much wider context have on these differences.

Notes

1 Ambivalence about Soviet Armenia has no doubt been heightened by recent unrest over the region of Ngorno Karabagh. Although the majority of its inhabitants are Armenian, Ngorno Karabagh is incorporated into the Soviet Republic of Azerbaijan. Recently, there has been a wave of strikes and agitation in Soviet Armenia as well as Ngorno Karabagh in respect of demands that the region be joined with the Armenian rather than the Azerbaijani republic. Protest within the USSR has been echoed in demonstrations by diaspora Armenians in support of the transfer.

Chapter 5

Fieldwork among the Armenians of London

I came to study the London Armenians having first selected the Armenians as the population amongst whom I wished to conduct research, and having ascertained that there were approximately 10,000 Armenians in Greater London. Having chosen the population for study and the locale in which I wished to conduct my fieldwork, my first, and by no means minor, fieldwork problem consisted of actually locating the Armenians within this setting. Before settling in London, therefore, I made three short reconnaissance trips to the city, first contacting the bishop of the Armenian Apostolic Church and then gradually expanding my contacts from this initial starting point. From these early contacts, I began to learn of the dispersed nature of the Armenian population and of the institutions of the Church and the Armenian House which I visited and where I met and talked to several other individuals. I then began to search for accommodation. In this I was helped by an indirect contact with an Armenian woman who was active in the community and who gave me some valuable background information about London Armenian associations and institutions, introduced me to some other Armenians and helped me to arrange accommodation in London which allowed me proximity to a few Armenian neighbours.

I finally settled in London in October of 1981 and continued to develop my contacts with Armenians, in some cases simply by telephoning individuals to whom I had been referred and arranging a meeting, as well as enrolling in a class provided in the Armenian Sunday School for adults learning Armenian as a second language, and visiting the churches and the Armenian House whenever possible. Through these institutions and the acquaintances I made there I was able to obtain regular information about the activities sponsored by the Armenian voluntary associations and I endeavoured to attend as many of these gatherings as was possible, in one case being invited formally to become a member of one of these associations. Gradually I began to get a more solid and detailed picture of how and when and where Armenians interacted with one another. Although searching for the Armenians was sometimes a frustrating task, it was a valuable experience in two respects particularly. First of all, I gradually became aware that the route that I had used to enter the community was not markedly different from that used by Armenians themselves, particularly those Armenians who had few or no previously established contacts among London Armenians. Secondly, it made me directly aware of the social anonymity of this ethnic collectivity and of the ease with which a fairly small population can be swallowed up in such a large metropolis as London.

As the framework of the voluntary organisations became less blurred, it became clear that the Armenians considered the voluntary associations and the gatherings which they generated to be a 'community' but that by no means all Armenians in Greater London participated in this community. Although I was able to establish contact with several individuals who were only marginally or not at all involved in the community, it proved extremely difficult (within the limitations of time and resources available to me) to make any systematic coverage of Armenians who were outside the community altogether. I decided, therefore, to restrict my study to those Armenians who were to some degree participants in the 'community', even if only sporadically.

By and large, I interacted with Armenians when they interacted with each other – during their leisure time, in their homes, or at association gatherings, although I was a frequent visitor to a neighbouring shop owned by an Armenian family. I continued in this manner until August 1982 when I left London, returning in September to complete some more interviews and to visit the church and the school once more.

In the Spring of 1982, after some six months of fieldwork had been completed, I undertook to carry out a series of structured interviews with twenty Armenian households, interviewing wherever possible all the adult members of each household. In some of these cases I had previously met one or more of the members of the households concerned, while in other cases I was referred or introduced to the households by Armenians with whom I was already acquainted. Although I devised and administered a brief and fairly straightforward questionnaire, this questionnaire was used as a starting point for discussion rather than as a rigid format for the conversation as a whole. The respondents were encouraged to expand on their answers and to raise whatever issues they felt were relevant. In all but two cases the interviews were conducted in the homes of the respondents, at a time chosen by them, usually with accompanying refreshments or a meal, and lasting from one to four hours but in most cases for at least two. Because the respondents either already knew me personally before the interview or knew of me from Armenian friends I was not treated as a strange and distant interviewer, but as a guest. Thus, although in the process of the interviews I found that a number of questions were not as specific as they should have been and that a number of issues had not been addressed in the questionnaire at all, this, for the most part, did not prevent the relevant information being gathered since the respondents themselves were quick to make the specifications and expansions themselves.

The interviews were helpful in two major respects. First, they allowed me to 'home in' on elements which had appeared in less formal observations and interactions with other Armenians. Specifically I was concerned to know how wide or narrow was the frame of reference within which individual Armenians worked to establish friendships in London: relationships established before arrival in Britain, inflection set, community activities, or domains outside the community altogether. Secondly, the interviews allowed me to deepen acquaintances already made or helped me to establish new ones.

What became clear in the course of the interviews was the importance of my previous and continuing participation in the community and encounters with Armenians. Many of the answers would have meant little or nothing to someone who had no previous knowledge of the community. For example, very commonly, when respondents referred to their or their friends' participation in the organisation of, or participation in, association gatherings, they referred to a particular gathering not by its official title, but by describing its content, or by reference to its date and location; quite often they referred to a particular association not by its title but by the names of members of it known to them, or in terms of the political party with which it was identified (e.g. Tekeyan, Ramgavar), or by a short-cut reference such as 'chorus' for the Ararat Song and Dance Ensemble. Without previous knowledge of the community, the flow of the interviews would have been impeded, with respondents constantly being required to try and remember and make references to gatherings or associations only by their official full title. Even where respondents were able to do this – and in many cases they were not – valuable information contained in these indirect references would have been lost. It is with some wariness, therefore, that I view a research methodology which relies exclusively on questionnaires or interview schedules without preceding or accompanying observation and/or participation. It is not only that the questions themselves could be the wrong ones to ask, but that the answers themselves might not assume their full intended meaning if the interviewer or principal researcher has little or no direct knowledge of the social context in which they are framed.

It is most probably clear from the above that I do not accept Sandra Wallman's contention that participant observation is not feasible in a dense urban setting (Wallman, 1982, p. 191). This is not to deny that the researcher will have to adapt the method to the exigencies of the setting in which he or she is located, both to its urban nature as well as to the particular characteristics of the specific urban locality within which he or she is working. But this necessity for situational adaptation is surely not a unique requirement of urban-based anthropological fieldwork but an ever-present aspect of participant observation in whatever setting it is employed as a methodological tool.

Which brings us to another suggestion which has been made in respect of urban anthropological studies. I refer here to the view that anthropologists must endeavour to focus more closely on the peculiar features of the city, conducting studies not *in* the city, but *of* the city (Hannerz, 1980). But it is difficult to understand why such a requirement should be particularly demanded of anthropological studies conducted within urban settings and not of studies conducted in other kinds of settings. With whatever population they have worked and in whatever setting the study was conducted, anthropologists have tended to look at places in terms of their effect on people, not in terms of their own intrinsic qualities. And this influence of environment is always a relative one in the sense that people organise themselves in respect of selective properties of their environment rather than of that environment as a whole. Perhaps one of the aspects that has come out most clearly in Barth's ecological approach to ethnicity is that groups of people who appear ostensibly to be sharing the same physical and socio-cultural environment may be organising themselves differently to take account of different features of that environment (Barth, 1969 *a*, 1969*b*).

As for the Pathans and the Baluch in rural Afghanistan, so for the Armenians; the experience of living and working in London does not necessarily throw up the same features of that city as it does for other ethnic groups within it or more generally for other Londoners. It is, therefore, to beg the question to suggest that anthropologists should focus on the city as their object of study. Which city? Which London? I have not, therefore, conducted a study of London as a city but a study of Armenians as they have experienced London.

But if the city on its own cannot form the subject of our study, neither should the focus of our analysis become too narrowly based.

> A network in this sense [of a social field defined in relationship to a particular individual] is always egocentric: it exists only and is defined with reference to a particular individual. As Barnes remarks, each person sees himself at the centre of a collection of friends. It follows therefore that the network is always 'personal', for the set of links that make it up are unique for each individual. [Epstein, 1969, p. 109)

There is, however, an analytic gap between the individual and his or her personal links and the social environment within which these links are contracted. Nor is that gap necessarily filled by an institutional analysis, the complement, Mitchell suggests, to network analysis (Mitchell, 1969, p. 49).

In the preceding chapters I have tried to show that within the Armenian community can be found a diversity of backgrounds, experiences, attitudes and interests. The London Armenian community is, therefore, by no means homogeneous nor even tightly integrated, and I have tried to draw attention to the internal social boundaries within it which influence the boundary between it and non-Armenians in this city. But it is none the less a community or social group both as Armenians themselves view it and in terms of the way in which they participate in it. The way in which Armenians organise their relationships within this community and define their role in it is not simply a product of their actual direct or even latent contacts with other Armenians. Neither is it only a product of shared institutions or norms, since these are not always shared and certainly not always or even usually agreed upon. Armenians are also influenced by their shared use of the community's facilities and participation in association gatherings, even though the specific nature of that use and participation may vary between individuals and between the subsections of the community. They are influenced by their common exposure to the literature, advertisements, and circulars which are an omnipresent adjunct to the gatherings of Armenians, even though their reaction to this exposure varies and sometimes greatly so. They are influenced by categorical evaluations of subgroupings of Armenians on the basis of nationality, age, or political orientation; judgements of individuals and groupings on the basis of public styles of presentation; experiences based on participation in Armenian communities elsewhere; and so on. All of this contributes to an awareness of the Armenian 'other' which goes beyond actual personal links with other Armenians. What is relevant here is not whether evaluations of that Armenian 'other' are equivalent between the respective appraisers, or whether that Armenian 'other' is actually encountered as such or is even present , but that it is felt to be present. And that presumed presence has a crucial influence on how Armenians evaluate that little slice of London which is their community and on how they define and explain their participation in that community. If the social environment in which Armenians operate is not London as a whole, neither is it their respective totals of personal links, for these links are mediated by a variety of more generalised inputs. Network analysis, by focusing on the individual as the unit of analysis is ill equipped to give us a sense of the social environment within which that individual is functioning. Nor, in its increasing tendency towards morphological analysis, is it equipped to tell us much about the quality of the relationships between Armenians, their content, or the values and meanings attributed to them by Armenians. A strict morphological analysis of the personal links of individual Armenians in London could lead one to the distorted conclusion that contacts between Armenians do not form a particularly significant aspect of their lives, much of which are taken up with encounters with non-Armenians. But this would be to disregard the very real commitment of many Armenians to maintaining and developing these contacts.

The focus of analysis in this study was, therefore, neither London as a city nor the Armenian as the centre of a personal network, but the Armenian in terms of his or her membership of an ethnic grouping in London. Which brings us back to the question of participant observation in the urban setting. The issue here is not whether participant observation can be conducted within this kind of setting for as this study has indicated, it can. Nor is the issue whether the antrhropologist is by definition a participant observer. As Wallman rightly points out, a discipline should not be defined by the methodologies which it employs (Wallman, 1982, p. 196). The issue is whether our interest in a man as a social being remains fundamentally a holistic one, that is to say that we are interested in how man relates to, and is in turn affected by his environment. If, as I have suggested, that environment is relative to the needs, perceptions, and organisation of particular societies or social groups, and that society or group is more than the sum total of its members and their respective involvements, then a quantitative calculation of the features of that environment or of the characteristics of the individuals operating with in it will not suffice to provide us with more than a glimmer of how these respective features and characteristics connect with one another; in short, of social process. To amplify that glimmer, we still, in most cases, need to observe and participate in that social process. The issue is not whether participant observation is anthropology in practice, but whether it remains still the most effective way we have of finding some of the answers to the kinds of questions which anthropologists ask of their research. The experience of conducting fieldwork among the London-Armenian community does not appear to have negated the assumption that it is.

Conclusion

I have analysed a process of ethnic community development in London which challenges some previous conceptions of ethnicity. The Armenians are dispersed in terms of residence, workplace, and educational establishment over a wide area of one of the largest conurbations in the world. Consequently, the Armenian community manifests itself in gatherings sponsored by voluntary associations which draw Armenians from their respective corners of the city to them rather than operating within the context of an already present clustering. This community is circumscribed by the instrumental involvements of its members at work, residential neighbourhood, and school, structuring itself to accommodate these commitments by operating within the leisure time of its members rather than structuring the commitments themselves.

The structure of this framework of voluntary organisations is highly decentralised, with a tendency towards the proliferation of associations in contrast to the much slower and smaller increase in centralising institutions or gathering places. But this proliferation increases the opportunities for Armenians to be involved directly in the organisation of their community and its activities, and with more activities provided by more associations in participation in this community as well.

Although assuming a moral unity of Armenians as a people with common origins and a common ultimate destiny, Armenians do not view their community as homogeneous. They not only recognise differences between them, they have incorporated this very heterogeneity into their image of the Armenian. It is in terms of these categories of difference that Armenians refer to and shape their concepts of the implications of being an Armenian, their projections of how the community should be run and developed and justify their consequent efforts to impress these views on their ethnic cohorts. It is through their arguments over different associations and kinds of Armenians that Armenians are involved in a continual process of defining their community both in terms of its content and its boundaries.

Circumscribed as it is, the organisation of the community has enhanced the initial social anonymity of Armenians as an ethnic category within the wider framework of London. This anonymity has served Armenians well, allowing them to operate with relative freedom through the socio-economic structure in which they are embedded. If Armenians do not necessarily want to be unknown to non-Armenians as a people, most do not want to be known in any negative way. They are concerned to pre-empt the development of a situation in which many West Indians and Asians in Britain find themselves today.

But the relative success of the integration of Armenians into the socio-economic structure of Britain has also had disadvantageous implications for their efforts at maintaining contact with one another. One of the most serious debates between Armenians is concerned with the extent of these implications for the perpetuation of Armenianness in Britain and the manner in which Armenians should respond to them. While most Armenians subscribe to a charter of identity which views the Armenian as an exile whose ultimate purpose is the reclamation of his or her 'lands' in Eastern Turkey, two major contrasting interpretations of this charter have developed, not only within the London Armenian community but also within the international Armenian diaspora.

On the one hand, the charter is treated as attributing an ultimate purpose to the perpetuation of Armenianness but with few immediate implications for the organisation of the community or for individual aspirations to successful settlement and advancement in London or the West generally. Opposed to this is a developing movement whose supporters argue that the more Armenians emigrate to the West and the firmer their integration into its respective countries and cities, the greater is the danger of the assimilation of Armenians into their host populations. Only if the 'lands' are seen as an immediate issue and Armenians directly organise and press for their reclamation can this destiny be avoided. Since this movement not only seeks to draw the attention of non-Armenians to the 'cause' but one of its manifestations has been a campaign of assassination and bombings in Western capitals, it threatens not only to raise the profile of Armenians as a collectivity within London but to do so in a negative way, a prospect dreaded by its opponents. Armenians in London may in the future have to adapt their self-presentation to the possible consequences of one kind of interpretation of their collectively shared charter. If Armenians are today debating over how visible they can afford to be, tomorrow may see as dynamic and multi-faceted a debate over how to deal with the consequences of categoric visibility.

Previously I pointed out that the social anonymity of London Armenians challenges the assumption that group differences need be recognised on both sides of the ethnic boundary. I also suggested that the Armenian case raises serious doubts about the generalisation frequently made in the literature on ethnicity that ethnic groups are interest groups competing for scarce resources inasmuch as the Armenian community has accommodated to the interests of Armenians in employment, housing, education, etc. rather than organising the deployment of these interests. And similarly the Armenian case indicates that the development of countervailing alignments and cross-cutting interests within and between ethnic groups does not necessarily entail a diminishing saliency of ethnic ties and consciousness. It may, in fact, as it does in the Armenian case, heighten this ethnic consciousness inasmuch as individuals are constantly forced to re-evaluate the nature of their commitments to and participation in, their community in the light of their commitments to investments outside it. Armenians, in other words, cannot take their or their fellow Armenians' commitment to the Armenian community for granted. It must be constantly reassessed and repledged in terms of that assessment, and much of the discourse between Armenians about what it means to be an Armenian relates to these assessments and to the attempts by Armenians to convince each other to make those pledges.

But if Armenians do not use their membership in the community to gain or to retain access to most of the resources which are important to them in their lives in London; if they have sought through maintaining a low profile to avoid making their ethnic identity predicative of their other involvements in the city; if Armenian ethnicity is for most intents and purposes a part-time ethnicity; one might legitimately ask, 'Why bother?' In trying to answer this question, I do not for a moment suggest that all ethnic groups are like the London-Armenian community, but the extreme compartmentalisation of Armenian ethnicity does suggest that possibly we need to re-orient our thinking on ethnicity and particularly on minority groupings. In so doing, it is helpful here to compare, even if only in a very general way, elaborations of social relationships based on achieved statuses with elaborations based on ethnic ascription. We are not particularly surprised when, for example, workers in a plant extend their relationships with each other to other spheres – domestic, recreation, neighbouring, etc., although these are not directly predicated by or formally necessitated by their working relationships. In other words, we are not surprised when people seek to deepen and extend their relationships with those with whom they come into interaction with, may even rely upon, in the fulfilment of their most fundamental requirements. Nor do we ask why they are interacting at all because their interaction, however extensive and varied it may have become, still owes its impetus to necessary instrumental functions.

However, when we come to deal with relationships based on ethnic ascriptions we have a situation which appears to be formally inverted from that described above. We have here the presumption of a social bond conceptually made before the establishment of an actual relationship of interdependence, a bond which Hannerz contends does not 'itself suffice as a definition of one's purposive involvement in a situation' (Hannerz, 1980 p. 152). However, inasmuch as the ascription of a social bond can go hand in hand with the performance of instrumental roles, the upside down nature of ethnic ascription has not been seen to be problematic. Rather the two have been seen as complementary; ethnicity providing the cement for the building blocks of economic and political interests. Ethnic ascription by asserting a claim to community provides what the attempts at extending and deepening achieved contractual relationships seek to accomplish: to make an instrumental tie more enduring, and hence, less precarious. Those who have taken a political approach to ethnicity have assumed that where ethnic ascription does not perform this function it becomes irrelevant. They have assumed that ethnicity cannot become compartmentalised from this function. But as the Armenian case shows it can, and it can because of the sense of possible community which ethnic ascription predicates. This is so whether generated out of corporate economic and political interests, such as those associated with Karen hill farmers of Thailand (Iijima, 1979); or out of territorial interests, such as those which may be associated with the Saami of Norway (Paine, 1982*b*); or out of discrimination and shared deprivation, such as that experienced by Negroes in Britain or the USA; or simply out of common regional derivations as is the case with many migrant groups. Once developed, it comes to assume an autonomy from the factors generating it.

By this I do not mean to imply that it operates in a socio-cultural vacuum. On the contrary, it is this autonomy which attributes to ethnicity its 'peculiarly reactive nature' (Wallman, 1979, p. 9) and allows it to adapt to the changing and perhaps diversifying interests of the membership of an ethnic category. But perhaps even more important is that this autonomy allows the sense of possible community to assume the status of a valuable resource in its own right.

One could go further and suggest that the feature of ethnic groups which I seek to stress here, i.e. the throwing up of social boundaries which define and signify their members' sense of communality, is by no means unique to this particular kind of grouping. In a sense, our concern with boundaries in respect to ethnic groups represents a far broader shift in the discipline of anthropology. If once we were satisfied to analyse the internal social structure of a group, we now no longer take as self-evident the structural limits of these groupings. In part, this reflects an increased sophistication of analysis as our realisation deepens that the local small groupings which we continue to make the focus of our studies are not and cannot be treated as socio-cultural isolates. They participate in wider social, political, and economic settings, and we are concerned therefore to reach an understanding of the way in which they manage their integrity as collectivities within these broader frameworks. But in part it is also due to trends originating outside the discipline in which small groupings are increasingly incorporated into and interlinked with larger and yet larger politico-economic units. It is, therefore, not only we, the analysts, but also the subjects of our attention who cannot take the definition and explanation of social group boundaries for granted. The larger the units become in which people are incorporated and the more remote and yet increasingly omniponent become the centres of power of these units, the more the need is felt to anchor oneself in smaller, more easily grasped and more immediately experienced social units. And yet because these smaller social units of neighbourhood, locality, occupation, ethnicity, etc. are affected by and dependent on their participation in larger metropoli-tan, state, and interstate structures, their viability and saliency are ever open to question. To survive as meaningful units of self-identification they must constantly strive to identify and validate the social boundaries which define them. Anthony Cohen's conclusion in respect to British rural cultures:

> The strength of local culture . . . does not necessarily diminish as the locality becomes increasingly precarious: quite often the reverse seems to be the case, when the maintenance of the culture becomes the effective *raison d'être* of the peripheral community. [Cohen, 1982, p. 7].

can equally well be applied to ethnic groups like the Armenians, or even to a more tightly articulated ethnic group like the Hausa of Ibadan who adopted the Tijaniyya religious order when their territorial and organisational auton-omy was threatened by their incorporation into the expanding city of Ibadan and the rise of Nigerian Federal Politics (Cohen, 1969). It is precisely because the Hausa, who held a monopoly of a particular economic sector, and the Armenians, who hold no such corporate or monopoly economic interests, are both involved in processes of ethnic boundary maintenance that the occur-rence and persistence of such ethnic boundaries cannot be generalised as an expression and informal organisation of such common interests. Their main-tenance can be valuable in their own right as providing a definition of community which makes it realisable.

However, operationalising this resource inevitably entails its own costs at the very least in terms of time and effort, as is the case with Armenians participating with any regularity in the activities which constitute their community. An ethnic community or group is the product of the appraisal of its active members and its eligible members of the cost of maintaining the sense of possible community as an operational resource *vis à vis* the cost of abandonning it and *vis à vis* the possibility of abandonning it in terms of the external constraints which may be brought to bear on such a tendency. Armenians, as we have seen, by virtue of their social anonymity, have relatively few such external constraints imposed upon them and there are Armenians in London who if they have not renounced their ethnic identity *per* se have not take up the possibilities that it allows for participation in and organisation of an Armenian community. But there are still sufficient

numbers of Armenians who seem to have judged that the cost of not maintaining membership in the community, and hence the community itself, in
terms of the more uncertain prospects of deepening and extending contractual relationships which do not rest on ethnic ascriptions, are greater than the
costs involved in participation in and maintenance of their community. But
even in this latter case, there has been an attempt to minimise the costs of
being an Armenian in the active sense by the avoidance of what Don
Handleman has called a hierarchial 'arrangement of membership sets' in
which 'all categorizations about a person may be allocated according to, and
interpreted in terms of, membership in a given category set' [Handleman,
1977, p. 193).

That is to say that Armenians have sought to avoid making their membership in the community contiguous with all or even most of the other roles they
perform in the city of London. Nor in this respect do Armenians appear to be
peculiar, at least among minority but non-territorially based ethnic groupings. As Cynthia Enloe points out:

> For an ethnic group that depends on the advanced sector of society for its own
> employment and livelihood, for an ethnic group whose wellbeing is directly
> affected by central decision-making, separation from the mainstream is a form of
> oppression, not communal liberation. [Enloe, 1973, p. 144]

In this vein, Trottier points out that the Asian-American movement, like the
Black-American movement, has been directed towards the claim of equal
participation in the mainstream of American society in contrast to the Indian-
American movement, which has a territorial component and has been
directed towards the right not to participate, the right for local autonomy
(Trottier, 1981, p. 301). But what Trottier or Trosper, who both deal with
this Indian-American movement, do not appear to have fully treated,
although they refer to it, are the two strands within this movement: an
urbanized 'tribe of all nations' strand; and a rural localised reservation strand
(Trottier, 1981; Trosper, 1981). While reservation Indians may have been
demanding greater political autonomy, it is unlikely that urbanised Indians
desire quite the same kind of autonomy for themselves with its overtones of
segregation if applied in an urban context. Thus, within the same movement,
it appears that an ethnic charter is being attached to different aspirations; in
the one case, a demand for local autonomy and state recognition of corporate
economic and political interests; and in the other, what is more likely, a
demand for equal status and the opportunity and wherewithal for participation in the politico-economic mainsteam.

If Asian-Americans and Indian-Americans are struggling against negative
stigmatising stereotypes, Armenians in London have not yet been subjected to
such stereotypes. If the former are reacting to the actuality of stigmatisation,
the Armenians are, in their management of ethnic identity and community,

reacting to the potential of the development of negative preconceptions which could limit or affect the nature of their involvement within London – economic, educational, residential, etc. The corollary of this is that not only has a concentration not been imposed upon Armenians within these particular spheres, but that they do not see such a concentration as a desirable possibility.

The peculiarity of London-Armenian ethnicity does not rest, therefore, in its tendency towards compartmentalisation but in the relatively few external checks imposed on this tendency in comparison with those imposed on their more visible and more stigmatised ethnic counterparts in Britain or in the USA. If there are Asian and Black-Americans or Anglo-West Indians, Pakistanis, Sikhs, etc. who do not want to be separated from the economic mainstream but to participate in it fully *and to* maintain their sense of ethnic identity, Armenians have so far already managed to achieve a fairly high degree of separation between their aspirations towards community and their aspirations towards successful participation in the socio-economic mainstream of Britain. The result, however, is a compartmentalisation not only of Armenian ethnicity but of the nature of the involvements of community participants in spheres outside the community. For having used their ethnic ascription to accomplish what others might seek to develop through achieved statuses, they have tended to pre-empt the extension and deepening of contractual relationships at work or in the neighbourhood towards a greater sociability, towards what they might term friendship. And this, in turn, reinforces the tendency to seek out such relationships within the community and for those with access to relationships formed outside Britain even within the inflection sets found in this community. Thus Armenians, may be correct that the British are 'cold', but the difficulty of making their relationships with the British with whom they regularly interact less contractual is no doubt compounded by the availability (and its utilization) of an ethnic ascription which allows for the development of a social bond which by definition, is not contractual.

I suggest, therefore, that the Armenians are not a peculiar or aberrant case but rather that their apparently unusual social anonymity and the circumscription of their community are means to achieve aspirations shared by no mean number of their more visible and more concentrated, but similarly minority and non-territorial-based, ethnic counterparts. I further propose that the very compartmentalisation of Armenian ethnicity should not be dismissed as a unique irrelevancy but rather should be taken to suggest that the needs for community, and/or relationships of a communal type, need to be treated as analytically separate, even if they are not always operationally separate, from the need for and means of acquisition of other equally important resources, of what have been referred to as 'interests' in the literature. Most individuals aspire to all of these resources. An individual may be able, or be required, to seek these resources through involvement with one set of people or one group, whether this be an ethnic group or another kind of grouping, but he or she may also attempt to acquire these different resources through involvements with different sets of people or groupings. Contiguity between these sets of interactional alters is no more a necessary aspect of ethnic groupings than it is of residential or occupational groupings.

Our starting point in the analysis of ethnicity and its persistence should not, therefore, be an apriori assumption of a particular level of integration between these different types of involvements. Rather, examining the factors influencing particular levels of integration in respect to particular ethnic groups should constitute the task of our analysis. By seeking to outline in the course of our analysis what is common to, but equally as important what is not common to, the members of an ethnic group, we might be able not only to arrive at a more flexible and less deterministic approach to the development of ethnic strategies, but also perhaps to avoid the unhappy tendency to treat ethnic groups as homogeneous chunks of humanity reacting *en masse* to the prevailing distribution of resources in their environment. Thus, we would not gloss over (as, for example, do Trottier and Trosper) potentially important differences of views, aspirations, and experiences within an ethnic group any more than we would gloss over the factors that make an ethnic group a group. Accordingly, I have tried in the foregoing chapters to show the factors influencing the development of a 'part-time' Armenian community; decentralised and circumscribed within one particular domain, accommodating to but not encompassing the interests of its members in other spheres. But equally I have tried to indicate that the present structure and spread of the Armenian community is not the product of a uniform collective response to the exigencies of life in London. It is the product of a continous discourse between Armenians in which differences of experience, interpretations, and aspirations are recognised and deemed important by the Armenians themselves. In the future these very differences may lead to a change in the way Armenians organise their community and present themselves and their identity to outsiders. In this respect I have focused on a particularly significant difference in interpretation of the charter which ascribes to the Armenian community its sense of moral unity, the manner in which Armenians have responded to this difference, and the possible consequences of one particular interpretation of that charter for the position of Armenians as an ethnic category and community in London.

Questionnaire used in household interviews

The questionnaire was made up of two sections. For the first set of questions only one member of the household was interviewed, providing the relevant information about him/herself and all the other members of the household, children and adults. For the second set of questions, each adult household member (15 years of age and over) was interviewed wherever possible.

Could you please give me the following details about each member of your household, including yourself?

1. Name
2. Relationship to respondent
3. Sex and age
4. Marital status
5. Where was each person born?
6. What is the occupation of each person and where does each work?
7. How many years of formal education has each person had?
8. Have you, or any member of your household, any formal qualifications or certificates? Please specify.
9. How many years of formal education has each person received in an Armenian educational establishment?
10. Address of household

An amended version of the previous set of questions was used for respondents either born in Britain or who were under the age of ten when taking up residence in Britain.

Name:
1. When you first came to this country did you have any friends or relations already here?

If so, were they
- (a) Armenians from Iran
- (b) Armenians from Lebanon
- (c) Armenians from Cyprus
- (d) Armenians from Iraq
- (e) Armenians born in Britain
- (f) English
- (g) Scottish
- (h) other: please specify

2. How did you meet people and make friends when you first came to this country?
   - (a) at work
   - (b) at school
   - (c) at an Armenian club or social event
   - (d) at an English or non-Armenian club or social event
   - (e) old friends or relations introduced you to new ones
   - (f) in your residential neighbourhood
   - (g) at church
   - (h) other: please specify

3. How would you compare the friends you have today with the friends you had in your first two years in this country?
   - (a) The same people
   - (b) you have kept your old friends but added new ones
   - (c) few of your friends today are the same ones you knew then

4. If you have made new friends since the first two years how did you meet them?
   - (a) at work
   - (b) at school
   - (c) at an Armenian club or social event
   - (d) at an English or non-Armenian club or social event
   - (e) old friends or relations introduced you to new ones
   - (f) in your residential neighbourhood
   - (g) at church
   - (h) other: please specify

5. Where would you normally socialise with these friends?
   - (a) at the Armenian House
   - (b) at the Armenian Sunday School
   - (c) at St Sarkis's or St Peter's Church
   - (d) at an Armenian association or club meeting or social event

(e) when you visit each other's homes
(f) at an English or non-Armenian club
(g) at a pub or restaurant
(h) other: please specify

6. Where did you meet your spouse?
    Country
    City
    Location

7. In the last month how many times have you visited
    (a) the Armenian House
    (b) St Sarkis's or St Peter's Church
    (c) the Armenian Sunday School

8. In the last 6 months have you attended any events organized by an Armenian club or association?
    (a) No
    (b) Yes: specify

9. Do you sit on any organising committee of an Armenian association or club?
    (a) No
    (b) Yes: specify

10. Do any of the friends you referred to before sit on any organising committee of an Armenian club or association?
    (a) No
    (b) Yes: specify

11. How many of your present friends are Armenian?
    (a) all
    (b) more than half
    (c) half
    (d) less than half
    (e) very few
    (f) none

12. Where do your non-Armenian friends come from?

13. How many of your Armenian friends speak the same Armenian dialect (inflection) as you do? (Reference is only to the major Eastern/Western division)
    (a) all
    (b) more than half

    (c) half
    (d) less than half
    (e) very few
    (f) none

14. Have you lived in any other countries apart from England and the country in which you were born?
    (a) No
    (b) Yes: specify where and for how long

15. How long have you lived in Great Britain?

16. How long have you lived in London?

References

Antreassian, J. (1981), 'The Armenian in America, A personal viewpoint', in R. G. Hovannisian (ed.), *The Armenian Image in History and Literature'*, California: Undena Publications, pp. 251–6.

Aregak (1965), Armenian Monthly, Special Issue, London.

Arlen, M. J. (1976), *Passage to Ararat*, London: Chatto & Windus.

Atamian, S. (1955), *The Armenian Community*, New York: Philosophical Library.

Bardakjian, K. (1981), 'Armenia and the Armenians through the eyes of English travellers of the nineteenth century', in R. G. Hovannisian (ed.), *The Armenian Image in History and Literature*, California: Undena Publications, pp. 139–54.

Barth, F. (1969a), 'Introduction', in F. Barth (ed.), *Ethnic Groups and Boundaries*, London: Allen & Unwin, pp. 9–38.

—— (1969b), 'Pathan identity and its maintenance', in F. Barth (ed.), *Ethnic Groups and Boundaries*, pp. 117–34.

—— (1981), *Selected Essays of Fredrik Barth*, vol. 1, *Process and Form in Social Life*, London: Routledge & Kegan Paul.

Bedoukian, K. (1978), *The Urchin: an Armenian's Escape*, London: John Murray.

Brotz, M. (1955), 'The outlines of Jewish society in London', in M. Freedman (ed.), *A Minority in Britain*, London: Vallentine, Mitchell, pp. 137–197.

Bryce, Viscount (1916), *The Treatment of Armenians in the Ottoman Empire*, documents presented to Viscount Grey of Fallodon, London: Hodder & Stoughton.

Burney, C. (1982), 'Avant les Arméniens: les Ourartéens guerriers et bâtisseurs', in G. Dedeyan (ed.), *Histoire des Arméniens*, Toulouse: Editions Privat, pp. 53–84.

Carswell, J. (1981), New Julfa and the Safavid image of the Armenians', in R. G. Hovannisian (ed.), *The Armenian Image in History and Literature*, pp. 83–104.

Cohen, A. (1969), *Custom and Politics in Urban Africa*, London: Routledge & Kegan Paul.

—— (1974a), *Two Dimensional Man*, London: Routledge & Kegan Paul.

—— (1974b), 'Introduction: the lesson of ethnicity', in A. Cohen (ed.), *Urban Ethnicity*, London: Tavistock Publications, pp. ix–xxiv.

—— (1981), 'Variables in ethnicity', in C. F. Keyes (ed.), *Ethnic Change*, Seattle and London: University of Washington Press, pp. 307–31.

Cohen, A. P. (1982), 'Belonging: the experience of culture', in A. P. Cohen (ed.), *Belonging: Identity and Social Organization in British Rural Cultures*, Manchester University Press, pp. 1–17.

—— (1985), *The Symbolic Construction of Community*, London: Tavistock Publications.

Constantinides, P. (1977), The Greek Cypriots: factors in the maintenance of ethnic identity', in J. L. Watson (ed.), *Between Two Cultures*, Oxford: Basil Blackwell, pp. 269–300.

Dedeyan, G. and Thierry, N. (1982), 'Le Temps de la Croisade (*fin XIè–fin XIVé siécle*)', in G. Dedeyan (ed.), *Histoire des Arméniens*, pp. 297–340.

Der-Karabetian, A. (1981), 'Image and self-image of Armenians in Lebanon: a psychosocial perspective', in R. G. Hovannisian (ed.), *The Armenian Image in History and Literature*, pp. 241–50.

Eidheim, H. (1969), 'When ethnic identity is a social stigma', in F. Barth (ed.), *Ethnic Groups and Boundaries*, pp. 39–57.

El Ghusein, F. (1917), *Martyred Armenia* (translated from the original Arabic), London: Arthur Pearson.

Enloe, C. H. (1973), *Ethnic Conflict and Political Development*, Boston: Little, Brown.

Epstein, A. L. (1969), 'The network and urban social organization', in J. Clyde Mitchell (ed.), *Social Networks in Urban Situations*, Manchester University Press, pp. 77–116.

—— (1978), *Ethos and Identity*, London: Tavistock Publications.

Foreign Office (1917), Germany, Turkey and Armenia, London: J. J. Keliher.

Freedman, M. (1955), 'Jews in the society of Britain', in M. Freedman (ed.), *A Minority in Britain*, pp. 201–42.

Garsoian, Nina G. (1981), 'The locus of the death of kings. Iranian Armenia – the inverted image', in R. G. Hovannisian (ed.), *The Armenian Image in History and Literature*, Malibu, California: Undena Publications, pp. 27–64.

Geertz, C. (1975), *The Interpretation of Cultures*, London: Hutchinson.

Hanleman, D. (1977), 'The organization of ethnicity', *Ethnic Groups*, 1, 187–200.

Hannerz, U. (1969), *Soulside*, New York and London: Columbia University Press.

—— (1980), *Exploring the City*, New York: Columbia University Press.

Hovannisian, R. G. (1967), *Armenia: on the road to Independence, 1918*, Berkeley, California: University of California Press.

—— (1981), 'Introduction', in R. G. Hovannisian (ed.), *The Armenian Image in History and Literature*, Malibu, California: Undena Publications, pp. 1–8.

Iijima, S. (1979), 'Ethnic identity and sociocultural change among Sgawkaren in Northern Thailand', in C. F. Keyes (ed.), *Ethnic Adaptation and Identity*, Philadelphia: Institute for the Study of Human Issues, pp. 99–118.

Keyes, C. F. (1981), 'The dialectics of ethnic change', in C. F. Keyes (ed.), *Ethnic Change*, pp. 4–30.

Krikorian, M. K. (1977), *Armenians in the Service of the Ottoman Empire, 1960–1908*, London: Routledge & Kegan Paul.

Lang, D. M. (1980), *Armenia: Cradle of Civilization,* (3rd edn.), London: Allen & Unwin.

—— (1981), *The Armenians: a People in Exile*, London: Allen & Unwin.

—— and Walker, C. J. (1978), *The Armenians*, Minority Rights Groups, Report No. 32, (revised edn).

Light, I. (1981), 'Ethnic succession', in C. F. Keyes *Ethnic Change*, pp. 54–86.

Mekhitarist Fathers (1978), *The History of my ancestors*, San Lazzaro, Venice: Mekhitarist Fathers.

Mitchell, J. C. (1969), 'The concept and use of social networks', in J. C. Mitchell (ed.), *Social Networks in Urban Situations*, pp. 1–50.

Nagata, J.(1981),'In defense of ethnic boundaries: the changing myths and charters of Malay identity', in C. F. Keyes (ed.), *Ethnic Change*, pp. 88–116

Nalbandian, L. (1963), *The Armenian Revolutionary Movement.* Berkeley and Los

Angeles: University of California Press.

Nansen, F. (1928), *Armenia and the Near East*, London: Allen & Unwin.

Oshagan, V. (1981), 'The self-image of Western Armenians in modern literature', in R. G. Hovannisian (ed.), *The Armenian Image in History and Literature*, pp. 201–20.

Paine, R. (1982a), 'The Stamp of Swat: a brief ethnography of some of the writings of Fredrik Barth', *Man*, 17 (2) June, 328–39.

—— (1982b), Norwegians and Saami: nation state and fourth world', in G. L. Gold (ed.), *Minorities and Mother Country Imagery*, St John's, Nfld: ISER Social and Economic Papers, No. 13, pp. 211–48.

Parkin, D. (1978), *The Cultural Definition of Political Response*, London: Academic Press.

Sabbagh, R. (1980), Armenians in London, Research Report, No. 2, mimeo, London: The Polytechnic of North London, School of Librarianship.

Sarkisian, E. K. and Sahakian, R. G. (1965), *Vital Issues in Modern Armenian History*, (translated and edited by E. B. Chrakian) Watertown, Mass: Armenian Studies.

Suny, R. G. (1981), 'Images of the Armenians in the Russian Empire', in R. G. Hovannisian (ed.), *The Armenian Image in History and Literature*, pp. 105–38.

Trosper, R. L. (1981), 'American Indian nationalism and frontier expansion', in C. F. Keyes (ed.) *Ethnic Change*, pp. 247–70.

Trottier, R. W. (1981), Charters of Panethnic identity: indigenous American Indians and Immigrant Asian-Americans', in C. F. Keyes (ed.), *Ethnic Change*, pp. 272–304.

Walker, C. J. (1980), *Armenia: the Survival of a Nation, London: Croom Helm*.

Wallman, S. (1979), 'Introduction: the scope for ethnicity', in S. Wallman (ed.), *Ethnicity at Work*, London and Basingstoke: The MacMillan Press, pp. 1–14.

—— and Associates (1982), *Living in South London*, Aldershot: Gower Publishing.

Watson, J. L. (1977), 'Introduction: immigration, ethnicity and class in Britain', in J. L. Watson (ed.), *Between Two Cultures*, pp. 181–213.

Werbner, P. (1980), 'From rags to riches: Manchester Pakistanis in the textile trade', *New Community*, 9 (1 and 2), pp. 84–95.

Index

Agregak Journal, 131–2
analytic frameworks
  circumstantialists, 5–6
  network analysis, 151–2
  political approach (interest groups),
    2–3, 4, 157
  primordialists, 5–6
  social boundaries, 4, 6–7, 40, 113–14,
    157
  symbolic analysis, 6–8
anniversaries
  24 April, 26, 131–3
  Armenian Independence Day, 26
anonymous ethnicity, 93, 95–6, 98, 103,
  112, 139, 149, 155, 158–9, 160–1
Antreassian, J., 90, 93–4, 130, 139, 141
Arlen, M. J., 121
Armenian associations and institutions
  characterisation, 33–4
  establishment of, 15–16
  trends in development of, 10–13
  uses of institutions, 17–18
Armenian attitudes, to
  apathy, 53, 103
  ascription, 107
  community commitment (doing),
    37–9, 46, 138
  continuity, 128, 130
  early origins, 125–8
  exile, 4–5, 123, 134, 155
  internal differentiation (individualist),
    42–3, 45–6, 48–50, 52–3, 54, 76,
    154
  moral legacy (duty), 5, 133
  political parties, 51–2

  support for armed struggle, 35, 134–5,
    136
  time conflicts, 104–7
Armenian customs, 109–12, 115
  cuisine, 109
  folk-dancing, 109–10
  naming, 97, 108
  songs, 110
Armenian genocide (the massacres), 26,
  131–2, 133–4, 136, 138, 141
  history of, 119–23
Armenian political movements
  ASALA, 26–7, 35, 132
  Dashnakstitiun, 1, 10, 23, 32–3, 34, 35,
    51, 71
  history of (ASALA and historic
    parties), 10, 23–7, 137
  Hunchak, 1, 10, 23, 51
  Ramgavar, 1, 10, 23, 31, 32–3, 51
Armenian population
  debate over estimates, 18–21
  length of residence in London, 79
  in London, 1, 78
  in North America, 94
  and residential location, 78–81
  using community associations, 56–61,
    69–70
  using institutions, 17–18
'Armenian Question', 35, 36, 123, 135,
  142
Armenian republic
  independent, 25
  Soviet Socialist Republic (SSR), 26,
    110–11, 141–4, 147 n. 1
Armenian schools, 85–6

Atamian, S., 23, 24, 121, 122, 141

Bardakjian, K., 119
Barth, F., 4, 5, 6, 151
Bedoukian, K., 122
borderline associations, 11
    Armenian General Benevolent Union
        (AGBU), 31–2, 71
    Armenian Scouts Association, 32
    Melkonian Alumni Association, 32,
        71
    Tekeyan Cultural Society, 29–31, 51,
        71
Brotz, H., 12
Bryce, V., 122
Burney, C., 115–16

Carswell, J., 118
Cohen, Abner, 2, 3, 4, 5, 6
Cohen, Anthony P., 6, 7, 158
collective ideology, 2–3, 4
community landmarks (gateways),
    17–18
Constantinides, P., 3
cultural charter, 155, 161

Dedeyan, G., 117
Der-Karabetian, A., 83, 89–90, 91
displaced Armenians, 139–41

Eidheim, H., 100
El-Ghusein, G., 122
Enloe, C. H., 159
Epstein, A. L., 3, 4, 151
ethnic ascription, 156–7, 160
ethnic entrepreneurism, 84–5
exogamous marriages, 87, 89–92

fund-raising, 28–9, 30
Freedman, M., 12

Garsoian, N. G., 116
Geertz, C., 6–7

Handleman, D., 159
Hannerz, U., 151, 156–7
homeland (our lands), 123–4, 127–8,
    130, 133–4, 137–8
    history of, 115–19
Hovannisian, R. G., 23, 25, 118, 119

Iijima, S., 157
informal relationships
    and country of origin, 98
    establishment of, 61–71, 85, 86, 100
    and inflection, 56–61, 71, 72–3
    a life history of, 64–5
    with non-Armenians, 106–7, 160
Ittahadist, 24

Krikorian, M. K., 118, 119, 121

Lang, D. M., 25, 94, 115–16, 117, 118,
    120, 121
language
    inflections, 1, 43–4, 46
    proficiency, 92, 96, 108–9
Light, I., 4
London Armenian magazines and
    newsletters
    Erebouni, 30
    Kayzter, 36
    Momentum, 34, 140–1

Mekhitarist Fathers, 128
Mitchell, J. C., 151

Nagata, J., 5
Nalbandian, L., 23, 24, 116, 117, 119,
    120
Nansen, F., 115–16, 121, 122, 123
non-political associations, 11
    Anahid Women's Association, 28–9
    Ararat Song and Dance Ensemble, 28
    Football Club, 28

Oshagan, V., 89
owner associations, 11
    Armenian House (Trust) 13, 15, 17,
        18, 72
    London Armenian Community
        Church Council (LACCC), 14,
        18–23, 28–9, 37, 38, 50, 73
    St Peter's Church, 14, 16, 18, 73
    St Sarkis's Church, 14, 18, 72

Paine, R., 4, 157
Parkin, D., 3, 6, 13
participant observation, 150–1, 153
part-time ethnicity, 3, 77, 113, 156, 161
political associations, 11, 16, 26
    Armenian National Committee, 33,

34, 51
Armenian Youth Federation, 33, 35
British Armenian Community
   Association, 35, 37
Committee in Defence of Armenian
   Political Prisoners, 35, 37
Navarsation Cultural Association, 33,
   35
Popular Movement for ASALA, 35–7

religion
   Armenian Apostolic Church, 1, 21, 22,
      88
   bishop, 21–2, 88
   Catholicos, 21, 25–6, 131–2
   secularisation, 87–9
   services, 18, 21–2, 86

Sabbagh, R., 102
Sahakian, R. G., 123

Sarkisian, E. K., 123
schools abroad, 92
socio-economic characteristics
   educational levels, 82–3
   occupations, 81–2, 98
stigmatisation, 100, 101, 139, 159–60
Sultan Abdul Hamid, 120, 121
Suny, R. G., 101

Thierry, N., 117
Trosper, R. L., 159, 161
Trottier, R. W., 159, 161

Walker, C. J., 23, 25, 94, 101, 102,
   115–16, 116–17, 118, 119, 120,
   121, 122, 123
Wallman, S., 150, 153, 157
Watson, J., 3, 114
Werbner, P., 3